Puppets, Puppetry and Gogmagog

Text and Illustrations by Deborah Hunt

Puppets, Puppetry and Gogmagog

Text and Illustrations by Deborah Hunt

Puppets, Puppetry and Gogmagog Copyright © 2013 by Deborah Hunt

All rights reserved. Printed in the United States of America. No part of this book may be reproduced, stored or transmitted in any form or medium; electronic, mechanical, photocopied, registered or by other means; with the exception of brief citations for reviews, without the written permission of the author.

Information:

Deborah Hunt

281 Convento St., San Juan, Puerto Rico 00912

maskhunt@gmail.com

First edition

ISBN 978-0-9853384-3-5

Text and illustrations: Deborah Hunt

Visual edition and graphic design: Mary Anne Hopgood

Other titles by Deborah Hunt:

Máscaras con máscaras

Masks and Masked Faces

Títeres, titererías y Gogmagog

| MASKHUNT MOTIONS | MASKHUNT MANUALS |

This manual is dedicated to

Guie Beeu, Dorian and Kian

... the next generations.

6	Contents
8	Introduction
10	Different Kinds of Puppets in this Manual
14	**Techniques, Recipes, Useful Information Before Starting**
14	Glue Recipes for Paper Mache
14	Other Glues for Other Processes
16	Using Paper Mache
17	Wiring the Puppets
18	How to Build a Stand for Sculpting a Clay Head
20	Basic Proportions of a Puppet Head
22	Eyes, Eyelids and Pupils
24	Geometric Shapes of Heads
27	**Paper and Cardboard Puppets**
28	Cardboard Fish
36	Paper Bag Puppet
40	Jigglers
43	Variation: Jiggler with **3** Dimensional Head
48	Cone Puppet
55	**Glove Puppets**
56	Basic Glove Puppet
67	The Hands
70	The Glove
73	Catalan Style Puppet
81	**Mouth Puppets**
82	Mouth Puppet Made with a Balloon and Cardboard
93	Mouth Puppet Over Clay Mold
97	**Rod Puppets**
98	Marotte
98	Different Ways of Making Heads and Attaching Them to the Sticks
100	The Facial Features
102	Variation: Marotte Over a Clay Mold
103	Variation: Marotte With the Puppeteer's Hand
105	Pop-up
111	Rod Puppet Manipulated from Below
113	The Shoulders
116	The Hands

Contents

120	The Basic Costume
123	The Control Rods for the Hands
125	The Turning Head Mechanism
127	Rod Puppet Manipulated from Above
130	The Feet, Boots and Shoes
132	Rod and String Puppet
133	The Central Rod
136	The Hands and Feet or Shoes
137	The Body/Costume
139	The Control
143	**Marionettes (String Puppets)**
144	Kathputli Style Marionette
145	The Body
150	The Arms
151	The Skirt
153	**9** String Marionette
156	The Two Parts of the Body
162	The Shoes
164	The Arms
165	The Hands
166	The Control
168	Stringing the Marionette
171	**Tabletop Puppets**
172	Sandbag Puppet
178	Thin Man
189	**Humanette**
195	**Puppets Made Over Plastic Containers**
196	Mouth Puppet Over Gallon Container
202	Variation: Gallon Container Cut Laterally
206	Two Headed Flip Puppet
211	Standing Puppet Over Liter Container
215	Bird Puppet Over Liter Container
221	**Giants**
222	Giant Made Over Wooden Frame
244	Variation 1: Flexible Arms and **2** Additional Puppeteers
245	Variation 2: Another Way of Using Clothes Dryer Tubing
246	Giant with Head and Body of Cane

A puppet is an inanimate object that represents a figure (human or otherwise) and is moved by a puppeteer in front of an audience.

Puppets have been with us for a very long time. The most ancient puppet to date was found near Brno in the Czech Republic; it is around 26,000 years old.

Puppets may have begun as articulated statues in religious rites.

They have been present on the roads, in villages, royal courts, carnival side shows and theatres across the ages. They paved the way for children's programming in television and today are present in films and music videos.

Puppeteers have been grouped with vagabonds, charlatans and tooth pullers. They have also been some of the most highly paid live entertainers in modern times. Puppeteers kept working when actors were forbidden to speak and when theatres were closed down.

They have spoken out against injustice and have scorned politicians. They have been censored and reviled. Puppets have made people laugh and cry for centuries.

They just don't stop. I celebrate their history and stubborn survival.

There are many, many kinds of puppets.

In this manual I offer construction methods for puppets I have built and used for different performances; in theatres, on the street and in unusual non theatrical spaces.

Some are tiny puppets made for intimate audiences of 6-12 people. Some are giants seen on an open field by thousands. I mostly construct in paper mache.

I remember thinking many years ago that one day I would build a wonderful puppet with many strings; a puppet that could do just about anything.

I would travel the world with my magical marionette performing puppet scale operas and very dramatic works in carnival like sideshows.

I would live with my puppet or puppets (because soon I would have many of them) in a caravan. The vision was perfect. Reality was another story.

One of the first puppets I built was a rabbit head with blinking eyes, a master of ceremonies for a glove puppet show.

I could have built a glove puppet rabbit

Introduction

but I wanted something bigger and I was hell bent on blinking eyes. It was one of the most tortuous building experiences because I did not really know what I was doing (not that that's a bad thing in and of itself) and it was finally extremely difficult to manipulate.

My hand cramped painfully and the blinking mechanism broke often. I became extremely frustrated.

I learned the hard way to ask myself at the beginning of each project the following questions:

What do I want the puppet to do? Where will I be performing? Who will I be performing the work for? Will I be alone or will there be other puppeteers? Do I need to change puppets quickly?

How can I simplify?

Some puppets can be made simply and quickly; most take a while to build.

A puppet is often a head, body, arms and legs and costume; a lot of parts that must come together; a lot of steps in a process before the magical moment of presentation.

Be patient. Try things. Risk failing. The art of puppet construction is the art of resolving problems. Enjoy it.

Above all a puppet is an object that must come alive.

When this happens, the public is drawn into an irresistible world; an uncanny world that has its roots planted in the early appearance of the human being on earth.

Let the invisible doorways open! Let the puppets come tumbling forth!

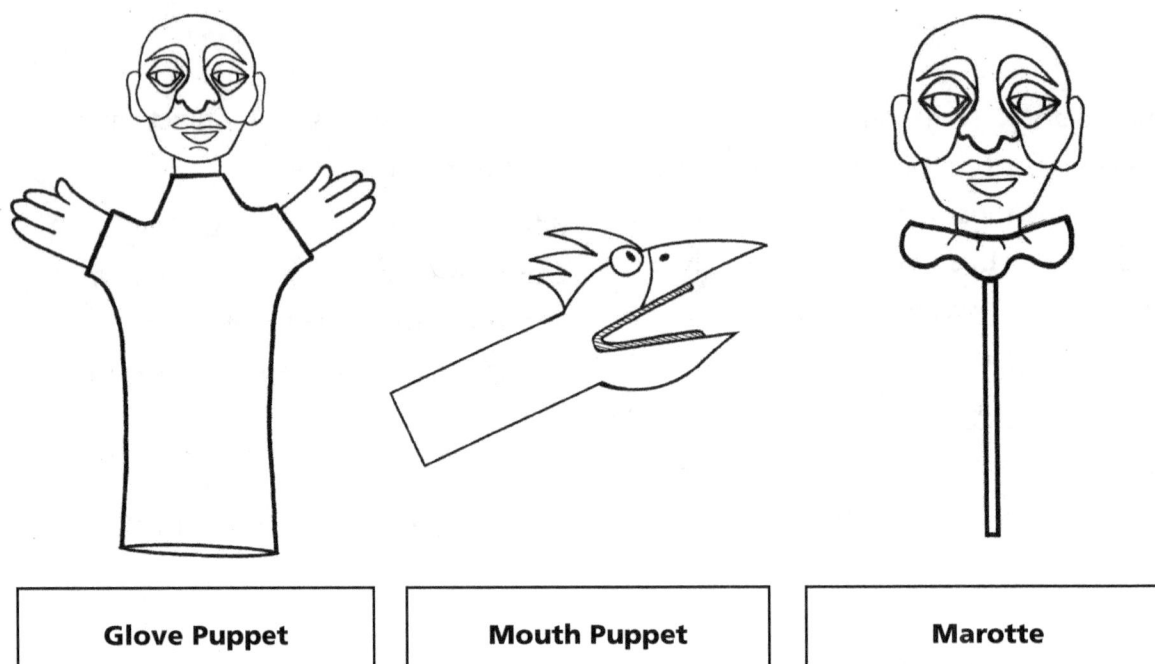

| **Glove Puppet** | **Mouth Puppet** | **Marotte** |

A glove (or hand) puppet is a puppet that is worn over the puppeteer's hand. The puppeteer may use various fingers to control the head and hands. The glove or costume covers the forearm of the puppeteer.

Glove puppets are made for dynamic action.

The puppeteer may use **2** puppets at once, one on either hand.

Like the glove puppet, the hand of the puppeteer fits inside a long sleeve that covers the arm to the elbow.

The thumb fits into and moves the lower jaw.

The other **4** fingers fit into the top part of the head.

This puppet is simply a head on a stick.

Different Kinds of Puppets in this Manual

Pop-up Puppet

Rod Puppet

Rod Marionette

The pop-up is an extension of the marotte. The rod moves up and down inside a cone. The hands are connected by a cloth attached to the head and the border of the cone.

The head is attached to a central rod. The costume is attached to the neck of the puppet and to the hands. A thinner rod is attached to each hand. The puppeteer controls the puppet by moving the hand rods in one hand and by turning the central rod secured to the head with the other hand.

The puppet is controlled from above by a central metal rod attached to the top of the head.

The hands are moved by strings attached to the top of the rod.

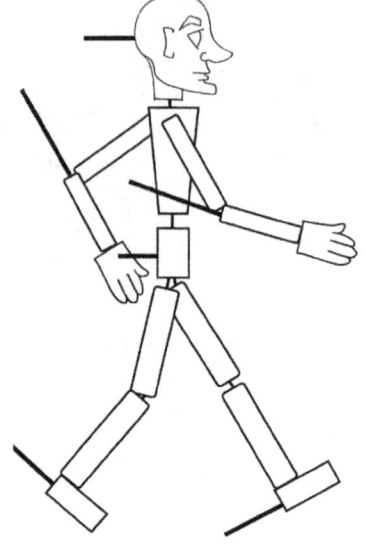

| **Marionette** | **Tabletop Puppet** | **Sandbag Puppet** |

This puppet is controlled by a number of strings attached to different parts of the body. The strings are connected to a control held above the puppet.

The puppeteer manipulates the marionette from above with the control.

The simplest marionette has **2** strings; the more complex **30** or more strings.

The puppeteer operates tabletop puppet in full view of the audience often on a table like surface.

The puppet may be operated by small horizontal rods from behind or (without rods) by direct contact with the hands of the puppeteer.

This puppet is basically a head attached to a bag of sand. It is operated by a rod attached horizontally to the back of head.

This puppet was invented by the French puppet company *Garin Trousseboeuf*.

Different Kinds of Puppets in this Manual

Humanette

Giant

A humanette consists of a small body suspended from the puppeteer's neck. The shoes of the humanette reach the playing surface. The head of the puppeteer is the head of the puppet. The hands of the puppeteer (sometimes worn with gloves) are the hands of the puppet.

Giant puppets are huge figures operated by one or more puppeteers.

Some are attached to a backpack system that is carried by the central puppeteer. The arms may be operated by the same puppeteer or carried individually by **2** other operators.

Other giants are supported by a wooden or metal frame that is carried by **1** puppeteer.

I prefer to build frame giants.

Puppets, Puppetry and Gogmagog

Glue Recipes for Paper Mache

There are many recipes for paper maché paste. These are **3** that I use.

Cellulose Wallpaper Paste

I generally use wheat or cellulose wallpaper paste in powder form. I have found it easier to buy in countries that use decorative wallpaper. I buy it from a hardware store.

I generally mix one part wallpaper paste with three parts water and stir it well with a whisk so there are no lumps. If I am making small quantities I fill a container with water, the volume of which is the amount of glue I want to end up with. I add the powder little by little until it feels thick enough. If it is too thick after **10** minutes I add a bit more water.

White Glue

This is not my favorite method because my fingers get extra sticky and it gets harder to handle the paper strips. It is also more expensive if you have to make bigger quantities.

Dilute the white glue with water; approximately **1** part glue to **2** or **3** parts water.

Cornstarch Glue

This method requires cooking so be careful. It is an economical way of making paste.

Take a cup of cornstarch and put it in a bowl (not plastic).

Add cold water; enough to make a paste. Keep adding water until you have something like pancake batter or thick cream.

Add a little less than 3 pints/1.7 liters of boiling water and stir vigorously with a whisk. The paste will turn more translucent when you add the hot water. Leave it to cool down. If you don't use it all, put it in the fridge so it won't go moldy. It will last about **3** days. You can also add some white glue to the mixture to make it more durable.

Other Glues for Other Processes

Carpenter's Glue

An aliphatic adhesive used especially for working with wood. It is safe and non toxic. Wood pieces will need to be held together under pressure (clamps or weights).

In this manual I will use this symbol for carpenter's glue.

Puppets, Puppetry and Gogmagog

Techniques, Recipes, Useful Information Before Starting

White Glue (School Glue)

A polyvinyl acetate adhesive used primarily for joining paper and wood materials. It is safe, non toxic and dries reasonably quickly (under an hour). It cleans up easily. It is not waterproof.

In this manual I will use this symbol for white glue.

Fabric or Craft Glue

I use a multipurpose adhesive for working polystyrene, plastic, wood, metal, glass, cardboard yarns, threads, beads, sequins, fabrics, or foamy material. Check the labels to see if the glue is appropriate for the material you are using. Unfortunately sometimes the glue doesn't do all it says. These adhesives are usually transparent. It is important to keep the top on the bottle when you are not using it. Use in a ventilated space.

In this manual I use this symbol for craft or fabric glue.

Epoxy

Epoxy glues are sold as two components that must be mixed to be used. They are water and solvent resistant. Bonding times vary from a few minutes to **24** hours. Some epoxies are toxic. Once the two components are mixed there is a limited time that the glue is useable. Epoxy is more expensive than other adhesives.

Use in well ventilated area; avoid contact with skin and keep away from fire or sparks.

In this manual I will use this symbol for epoxy glue.

Hot Glue

Hot glue (hot melt adhesive (HMA)) is a thermoplastic adhesive sold in cylindrical sticks. The sticks are introduced into a hot glue gun where it passes over a heating element and comes out the nozzle of the gun as a very hot liquid. It dries very quickly. Have all materials ready at hand. Be careful! Hot glue can cause burns.

In this manual I will use this symbol for hot glue.

Puppets, Puppetry and Gogmagog

Using Paper Mache

Paper mache comes from the French (papier-mâché) or "chewed paper". It occurs when paper pieces or paper pulp is bound with glue. It is a very ancient technique. Its strength comes from overlaying pieces of paper saturated with glue.

In this manual, paper mache refers to torn strips of paper. The paper is never cut with scissors because it leaves hard edges.

Newspaper has a grain. If you take several sheets of newspaper and tear from the fold downwards (with the grain) you will easily get strips.

I alternate the newspaper layers with brown craft paper. This way I am sure that each layer is complete. In the old days we saved our brown paper grocery bags. Now they are harder to find because almost every store uses plastic bags. So I buy rolls of craft paper.

Because this paper is thicker it is good to worry or scrunch the brown paper with the glue; then it can be applied easily.

Where you have larger areas to cover, use larger pieces or strips of paper; where you have corners or recesses in the molds, use smaller pieces of paper. Be patient.

The last layer is the surface you will paint, so it should be as smooth as possible (unless you want texture). I generally do all the layers at once. If I have to leave a mask during the mache process, I try to have at least **2** layers completed.

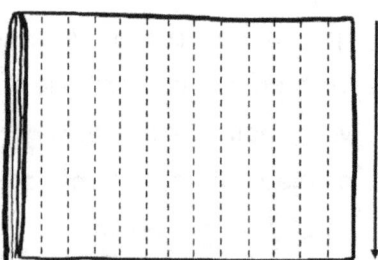 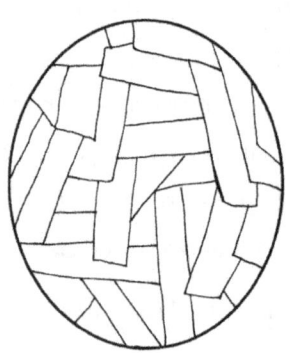

Wiring the Puppets

1

There is a tendency for the borders of paper mache to curl under when they are dry.

This wiring technique makes the borders a lot stronger and they will last for years.

I use annealed steel wire that is used for tying rebar on building sites. It is strong, flexible and economical.

Where necessary, clean out any excess petroleum jelly with a rag, paper towel or scrunched up newspaper.

2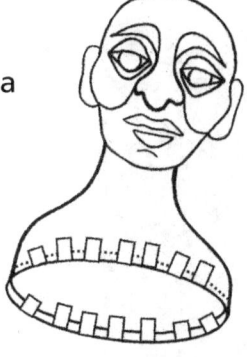

Using wire cutters cut a piece of wire a little longer than the circumference of the border of the opening.

Have ready previously cut pieces of duct tape about 2 inches/5cm long. I generally stick the ends of my pieces of duct tape to the back of a chair close to me.

Lay the wire around the inside edge of the opening and hold in place with the duct tape.

3

If you find that the duct tape is not sticking to the inside of the opening, it is because there is still a residue of petroleum jelly. Don't worry.

Over each piece of tape place a clothes pin (around the whole rim of the opening). These will keep the pieces of tape in place until you mache over them in the next step.

4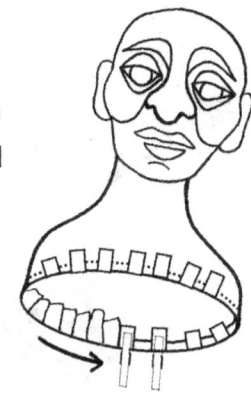

Have at hand some thin strips of newspaper and brown paper.

First mache the newspaper strips over the border of the opening, removing the clothespins as you go. It is important to completely cover the duct tape on the inside and outside of the opening.

When you have finished the first round of newspaper strips, repeat the process with the brown paper strips. Let dry.

Techniques, Recipes, Useful Information Before Starting

Puppets, Puppetry and Gogmagog

17

How to Build a Stand for Sculpting a Clay Head

Materials:

a piece of wood 12x12x1 inches/30x30x2.5cm, 1 inch/2.5cm dowel (an old broomstick will do), ¼inch/6mm dowel, a small bock of wood 4x4x2 inches/10x10x5cm, wood glue.

Tools:

drill, drill bits, wood screws.

1

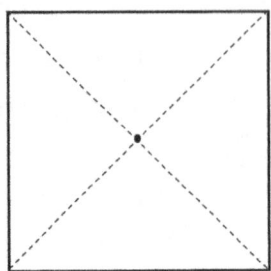

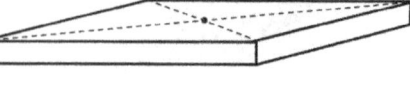

Cut a piece of wood which measures 12x12x1 inch / 30x30x2.5cm.

Find the centre point.

2

Cut a piece of broomstick, approximately 14 inches/ 35cm long.

3

Cut a small block of wood 4x4x2 inches/10x10x5cm.

Find the centre point.

Drill a hole through the centre the width of your broomstick. Check that it is a good fit.

I use this kind of drill bit for this.

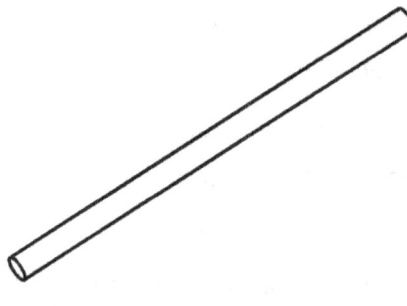

4

Glue the small block to the base with carpenters glue. Put something heavy on top until it dries.

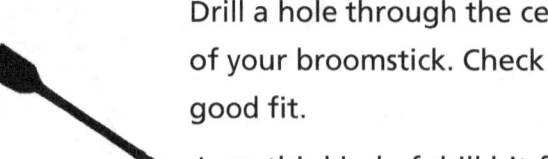

5

Drill a wood screw from the bottom of the base into the small block.

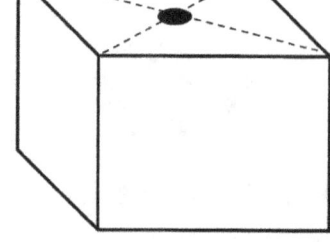

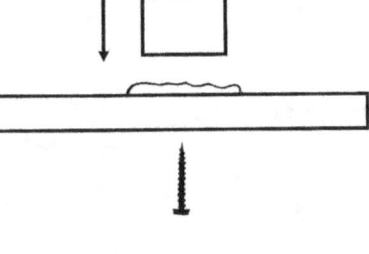

Drill **2** holes (the size of a smaller dowel) in the top of the pole. The first about 1 inch/2.5cm from the top and the second ½ inch/13mm lower and in the opposite direction.

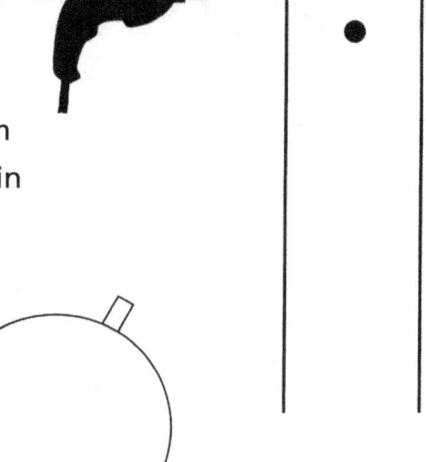

Fit **2** smaller dowels into and through the holes in the pole, gluing them into place.

Bird's eye view.

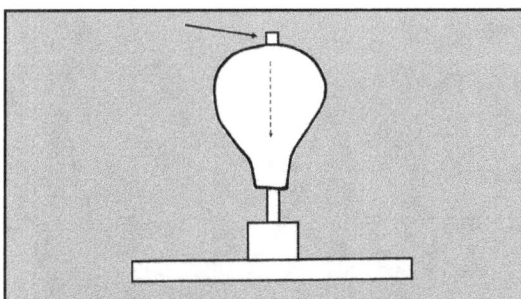

The smaller dowels prevent the clay slipping down an otherwise smooth pole. This can happen sometimes when the heads are large.

Put some glue on the bottom of the pole and force it into the hole in the small block. Let dry.

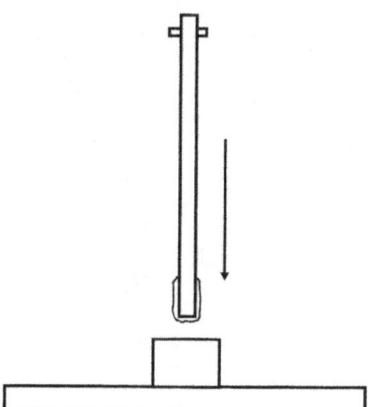

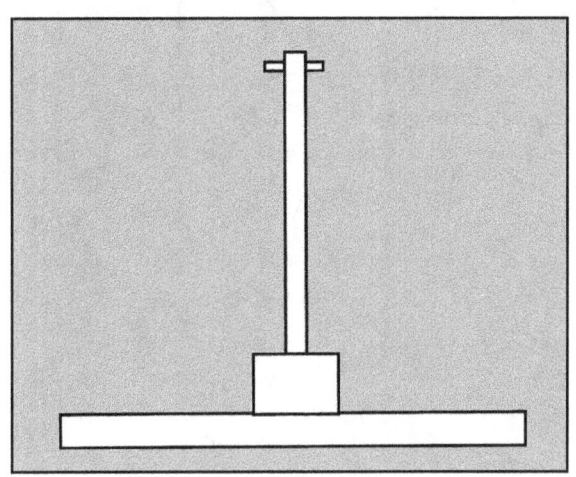

Puppets, Puppetry and Gogmagog

Basic Proportions of a Puppet Head

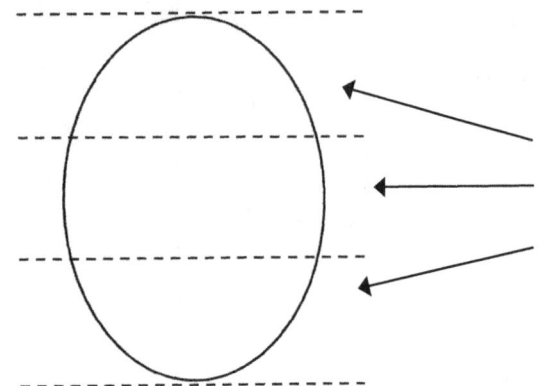

The face is divided horizontally into **3** equal parts.

Hairline to eyebrow.

Eyebrow to tip of nose.

Tip of nose to chin.

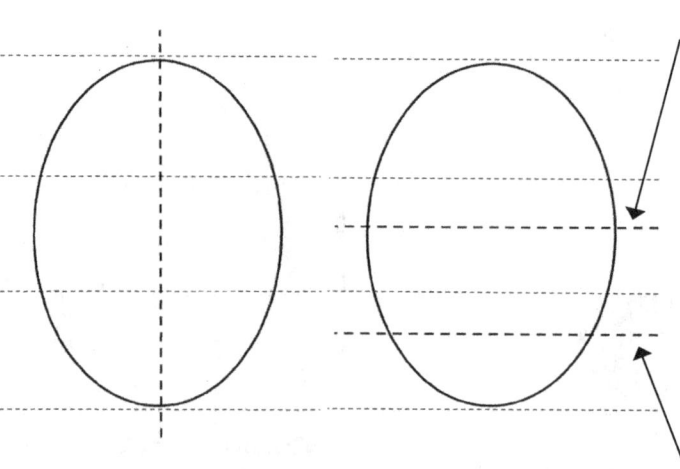

The face is divided vertically into **2** equal parts. This will give you a guideline for the nose.

The eyes generally lie a little higher than halfway in the middle third of the face.

The middle of the mouth generally lies a little higher than halfway in the bottom third of the face.

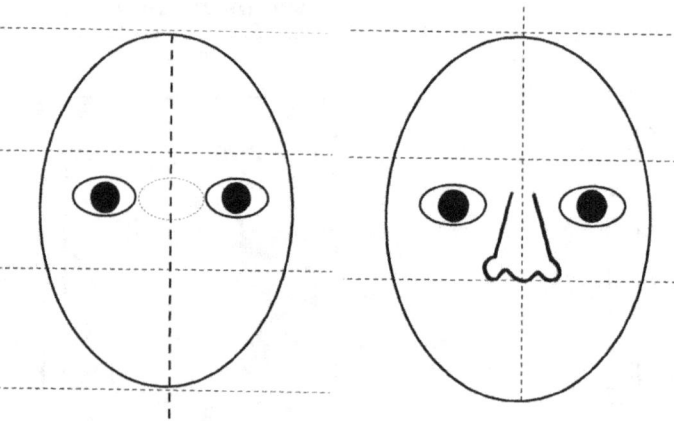

Placement of eyes. Generally spaced one eye width apart.

Placement of nose. The nose begins between the eyes and ends where the lower third of the face begins.

20

Puppets, Puppetry and Gogmagog

Techniques, Recipes, Useful Information Before Starting

Ear lies from mid eye to top of lip. Lobe may reach middle of lip line.

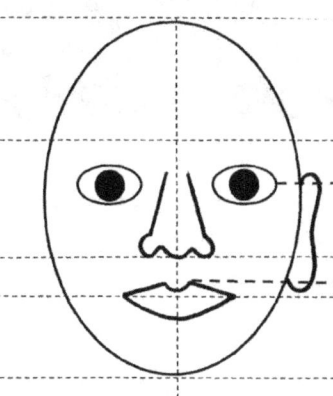

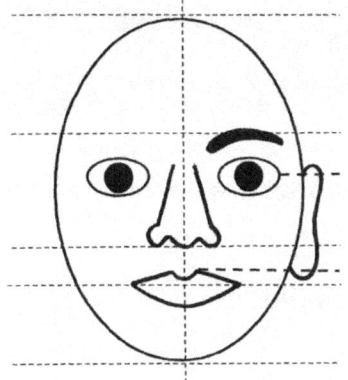

Eyebrows are positioned at the top of the middle section of the face.

This is more or less an "average" face. Good proportions for puppet faces that are not so exaggerated.

However it is good to **EXAGGERATE!**

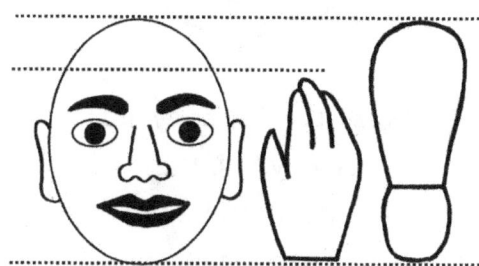

The size of the hand is more or less from the chin to the middle of the forehead.

The foot is more or less the height of the head.

It is often better to make the hands and feet of a puppet bigger.

Experiment.

The head is approximately 1/5 of the height of the puppet. These are "normal" proportions.

Break the rules if you like!

Puppets, Puppetry and Gogmagog

21

Eyes, Eyelids and Pupils

The eyes of a puppet are very important. Nearly always they must be seen from a distance. I prefer to exaggerate the size.

Here are some eyelids to consider.

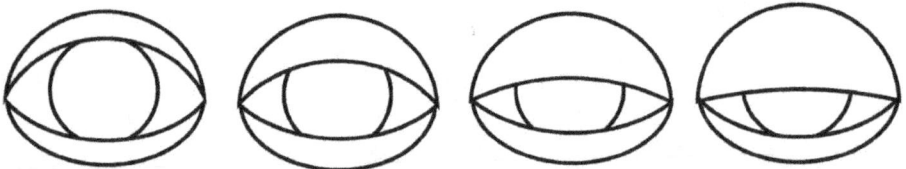

The upper eyelid. The larger and heavier it is, the more drowsy the effect.

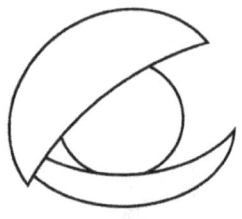 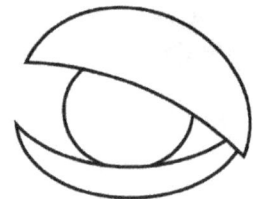 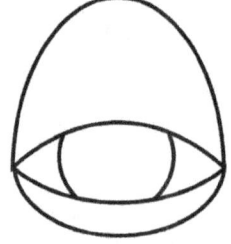

If the upper eyelid slopes towards the outside of the eye, the puppet will seem drowsy or dreamy, even a little lazy.

If the upper eyelid slopes towards the inside of the eye, a more malicious effect will be created.

If the upper eyelid is very tall, the effect can be one of superiority, or disdain.

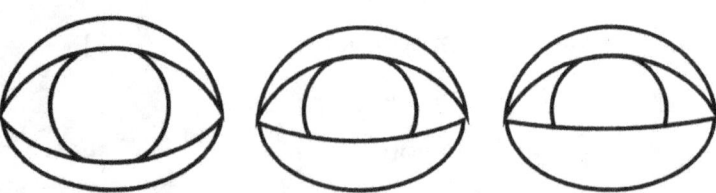

The lower eyelid. The larger it is, and the more it covers the eyeball, the more timorous the effect. It can be seen to be crying.

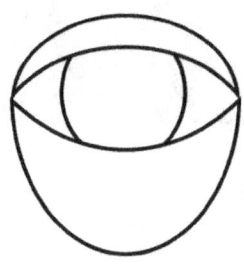 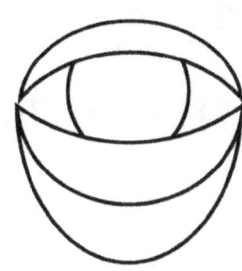 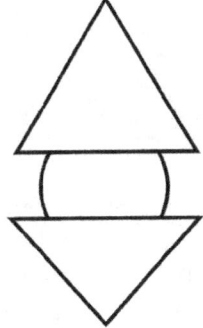 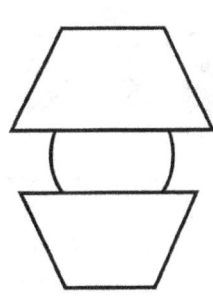

Try bags under the eyes for a tired and older effect.

Try a double bag.

Here are geometric shaped upper and lower eyelids.

The Pupils

The size of the pupils gives a lot of information. Tiny pupils give a feeling of shock, of fright. The larger pupils give a dreamy feeling. Experiment later on at the painting stage.

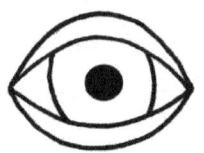 

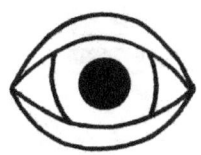 

Another Way of Creating Eyes

I keep a collection of wooden balls of different sizes. Some of them already have holes drilled in them.

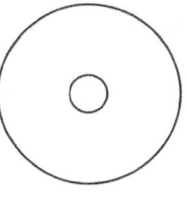

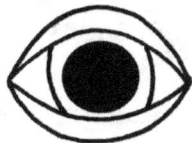 

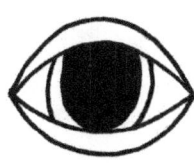

Puppets, Puppetry and Gogmagog

Geometric Shapes of Heads

The Geometric Shapes	Features Placed Evenly According to the Principles of Face Proportions	Features Concentrated in Lower Part of Face	Features Concentrated in Upper Part of Face	Features Placed Freely
○				
○				
○				
○				

24

Puppets, Puppetry and Gogmagog

Techniques, Recipes, Useful Information Before Starting

The Geometric Shapes	Features Placed Evenly According to the Principles of Face Proportions	Features Concentrated in Lower Part of Face	Features Concentrated in Upper Part of Face	Features Placed Freely
(oval)				
(triangle pointing up)				
(triangle pointing down)				
(square)				

PLAY AROUND! EXPERIMENT! INVENT!

Puppets, Puppetry and Gogmagog

25

Warning:
some of the steps include the use of tools and materials that have the potential to cause damage to property and/or bodily injury. Your safety is important and it is your sole responsibility.

These puppets are made of simple household materials. They are quick to make and easy to manipulate; a good place to start.

Paper and Cardboard Puppets

This fish can be made from a cardboard box. It moves simply and undulates. It can be made quite small or much larger for use in an outdoor procession.

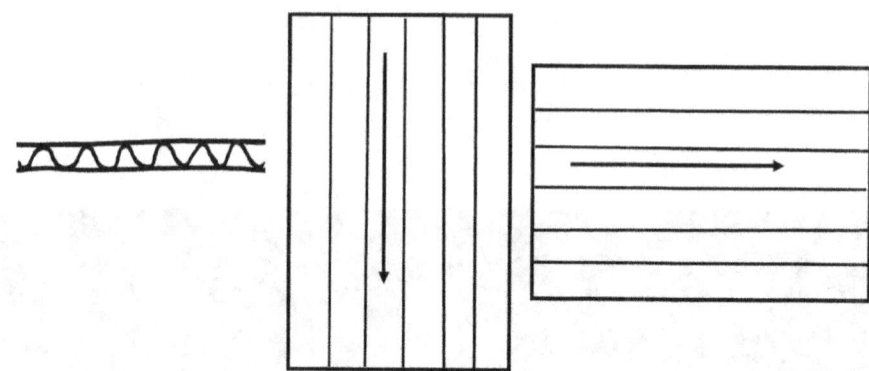

This fish puppet is made with corrugated cardboard.

Corrugated cardboard has flutes or "tunnels" that run in one direction.

You should always take into consideration which way you want the flutes to run; vertically or horizontally.

For the fish puppet I used single corrugated cardboard and place the template with the flutes running **vertically**.

Materials:
1 corrugated cardboard box, a pencil or magic marker, hot glue sticks, kebab sticks, duct tape, newspaper, brown paper, paper mache glue, acrylic paints.

Tools:
scissors, utility knife, hot glue gun, paint brushes.

1 To make the template, start with an oval shape and then draw the features around it.

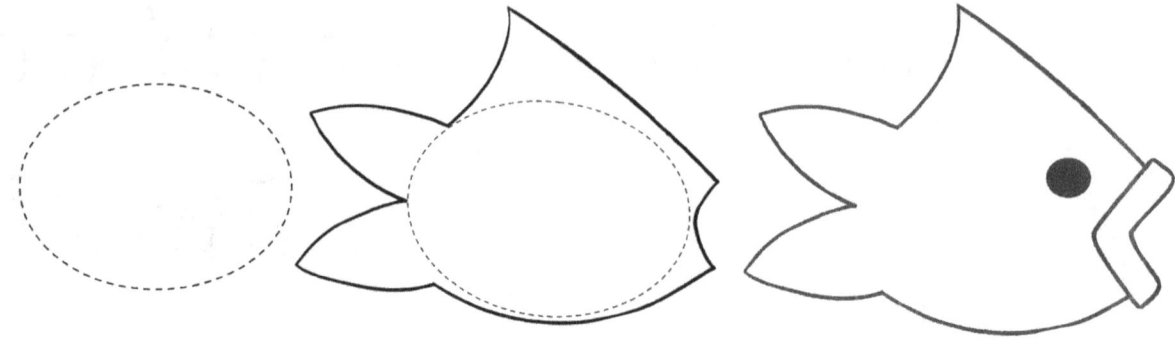

Puppets, Puppetry and Gogmagog

Here are some fish shapes to think about

Cardboard Fish

Place the corrugated cardboard with the flutes running vertically.

Draw your fish shape.

Cut out with scissors.

You can also use a utility knife.

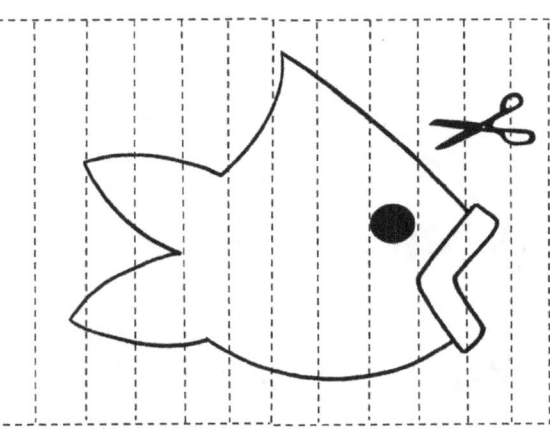

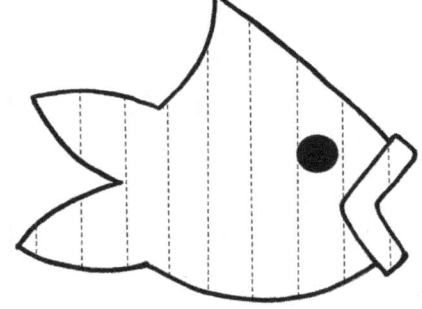

Puppets, Puppetry and Gogmagog   Paper and Cardboard Puppets

3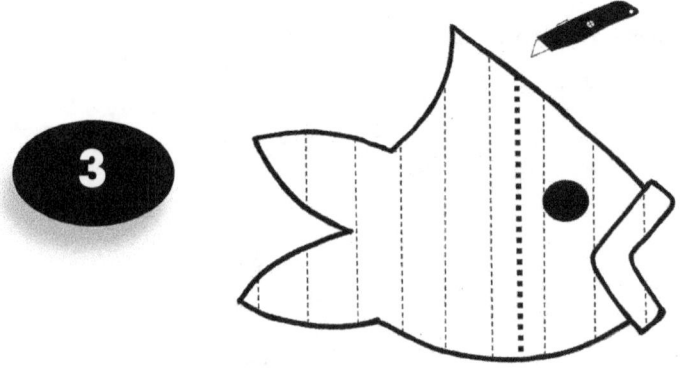

Lightly score a vertical line on the cardboard just behind where the eye might be painted later on.

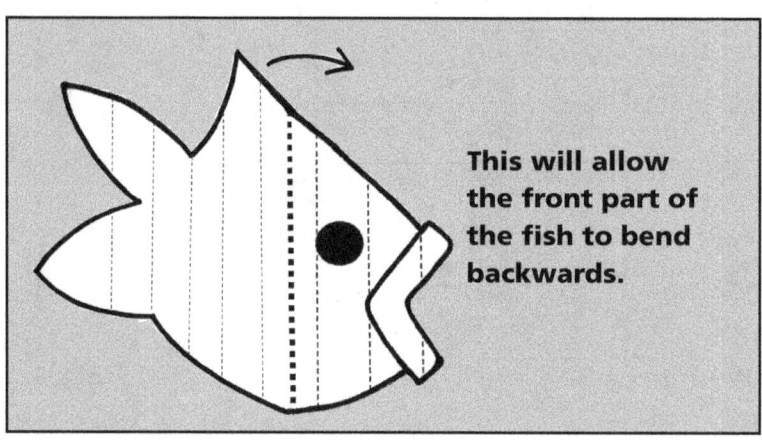

This will allow the front part of the fish to bend backwards.

4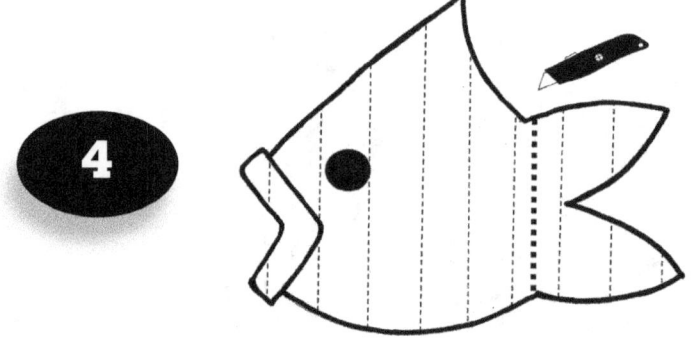

Turn the fish over.

Lightly score another vertical line just in front of the tail.

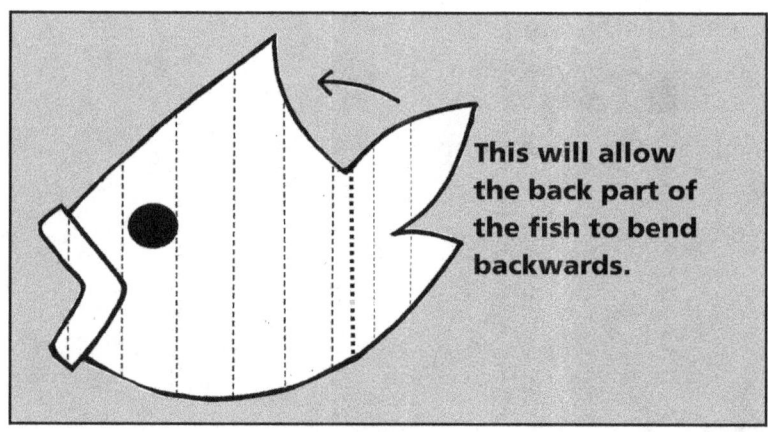

This will allow the back part of the fish to bend backwards.

5

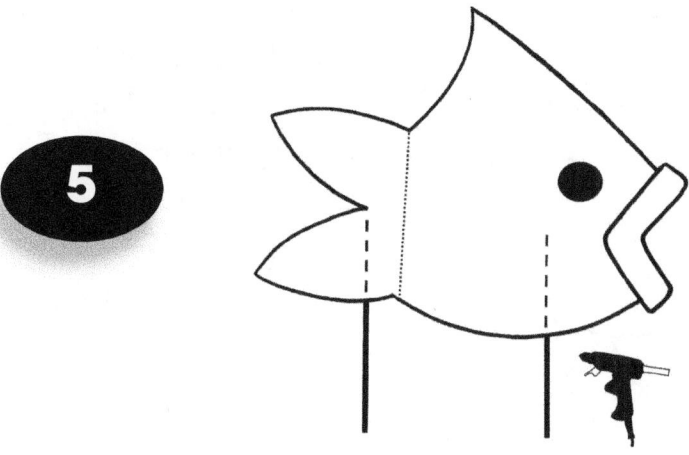

If the fish is small, insert **2** dowels into the vertical flutes near the front and back of the fish as shown.

These dowels are the controls for moving the fish.

Glue them in with hot glue.

Be careful; hot glue can cause burns.

Variation

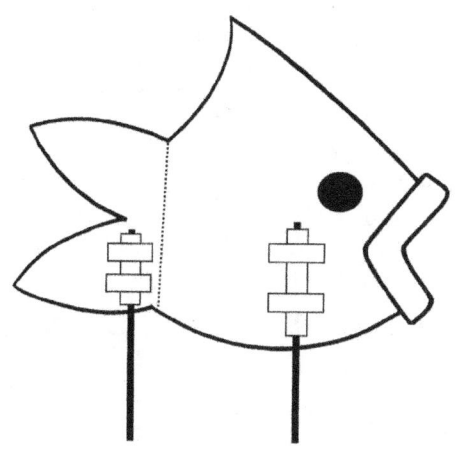

If the fish is bigger and the flutes are too small for the dowels you want to use, duct tape the dowels securely on to one side of the fish.

Apply **2** layers of paper mache (**1** newspaper, **1** brown) over the taped areas.

Let dry.

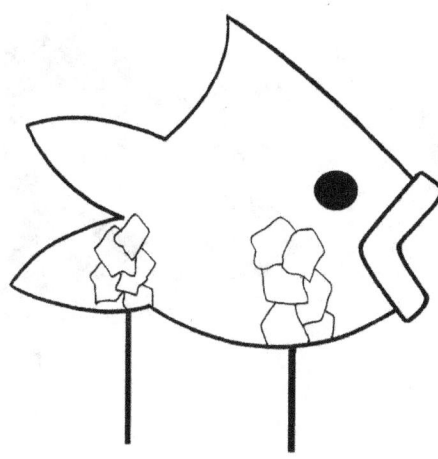

Cardboard Fish

Puppets, Puppetry and Gogmagog   Paper and Cardboard Puppets   **31**

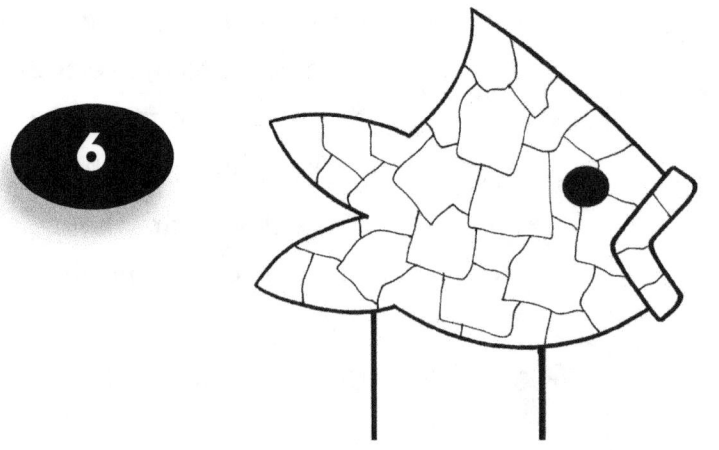

If you have the time and want to make the fish stronger, apply **1** layer of brown paper mache over the fish, front and back.

Let dry.

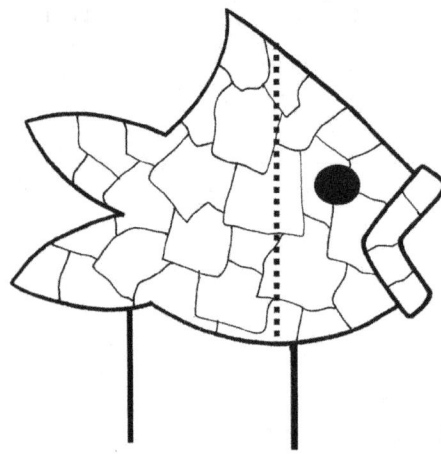

Don't apply too much mache over the score lines. You still want your fish to to be able to undulate.

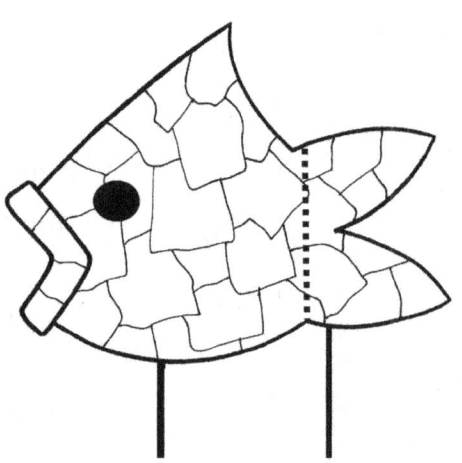

Paint your fish front and back.

Apply a white base coat first.

Variation

Follow steps **1** and **2** of the previous fish.

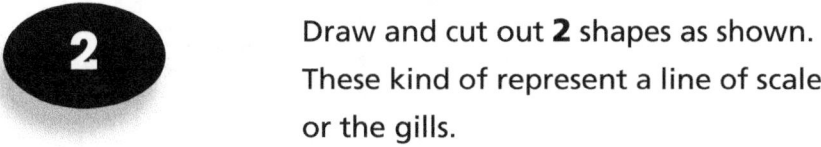

Draw and cut out **2** shapes as shown. These kind of represent a line of scales or the gills.

Glue with white glue or hot glue **2** pieces of light cloth over the openings.

The colour of the cloth would depend on the colours you wish to paint the fish afterwards.

If you use hot glue, be careful. Hot glue can cause burns.

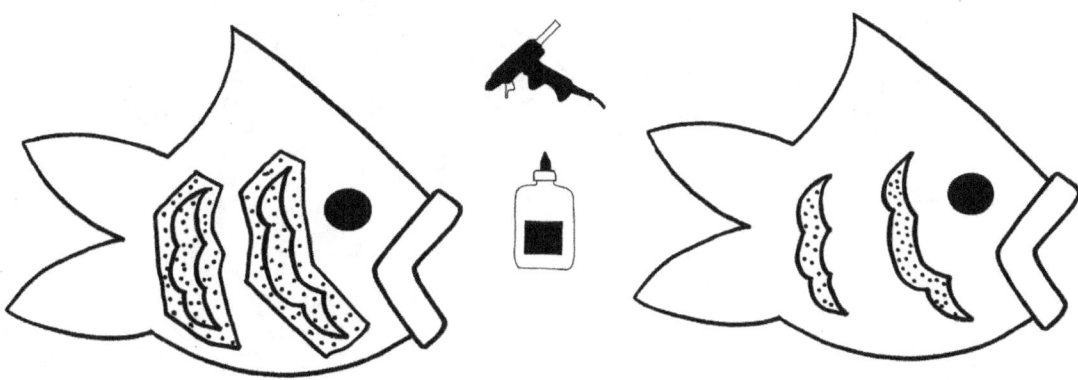

Cardboard Fish

4 Duct tape the dowel control sticks onto the fish. Don't cover the cloth insets.

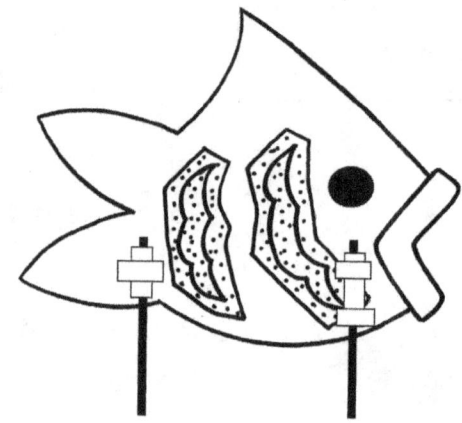

5 Apply **2** layers of paper mache (**1** newspaper, **1** brown) over the tape, covering it completely.

Let dry.

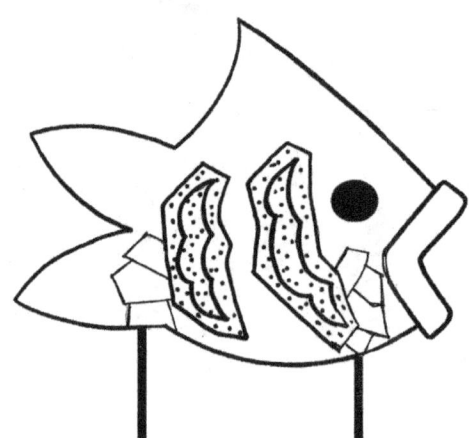

6 If you have the time and want to make the fish stronger, apply **1** layer of brown paper over the fish, front and back.

Do not cover the cloth insets.

Let dry.

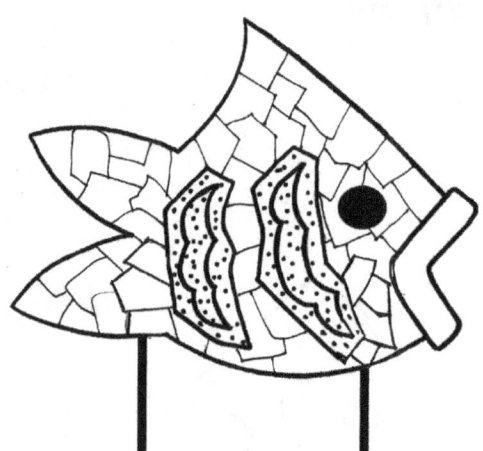

Paint your fish front and back.

Apply a white base coat first.

Cardboard Fish

| **Gallery of Possibilities** |

Puppets, Puppetry and Gogmagog — Paper and Cardboard Puppets

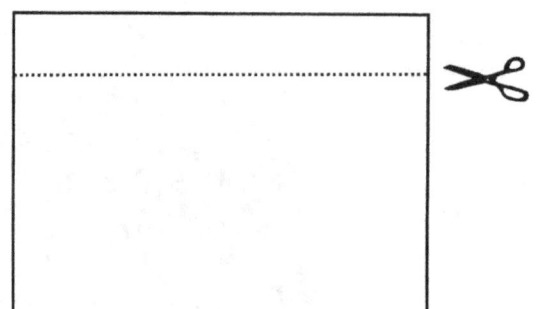 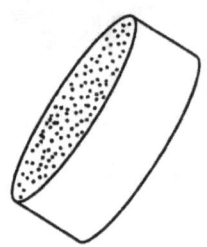

The paper bag puppet is made directly over your own hand. It is helpful to work with a partner.

Materials:

cardboard, pencil or magic marker, a small paper bag that fits over your hand, masking tape, newspaper, brown paper, paper mache glue, acrylic paints.

Tools:

scissors, stapler, paint brushes.

1 Make the cuff. Cut a strip of cardboard about 1 ½inches/38mm wide and long enough to go around the widest part of your hand.

Staple and/or tape it into circle.

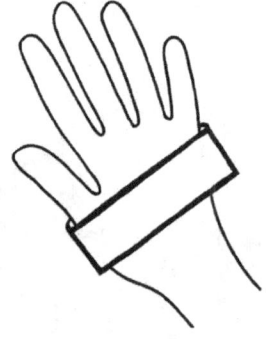

Be sure you can slip your hand in and out of the cuff.

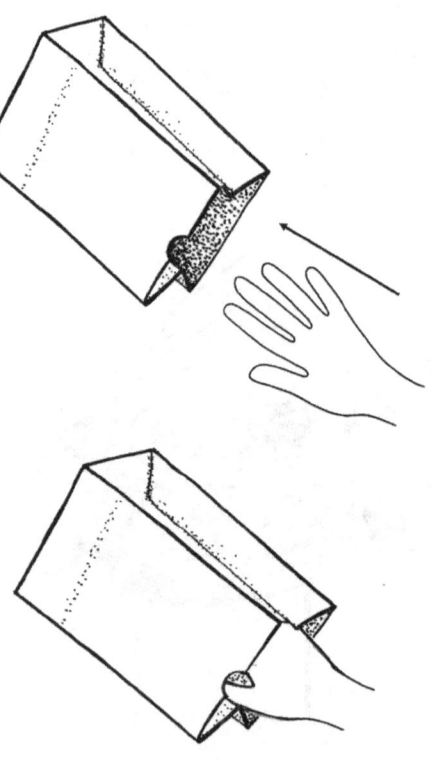

2 Slip your hand into a small brown paper bag.

Puppets, Puppetry and Gogmagog

3 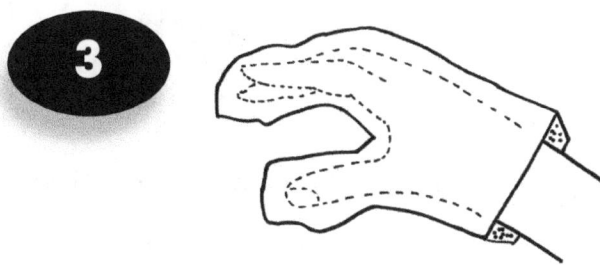 Work the bag around you hand, scrunching the paper around your thumb and then around the other **4** fingers.

4 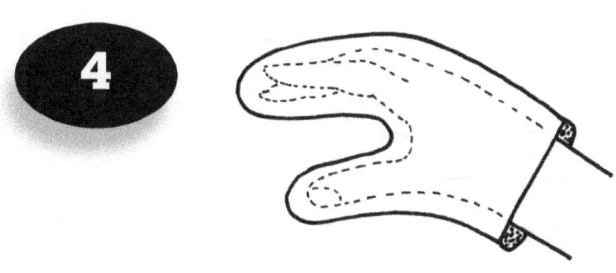 Try to smooth the paper around the thumb area and separately around the rest of the fingers.

It will look rougher than the illustration.

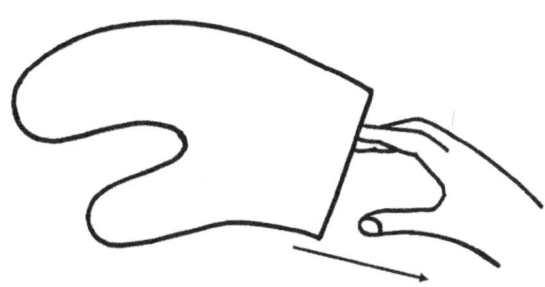 **5** Gently take your hand out.

6 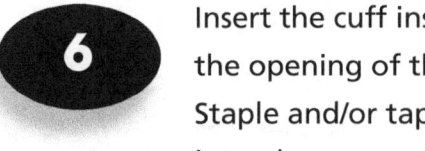 Insert the cuff inside the opening of the bag. Staple and/or tape it into place.

The bag itself will probably open up a bit. Don't worry.

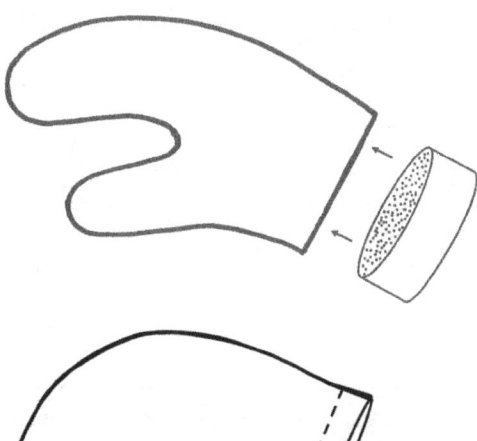

Paper Bag puppet

Paper and Cardboard Puppets

37

Puppets, Puppetry and Gogmagog

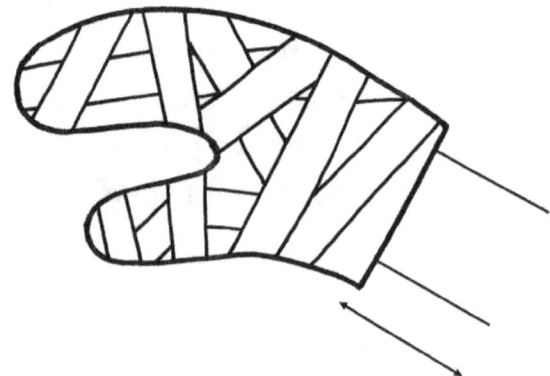

Tape the bag loosely around your hand.

Check that you can still move your hand in and out of the bag.

Have strips of newspaper and brown paper and the paper mache paste already at hand.

Apply **2** layers of paper mache (**1** newspaper, **1** brown) over the glove/bag.

If you cannot do this yourself, have someone help you.

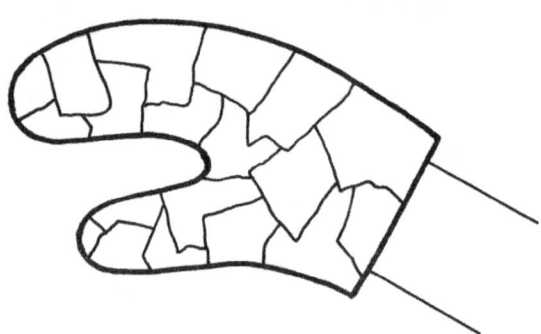

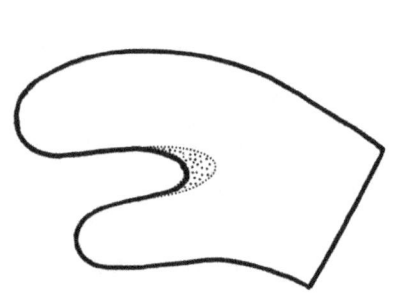 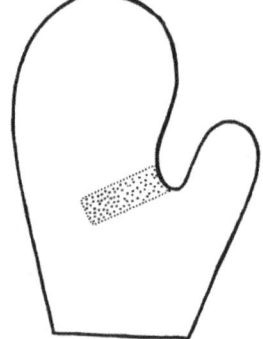 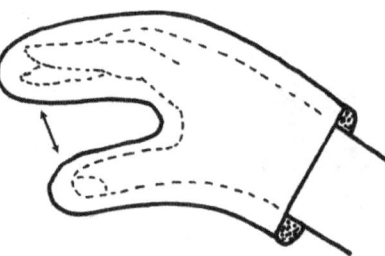

Do not put too much mache around the shaded areas indicated in the illustrations.

When dry you will be able to open and close your hand a little.

Puppets, Puppetry and Gogmagog

 When you have finished with the paper mache process, very gently extract your hand from the mached bag.

The bag may collapse a little or even tear. Don't worry.

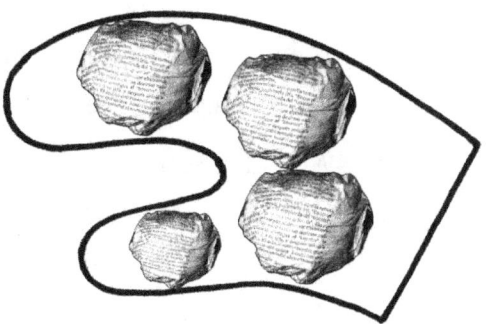

 Have some small balls of newspaper at hand and gently introduce them into the wet mached glove.

Let dry. Remove the balls of newspaper from the inside.

 Paint your puppet.

Paint a white undercoat first.

Paper Bag Puppet

Gallery of Possibilities

They jiggle and they jangle. Their hips move from side to side. A cardboard puppet that is very easy to manipulate.

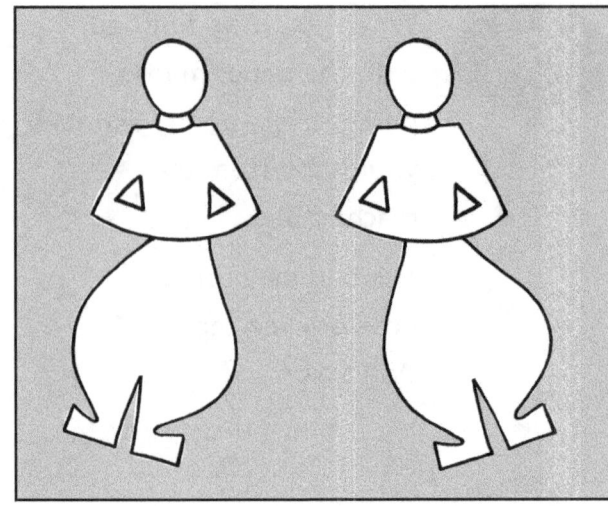

The jigglers are puppets made in **2** parts. They can be made from heavy paper or light cardboard, such as cereal box cardboard.

When the control at the back of the head is lightly twisted, the bottom part of the puppet swings from side to side.

Materials:

cardboard (cereal box weight), a flexible drinking straw, masking tape, magic markers or coloured pencils or paints, a small metal washer, string.

Tools:

scissors.

1 Cut **2** shapes similar to the illustrations. Later you can invent your own body parts.

Note that the waist of the trousers should be narrower than the base of the head and torso part.

2 Paint or color each part.

You may want to simply go through the process of construction and then make another one which you will colour in at this stage. It is easier to colour now than later on when the puppet is assembled.

Puppets, Puppetry and Gogmagog

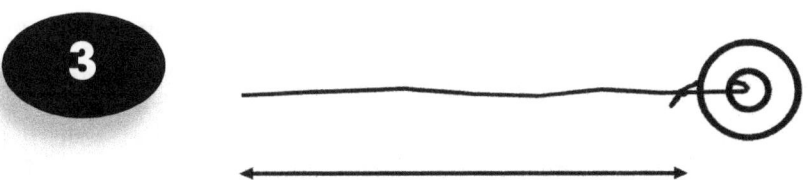

Attach a piece of string approximately 18inches/45.5cm long to a small washer.

The washer functions as a weight and helps with the movement of the puppet.

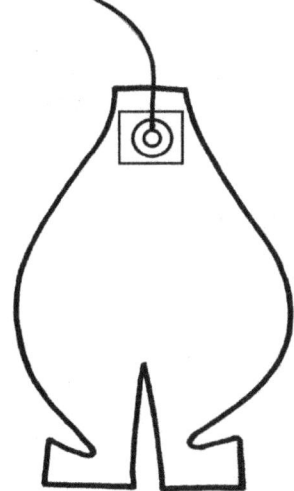

Tape the washer firmly to the back of the trousers, close to the waist line.

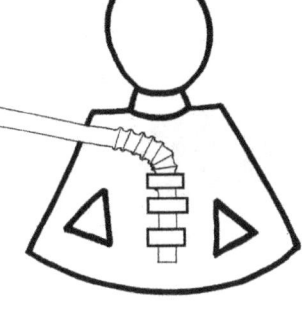

Tape a flexible straw to the back of the head/torso; just above the waistline.

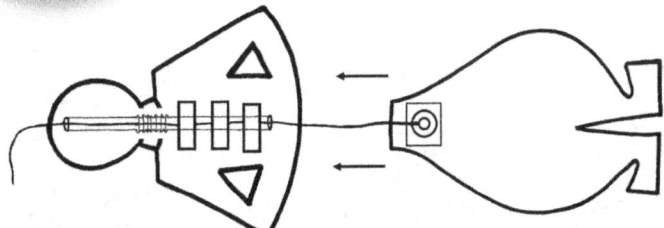

Thread the string through the straw as shown.

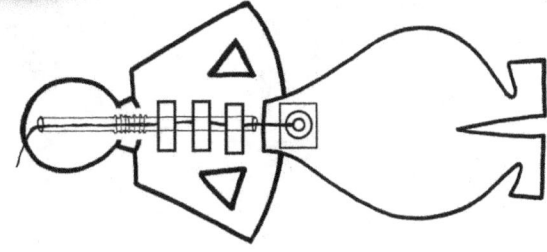

Pull the string gently until the trouser part is sitting on top of the bottom part of the torso. Leave a small space between the top of the trouser and the bottom of the straw. This allows for the movement of the puppet later on.

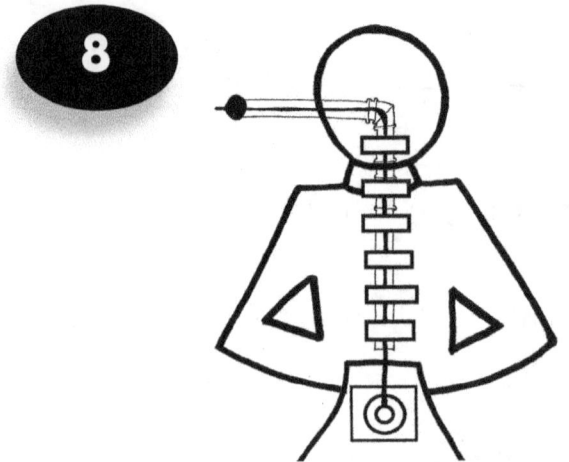

8

Stretch the straw up towards the head. Tape it firmly in place.

Bend the straw at a right angle. This creates your control.

Tie a big knot at the end of the straw; pulling the string taught but keeping the space open between the top of the trousers and the bottom of the straw.

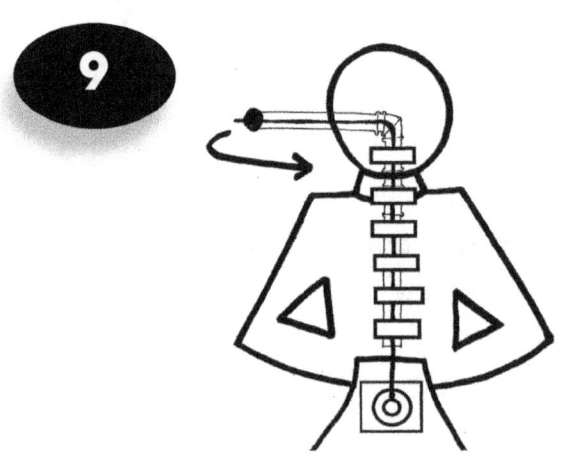

9

Twist the straw perpendicular to the back of the head.

Voilá.

Gallery of Possibilities

42

Puppets, Puppetry and Gogmagog

Variation: Jiggler with 3 Dimensional Head

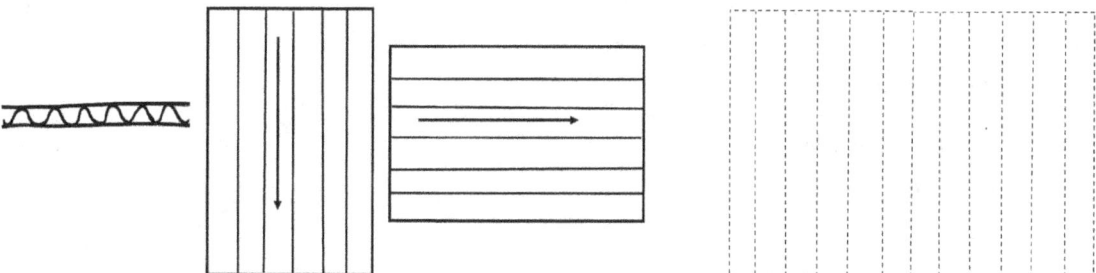

Additional materials: a package of air dry clay, **1** plastic egg.

The **2** body parts for this puppet are made of corrugated cardboard.

Corrugated cardboard has flutes or "tunnels" that run in one direction.

You should always take into consideration which way you want the flutes to run; vertically or horizontally.

For this puppet I use single corrugated cardboard and place the template with the flutes running **vertically**.

1 Draw and cut out with scissors or utility knife the torso of the puppet.

2 Draw and cut out with scissors or utility knife the legs of the puppet.

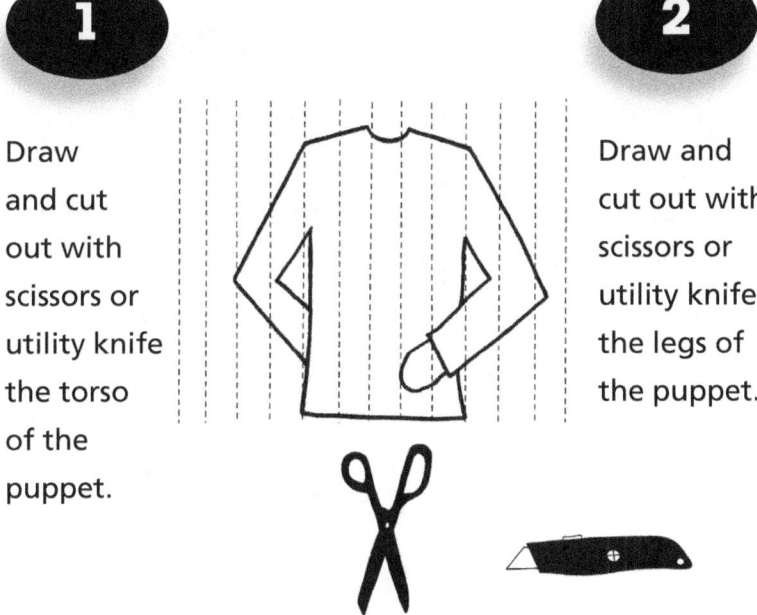
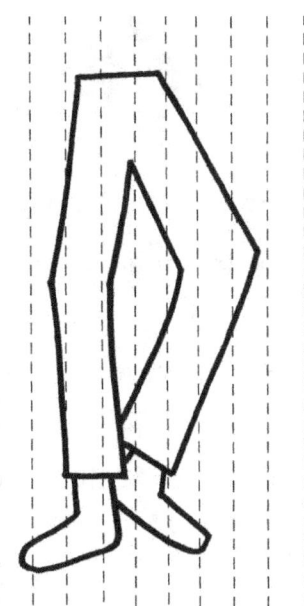

Puppets, Puppetry and Gogmagog   Paper and Cardboard Puppets

Mache over a plastic egg with a good layer of brown paper and wallpaper paste.

The size of the egg should be in proportion (or a little larger) to the cardboard torso and pants.

Let dry.

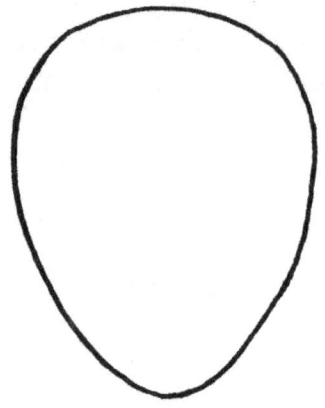 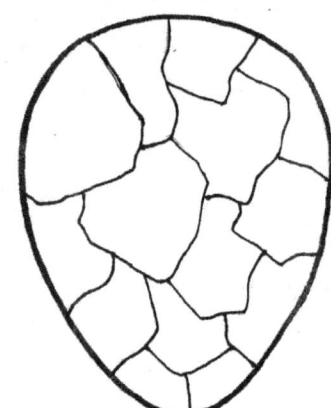

4

Take a small quantity of air dry clay and knead it a little.

See page **132** for more information about air dry clay.

Create the features of the face over the dry mached egg.

5

Paint the head once it is dry.

Paint an undercoat of white first.

This is also a good time to paint the cardboard torso and legs.

It is more difficult to paint after the puppet has been assembled.

6

Thread a long upholstery needle with a good amount of string.

Tie a big knot at the end.

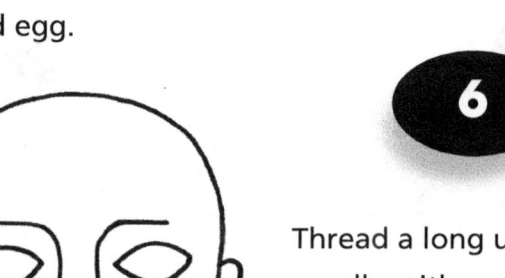
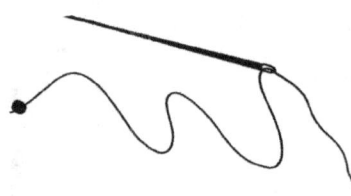

Puppets, Puppetry and Gogmagog

Lay the legs face down on a table.

Insert the needle into the cardboard, and along the central flute of the corrugated cardboard.

The needle should not pass through to the other side of the cardboard.

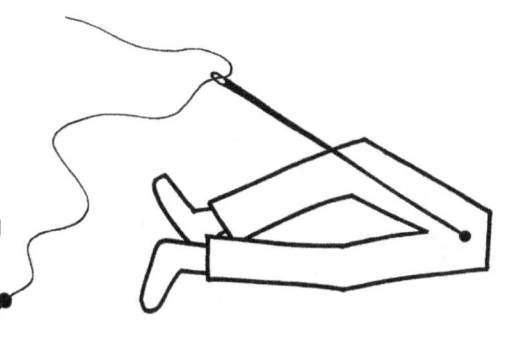

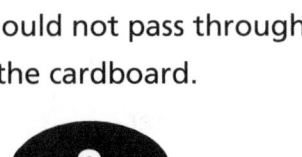

Push the needle until it comes out of the flute and pull the string through until the knot stops at the top of the legs.

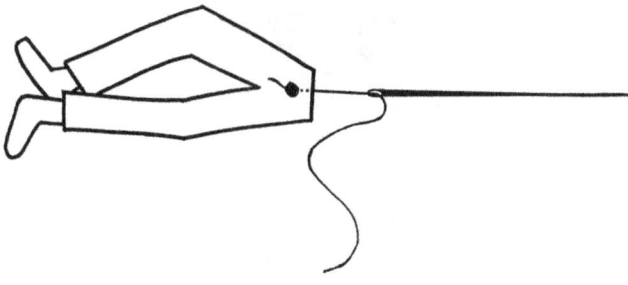

Leave a small gap and make another knot as shown.

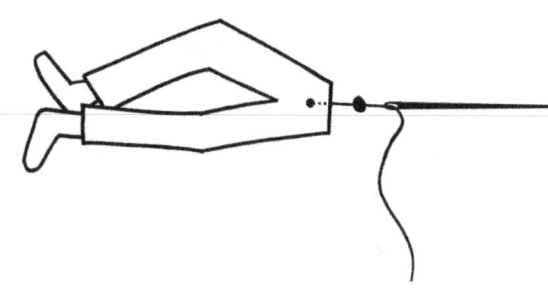

Place the torso face down on the table in line with the legs.

Introduce the needle more or less at a midpoint of the waistline as shown. The needle should not pass through to the other side of the cardboard.

Push the needle along the central flute of the corrugated cardboard until it emerges from the middle of the neckline.

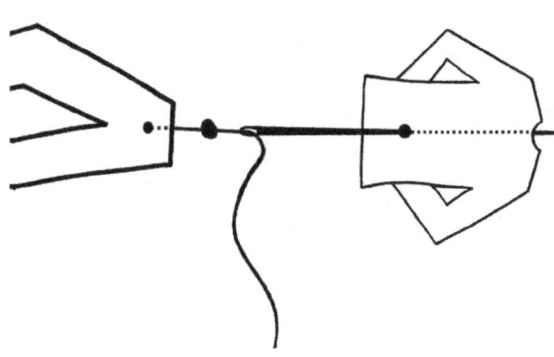

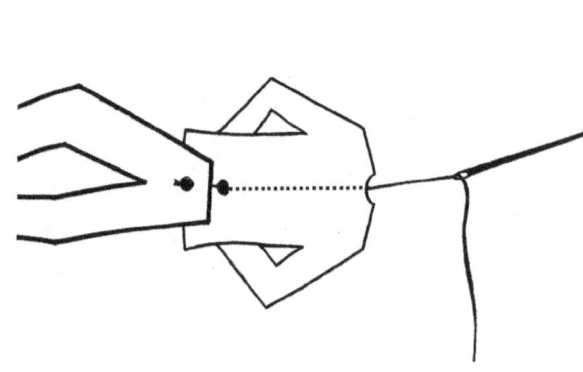

Pull the needle out and pull the string gently until the leg part is lying on top of the torso.

The second knot will stop it going any further.

Lay the head sideways as shown in line with the rest of the body.

Mark **2** points (top and bottom) on the head as shown with a marker. Use the needle to make holes at each point marked. You can make them bigger with a sharp nail.

Push the needle into the point marked at the bottom of the head.

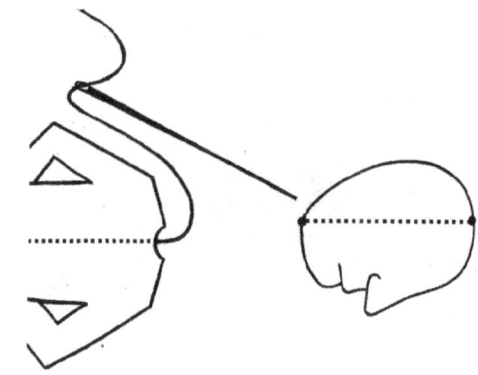

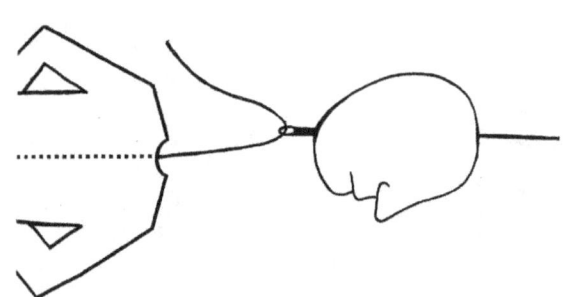

Keep pushing the needle toward the top of the head and through the hole at the top of the head. Pull the string until the head is close to the neckline of the torso.

46

Puppets, Puppetry and Gogmagog

14

Once the head is close to the neck line, tie a large knot at the top of the head.

15

Hot glue a thin dowel into the back of the head as a control.

The dowel should enter the head about 1 inch/2.5cm.

Be careful. Hot glue can cause burns.

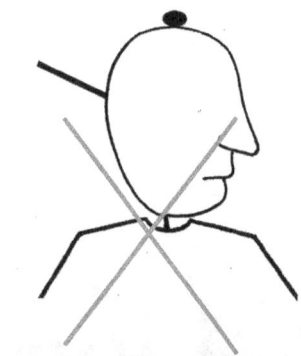

Be careful the control stick is not angled upwards.

16

Add hair or a hat to the top of the head to cover the large knot.

This is a more complex puppet with a turning head and arms that can be manipulated using small sticks as controls.

Materials:

cardboard, masking tape, pencil or marker, newspaper, brown paper, paper mache glue, a short piece of coloured ribbon, string, kebab sticks or short dowels, hot glue sticks, acrylic paints.

Tools:

scissors, utility knife, stapler, hot glue gun, upholstery needle, paint brushes.

1 Cut a large half circle of cardboard. The radius should be at least 7 inches/18cm.

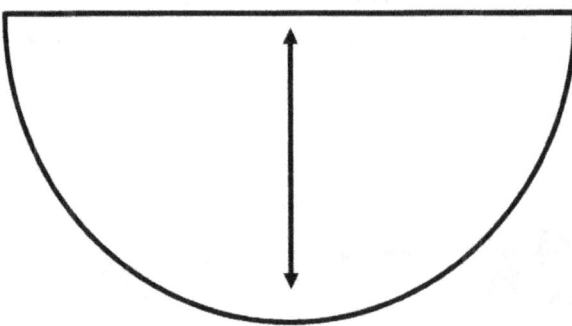

2 Create a cone as shown in the illustration and tape it securely.

For this puppet it is better to have a taller, thinner cone.

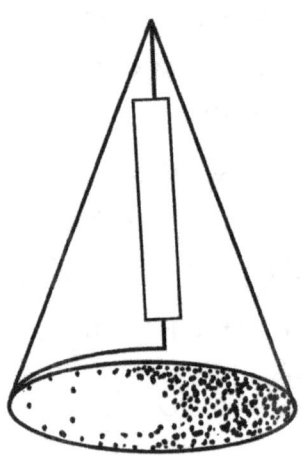

3 To make the cone stronger, apply **2** layers of paper mache (**1** newspaper, **1** brown) over the cone and around the border of the opening.

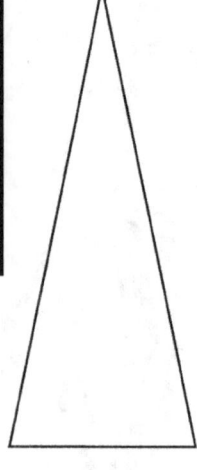
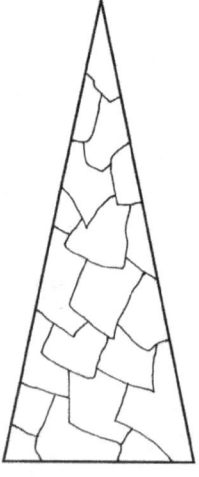

48

Puppets, Puppetry and Gogmagog

4

Mark a circle around the cone, a little higher than halfway up.

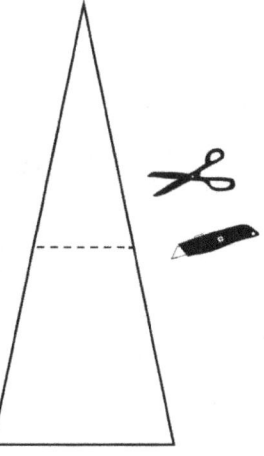

5

Cut along the marked line with scissors or utility knife.

The cone is now is **2** pieces; the head and the base.

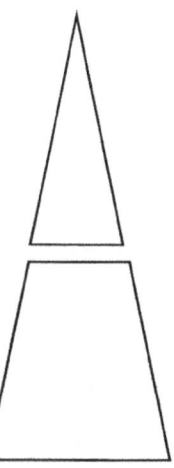

6

Cover the top of the base of the cone with masking tape.

Bird's eye view.

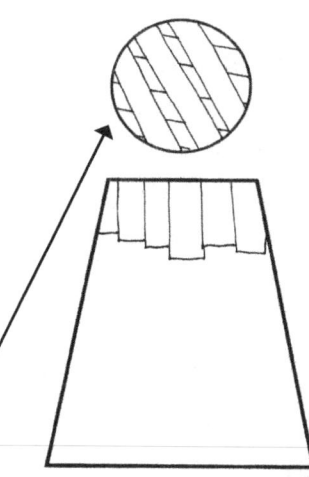

7

Apply **2** layers of paper mache (**1** newspaper, **1** brown) over the tape.

Let dry.

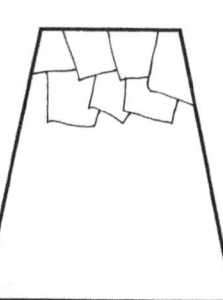

8

Cover the bottom opening of the top half of the cone with masking tape.

Bird's eye view.

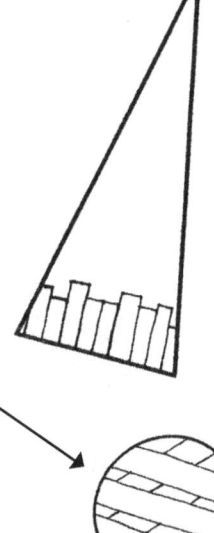

9

Apply **2** layers of paper mache (**1** newspaper, **1** brown) over the tape.

Let dry.

Cone Puppet

There are now 2 mached parts.

10 Mark a circle around the cone, a little higher than halfway up. The bottom part will form the head of the puppet.

11 Cut along the marked line with scissors or utility knife.

12 Cover the top opening of the head with masking tape.

Bird's eye view.

13 Apply **2** layers of paper mache (**1** newspaper, **1** brown) over the tape.

Let dry.

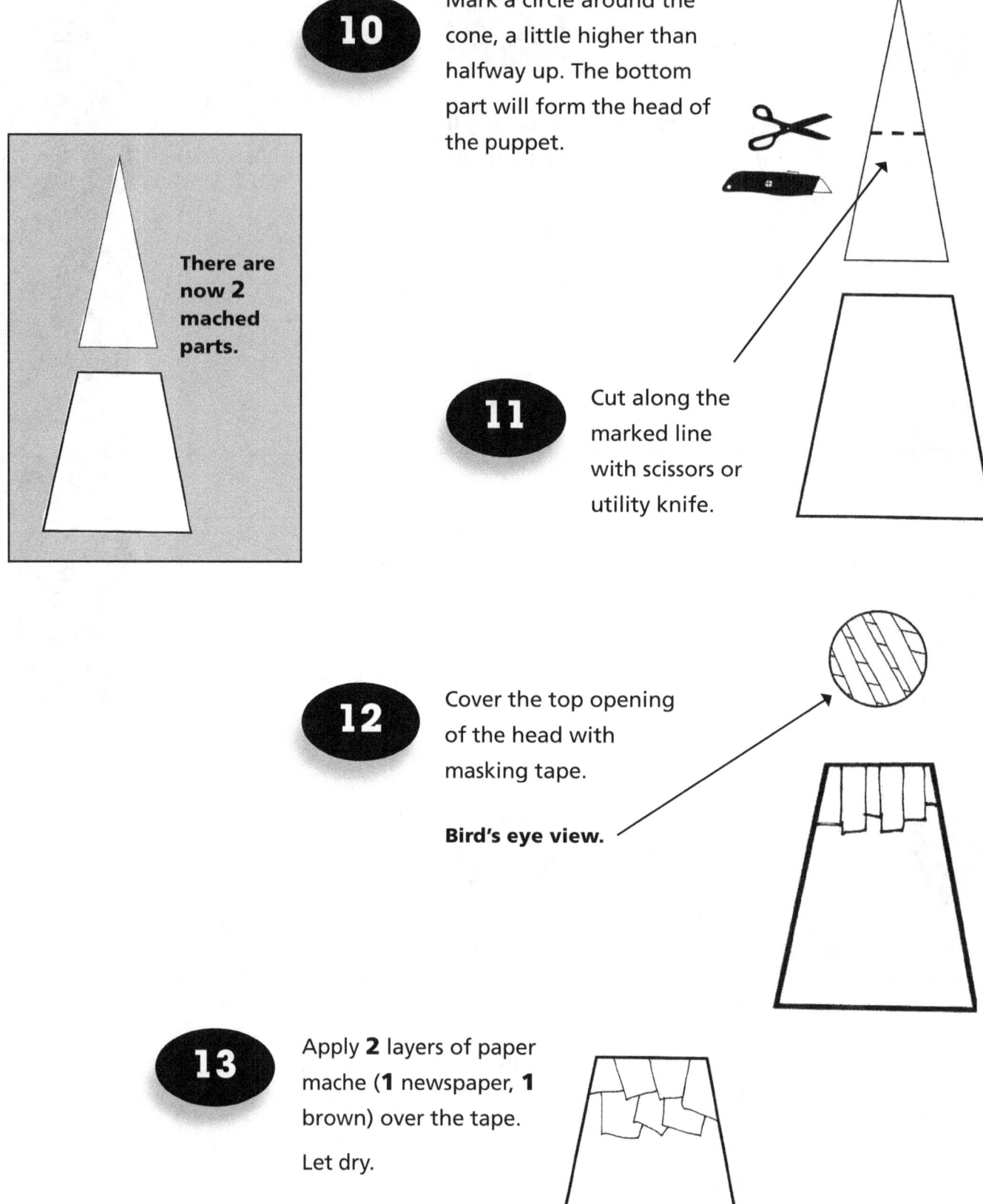

Puppets, Puppetry and Gogmagog

Cone Puppet

Paint the head and body of the puppet.

Paint an undercoat of white first.

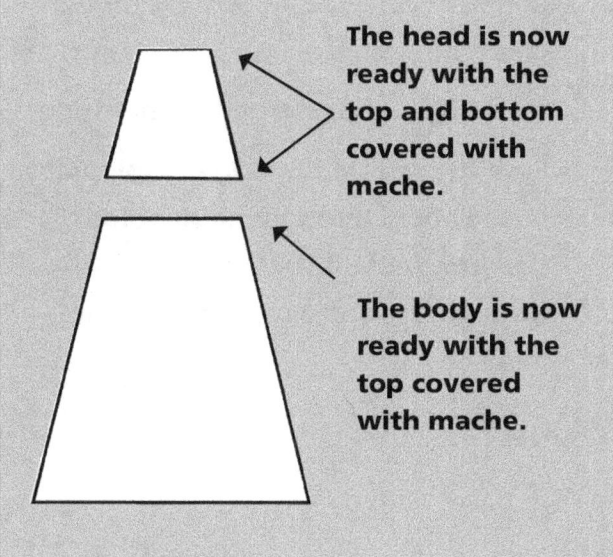

The head is now ready with the top and bottom covered with mache.

The body is now ready with the top covered with mache.

15

Before the puppet is assembled, the arms need to be made.

Try gluing a length of ribbon over the top of the body. Let the ribbon arms hang equally over the sides.

Let dry.

16

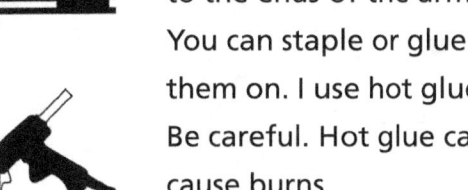

Cut small cardboard hands and attach them to the ends of the arms. You can staple or glue them on. I use hot glue. Be careful. Hot glue can cause burns.

Puppets, Puppetry and Gogmagog   Paper and Cardboard Puppets   **51**

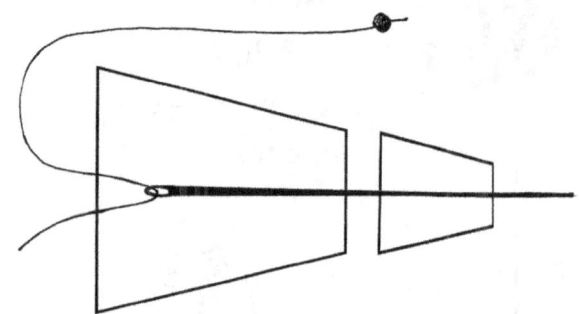

17

Assemble the puppet using an upholstery needle and strong thread or string.

Tie a big knot at the end of the string.

Push the needle through the midpoint of the body; through the ribbon of the arms (not illustrated here), then through the bottom and top of the head.

18

Pull the string, bringing the head and body together.

Make sure you leave a tiny amount of space between the two to allow the head to move from side to side.

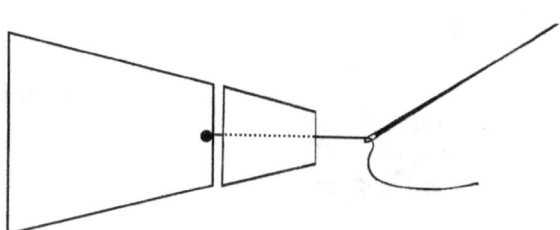

19

Tie a big knot at the top of the head and cut off the excess string.

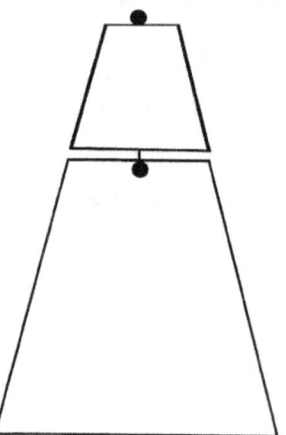

From the front the puppet will look like this.

20

Make a hole in the midpoint of the back of the head.

Hot glue a small dowel horizontally into the hole. Let it enter about 1 inch 2.5cm into the head.

This is the control for the puppet.

Be careful. Hot glue can cause burns.

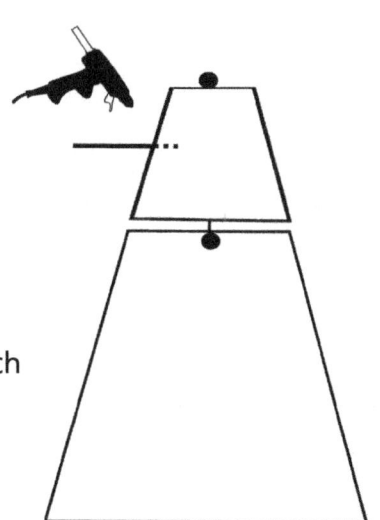

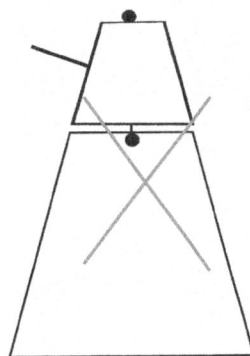

Make sure you do not slant the stick upwards.

21

Attach a smaller dowel or stick (I use kebab sticks for the smaller puppets) to the back of each hand.

These form the controls for the hands.

I use hot glue for this. Be careful. Hot glue can cause burns.

Create hair or a hat to cover the knot at the top of the head.

Cone Puppet

This puppet is made for action. It is generally seen inside a small puppet theatre. The glove puppet is operated in front or above the head of the puppeteer. A puppeteer may manipulate 2 glove puppets at once; having discussions, dancing, fighting and chasing.

A glove puppet is manipulated by inserting the hand inside the glove or body of the puppet. Generally one finger controls the head and the other fingers control the arms.

Glove Puppets

The following instructions on how to create a head over a clay mold can be used for other puppets further on in the manual.

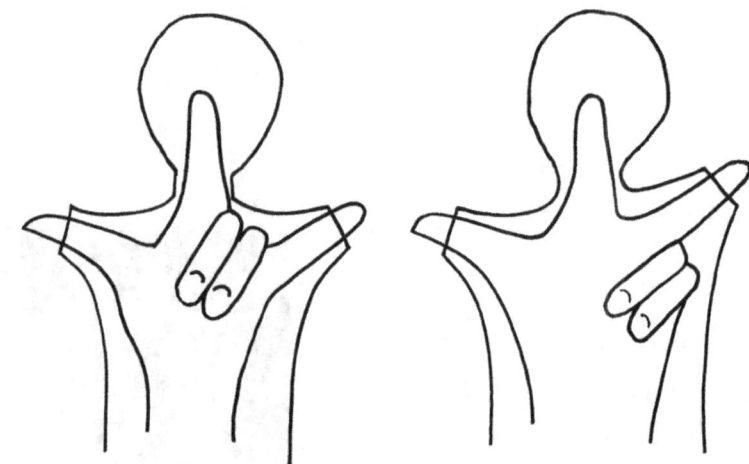

I generally make glove puppets that are operated using either of the two hand positions shown above.

Materials:

clay, *vaseline*, small wooden balls for eyes (optional), newspaper, brown paper, white glue, fabric glue, paper mache glue, paints, duct tape, cardboard, masking tape, foam material or felt for the hands (choose your colour), sewing thread, polyfill, cloth for the glove (or costume) of the puppet.

Tools:

clay cutter, sculpting stand, utility knife, scissors, sewing machine, sewing needles, paint brushes.

The Head

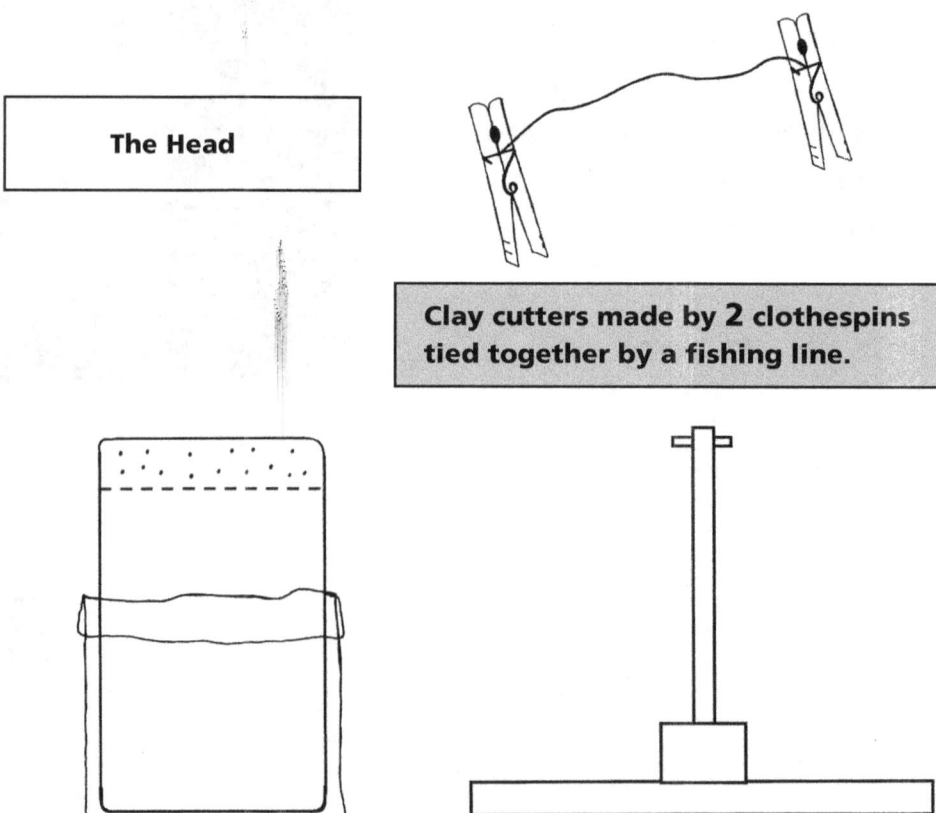

Clay cutters made by 2 clothespins tied together by a fishing line.

To mold the head I use water based clay, clay cutters and the puppet head sculpting stand (pages **18-19**).

Basic Glove Puppet

1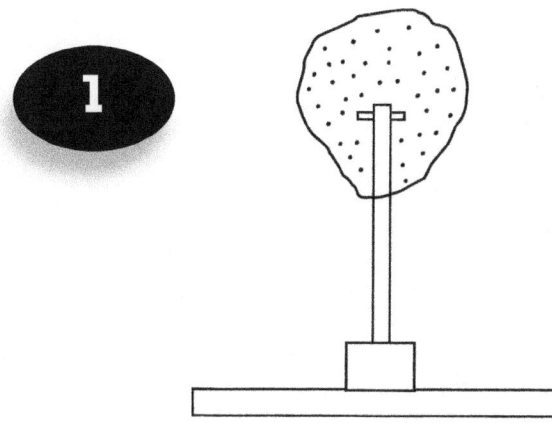

Form an oval shaped mass of clay on the top of the stand.

Add enough clay to more or less create the size of head you want.

Pack it together firmly.

2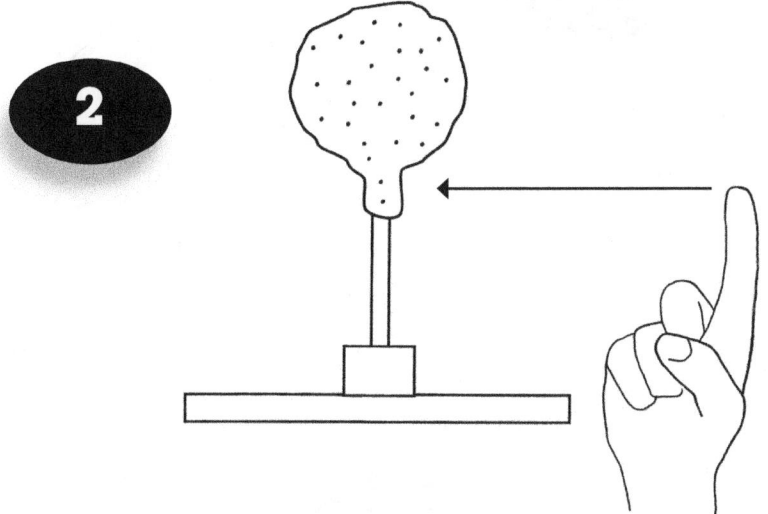

Add a neck.

Be sure the width of the neck is a little larger than the width of your index finger.

3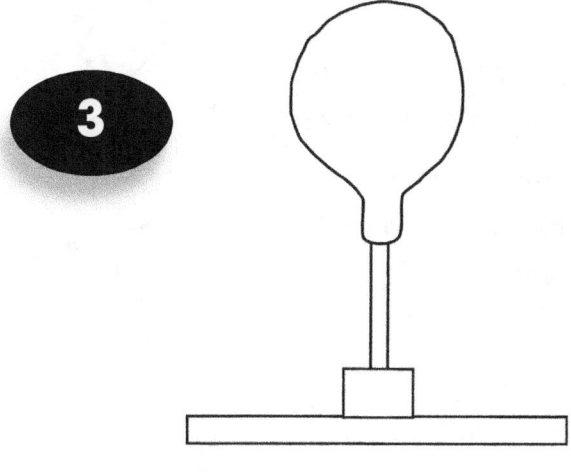

Smooth the head and neck, getting closer to the shape you want to create.

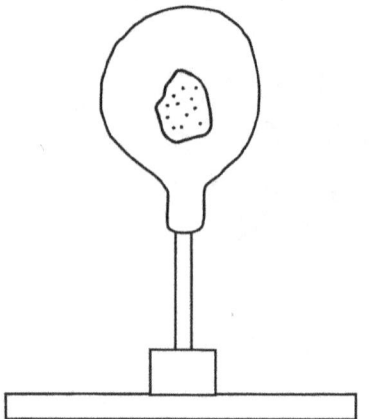
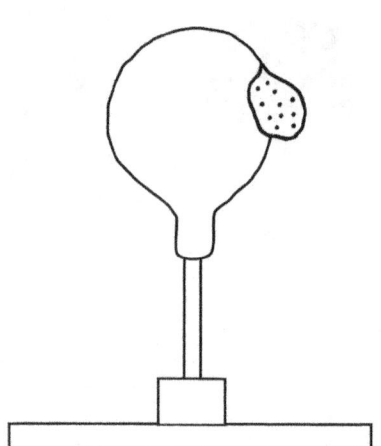

Add clay for a nose.

Check the profile for placement.

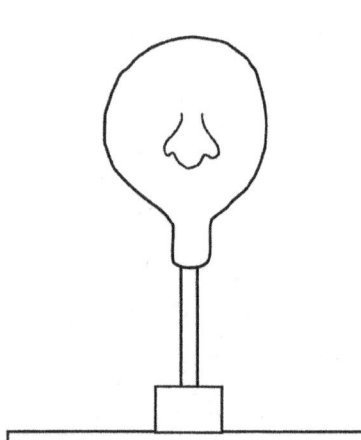
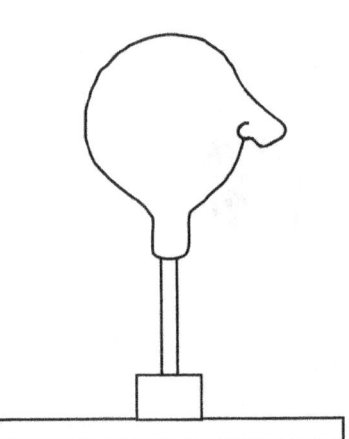

Work and refine the nose.

Check the profile.

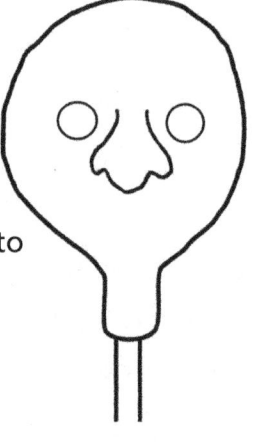
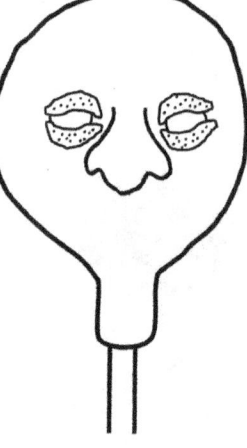

Sometimes I like to have quite detailed eyes and so I press small wooden balls into the clay. Over these I work the eyelids.

Make thin sausages shapes of clay and place them on top of and below the eyes.

Smooth them onto the clay head so they won't fall off.

> **Before proceeding with the eyes, refer to pages 22-23; eyes, eyelids and pupils.**

Puppets, Puppetry and Gogmagog

Work and refine the eyelids until you are happy with the expression.

Remember you will be applying **4** layers of paper mache so the shapes may lose definition.

Make your features as clean and defined as possible.

Basic Glove Puppet

Variation for the Eyes

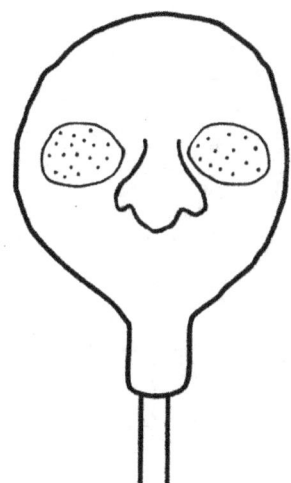

Add **2** oval balls of clay to create mounds for the eyes.

At the painting stage later on you can paint the eyes, eyelids etc.

Smooth the oval mounds so that they blend well into the rest of the head.

Continue with the next steps of sculpting the head.

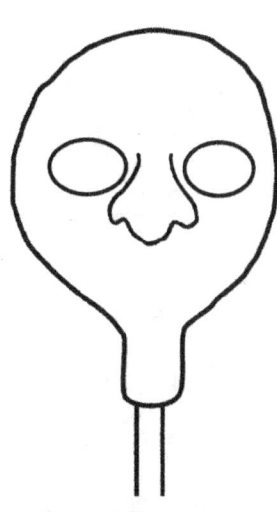

Check that the eyes are looking to the front.

Keep modifying the shape of the head. Perhaps add more clay to define better the jaw.

If you need to make the neck thicker in proportion to the head, do so now.

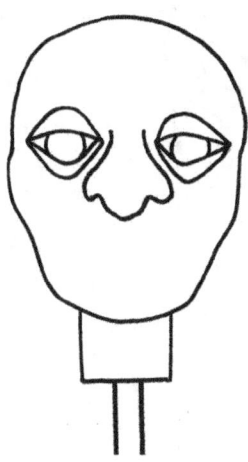

Add clay for the upper and lower lips.

I generally start with **2** trapezoid shapes.

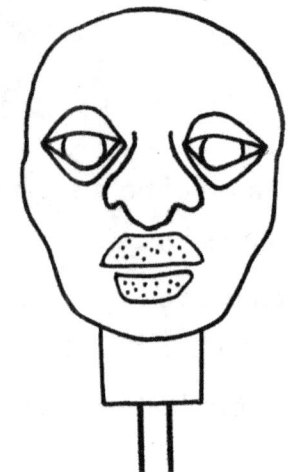

Work and refine the lips.

Pay attention to the area between the top lip and underneath the nose.

Pay attention to the area between the bottom lip and chin.

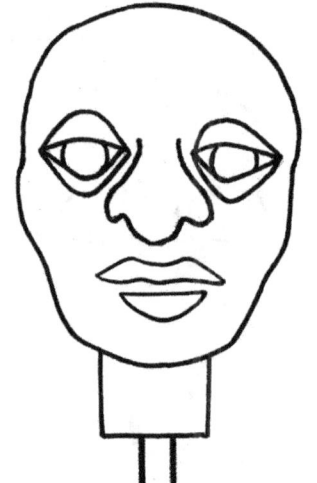
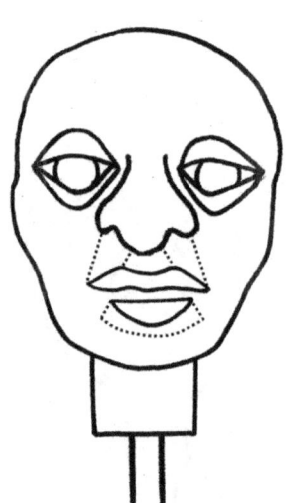

Add clay for the brow, cheeks and chin.

Work and refine them until you are satisfied.

Every now and then, check the profile of your head.

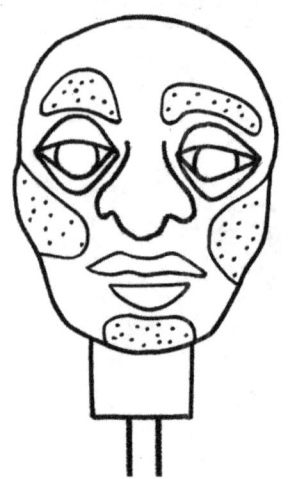
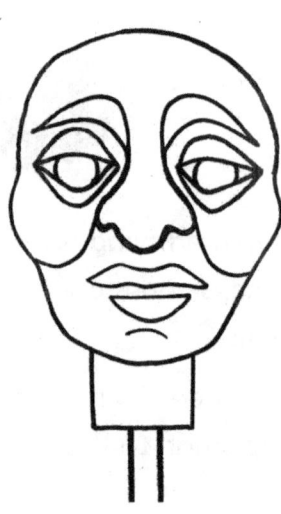

Basic Glove Puppet

13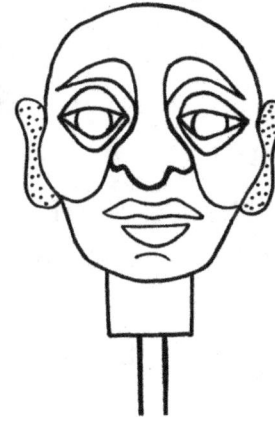

Add clay to create ears.

14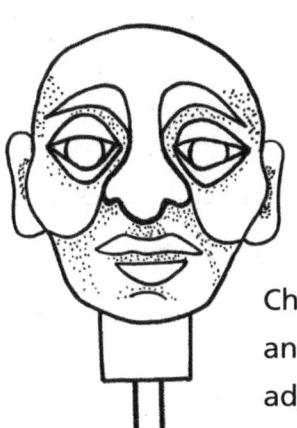

Work and refine the features until the head is finished.

15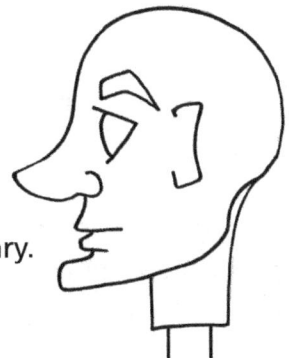

Check the profile and make any adjustments necessary.

16

Add a thin layer of *vaseline* or petroleum jelly all over the head and neck.

This acts as a release agent once the paper mache is dry.

17

Apply **4** layers of paper mache alternating newspaper and brown paper.

Make the mache as smooth as possible.

Pay attention to the final layer. This will be the surface you paint later on.

Let dry.

Puppets, Puppetry and Gogmagog — Glove Puppets

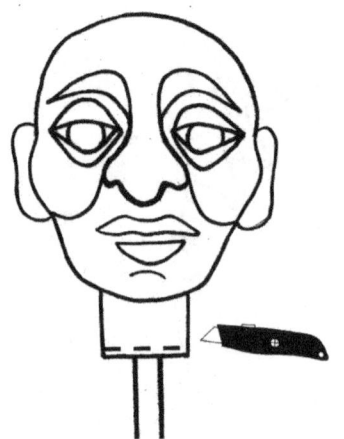
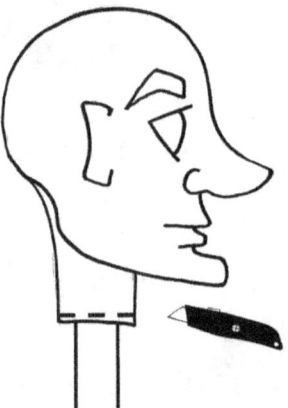

18

When the mache is dry, cut a line around the bottom of the neck as close to the border as possible.

Two Ways of Cutting the Dry Mached Head Off the Mold

Variation 1

1

Cut a line from the back of the neck up and over the head to the tip of the nose.

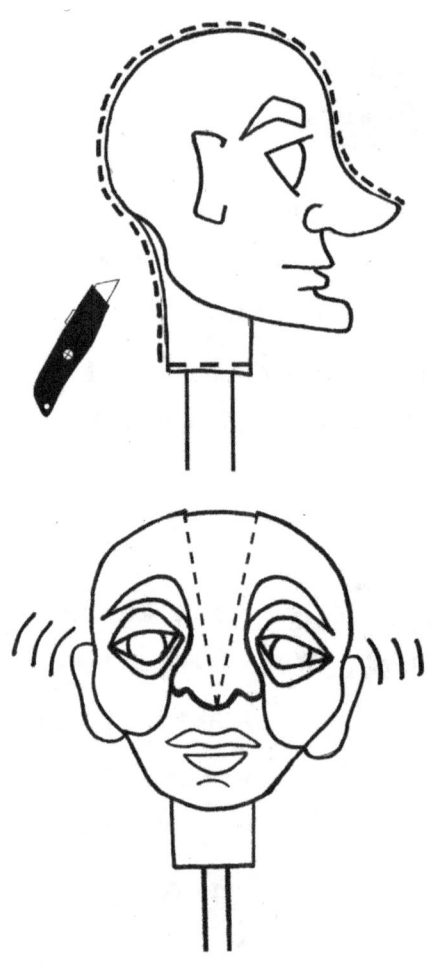

2

Open the mached head from the back and wiggle it off. You may have to extend the cut further on down the nose.

You may lose the clay ears at this point.

Don't worry. The clay left in the ears can be dug out later.

Puppets, Puppetry and Gogmagog

Basic Glove Puppet

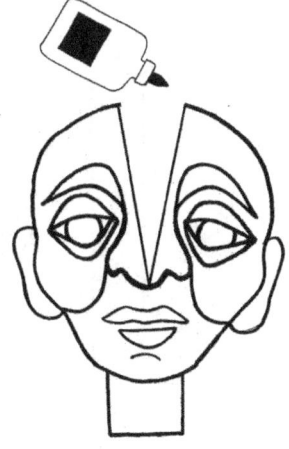

Apply white glue along the edges of the cuts.

Tape the borders of the cuts together with small pieces of duct tape.

Have the pieces of tape already cut beforehand.

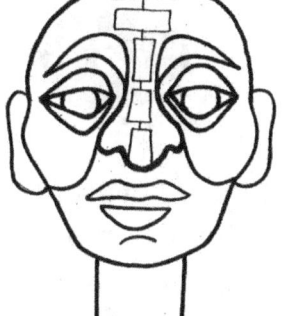

Apply **2** layers of paper mache (**1** newspaper, **1** brown) over and beyond the tape.

Make sure all the tape is covered and the mache is smooth.

Let dry.

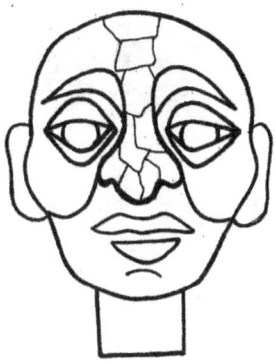

Variation 2

Cut the mache from ear to ear, starting from the bottom of the neck, over the top of the head and down through the ear on the other side.

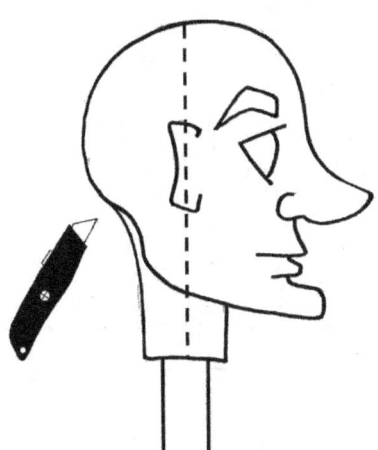

Puppets, Puppetry and Gogmagog

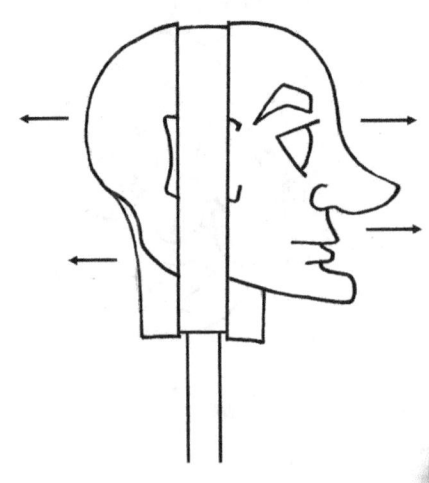

Pry the two halves of the mached head off the mold.

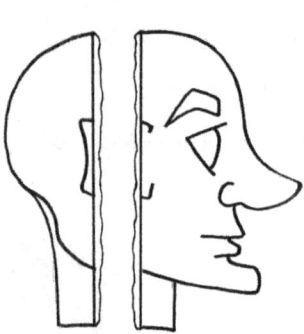

Apply white glue around the borders of both halves of the head.

Tape the **2** halves of the head together with small pieces of duct tape.

Have the pieces of tape cut beforehand.

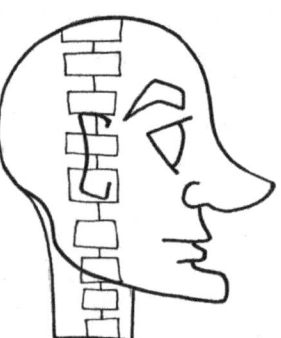

Apply **2** layers of paper mache (**1** newspaper, **1** brown) over and beyond the tape.

Make sure all the tape is covered and the mache is smooth.

Let dry.

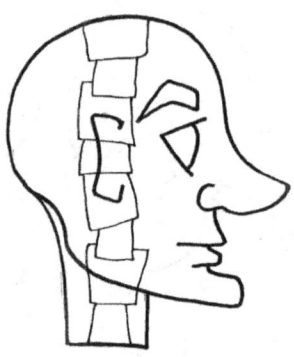

Puppets, Puppetry and Gogmagog

The Tube for the Neck

Make a tube of cardboard that fits around your index finger.

It should be approximately the length of your finger.

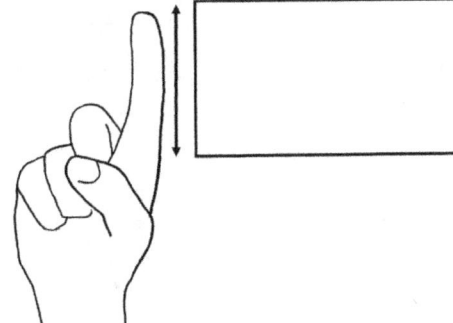

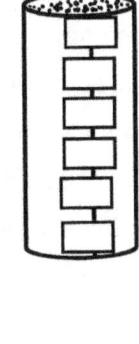

It is important that your index finger can enter and leave the tube easily.

It is also important that the tube can enter the opening of the neck.

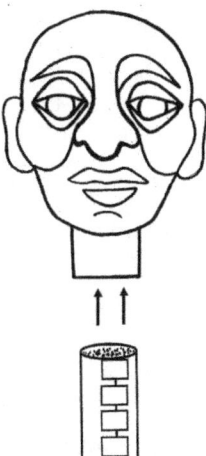

What happens if the tube fits your finger well but is too small for the neck of the puppet head?

You can always add more cardboard around the outside of the tube, but this extra bulk may impede your index finger from moving freely.

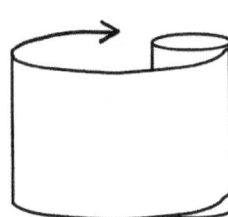

Basic Glove Puppet

Puppets, Puppetry and Gogmagog   Glove Puppets   **65**

You can also create a tube shaped like a funnel; smaller where it has to fit over your index finger and wider where it must fit into the neck.

This is the placement of finger, tube and neck opening.

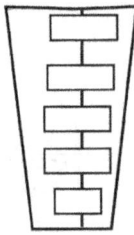 Apply some white glue to the outside of the tube.

Push the tube into the neck hole until the bottom of the tube and neck hole are together.

Let dry.

21 Paint the head and neck of the puppet.

Paint an undercoat of white first.

Puppets, Puppetry and Gogmagog

The Hands

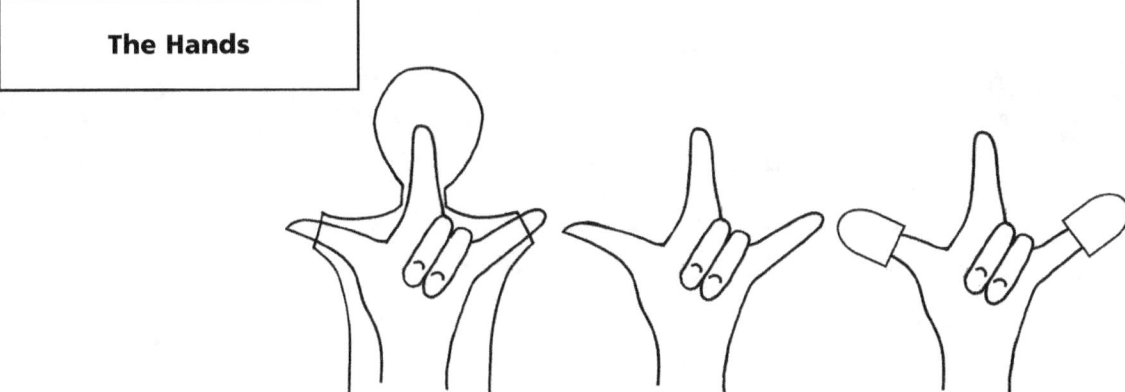

I like using this hand position in my glove puppets.

The illustrations show the hand inside the glove, the hand alone and the position on the fingers where the hands of the puppet will be placed.

In this case the puppet hands will go on the thumb and small finger.

If you choose to use this other hand position; the hands of the puppet will fit on the thumb and middle finger.

Here are some designs for hands that can be made with felt or foam material.

Basic Glove Puppet

22 Make **2** tubes of cardboard (one for each finger.)

The thumb tube will be bigger.

They should each slide on and off your fingers easily; but they should not be too big.

23 Make a pattern for your puppet hands.

Place each tube on a piece of paper and draw the outline of the hand shape you have chosen.

The pattern should allow for gluing or sewing the hand parts together, especially at the sides.

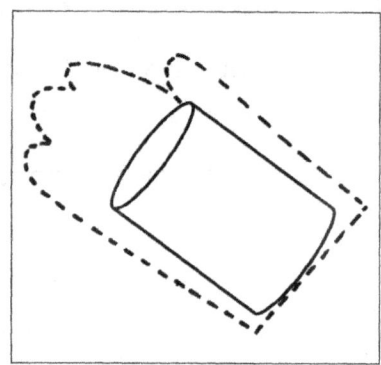

Choose the cloth you want for your hands. I use foam material a lot so I choose a colour close to the colour I have painted the face. Later I paint over the hands if necessary.

24 Pin your patterns on the cloth and cut **4** shapes (**2** for each hand of the puppet).

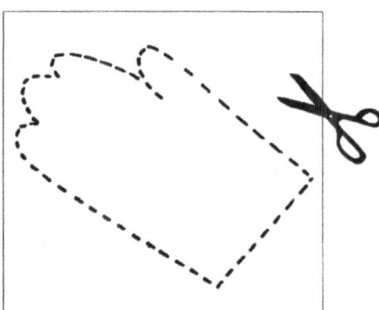

25 Apply a small amount of fabric glue on to one half of the hand and place the tube on top.

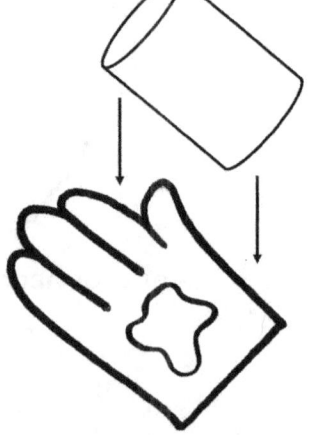

Puppets, Puppetry and Gogmagog

26

Apply a thin line of glue around the edge of the hand and on top of the tube.

Place the other half of the hand on top and press firmly around the edges.

From time to time keep pressing the edges together as the glue dries.

Repeat for the other hand.

27

So that the fingers of the puppet hand don't look flat, push a little *polyfill* up through the tube and into the finger space.

Do this once the hands are completely dry.

28

Check that your puppet hands fit well on your thumb and finger.

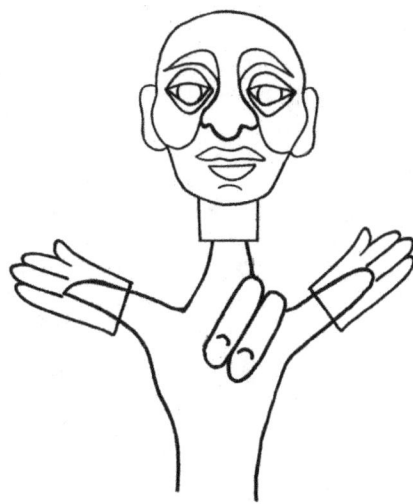

Basic Glove Puppet

The Glove

29

First, make a pattern for the glove body.

Place a large piece of paper on a table.

Lay your hand down on the paper. With the puppet head and hands on your hand, draw a line around the puppet where the glove will go. See the illustration.

Allow extra for seam allowance when sewing.

Cut the pattern out.

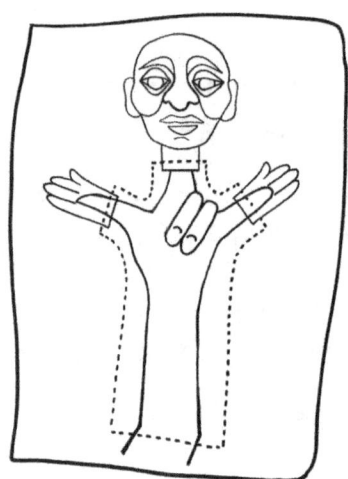

30

Pin your pattern onto **2** thicknesses of cloth and cut around it.

You should have **2** pieces of cut cloth; a front and a back.

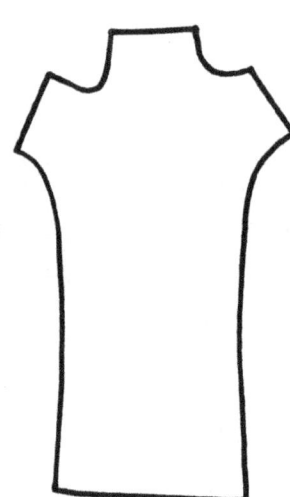

31

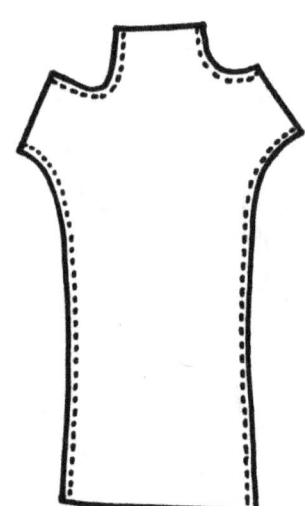

Sew right sides together (by hand or machine) or glue with fabric glue.

Leave the neck open and the sleeves open at the ends.

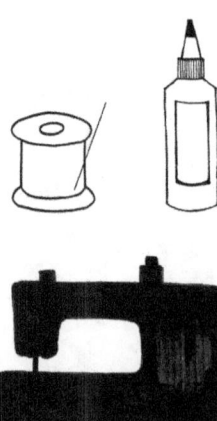

Puppets, Puppetry and Gogmagog

Turn the glove right side out and sew (or glue) a small hem close to the border of the bottom of the glove.

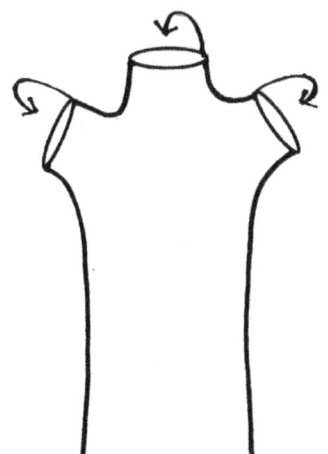

Fold a little the edge of the neck and sleeve openings towards the inside of the glove.

Sometimes I iron the folded edges flat.

This is to give a better finish once the head and hands are glued into the glove.

 Apply glue around the neck of the puppet head.

Carefully insert the neck of the puppet into the neck opening of the glove.

Press the cloth firmly around the neck of the head.

Let dry.

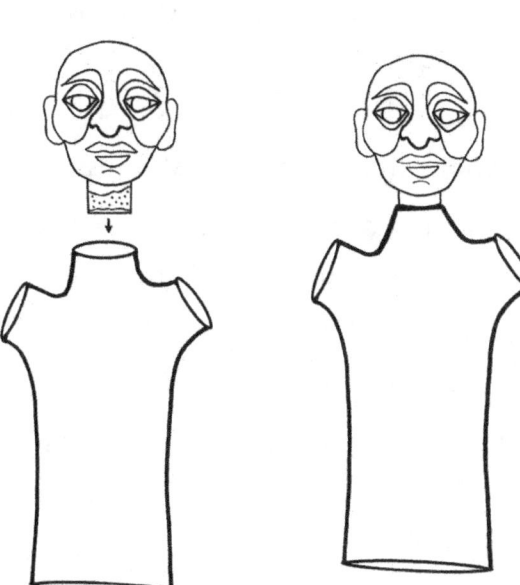

Basic Glove Puppet

Puppets, Puppetry and Gogmagog   Glove Puppets

71

 Apply glue to the outside borders of the hands.

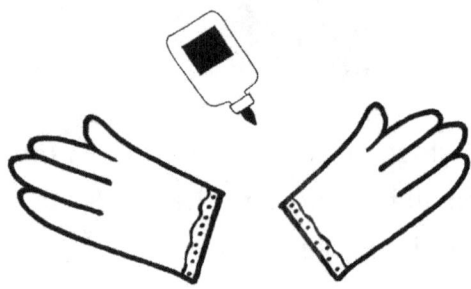

Carefully insert each hand (thumbs up) into the sleeve openings.

Press the cloth firmly around each hand.

Let dry.

Add hair or a hat or other details to your puppet.

You can add other elements of costume over the basic glove.

Be careful never to limit the movement of the puppet with very bulky costumes.

For puppet costume patterns and accessories I refer you to a free pdf so generously created and shared by Christy Graunke.

Here is a link to the pdf.

http://www.puppetpub.com/costumes.html

Catalan Style Puppet

This puppet is made with shoulders that accommodate **3** fingers of the puppeteer. The hands have extensions so that manipulation is possible. The movements of the arms and hands seem to be more graceful. This puppet is traditionally carved of wood.

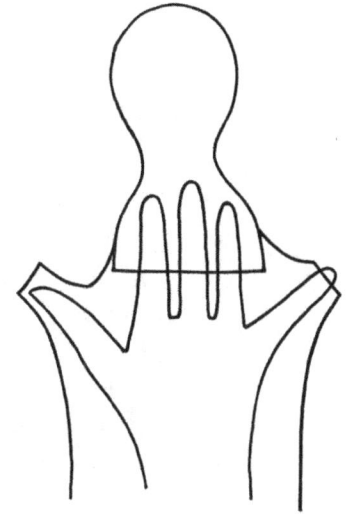

The materials and tools are the same as the Basic Glove Puppet.

The Catalan style glove puppet has a distinct head and shoulders from other glove puppets. You will need to add more clay for neck and shoulders.

Remember to make the shoulders wide enough for your three fingers.

If you make the shoulders too wide you will have to pad the space later on.

1

Create the head and shoulders in clay following the steps of the **Basic Glove Puppet** on pages **57-64**.

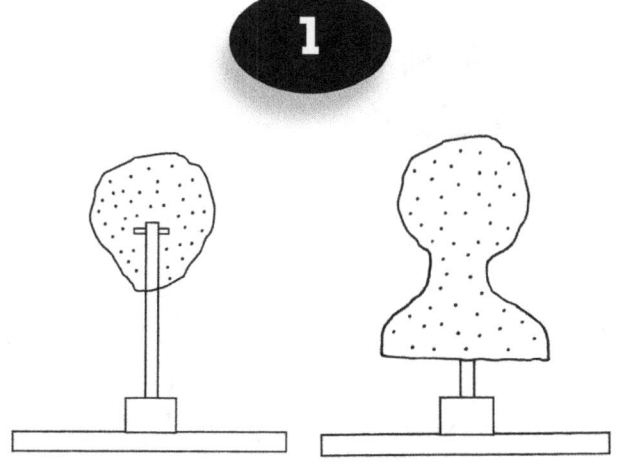

Puppets, Puppetry and Gogmagog

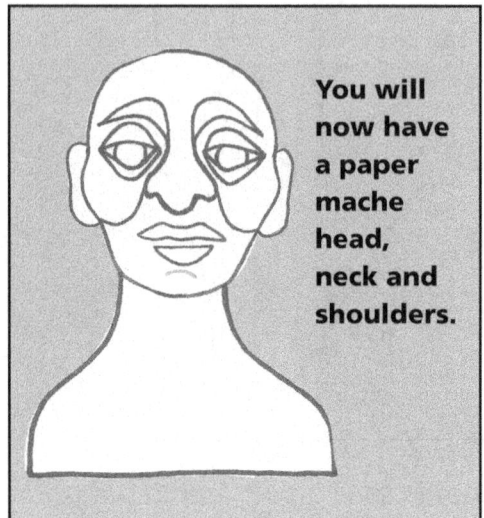

You will now have a paper mache head, neck and shoulders.

Follow the steps for wiring the shoulder opening on page **17**.

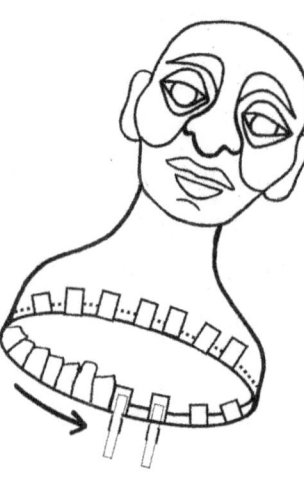

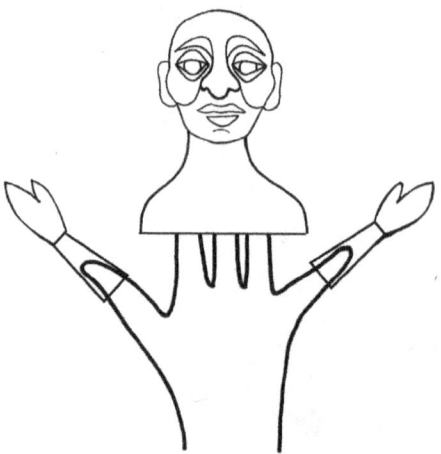

You are now ready to make the hands of the puppet.

Note that the tubes for this puppet are longer than the tubes for the basic glove puppet.

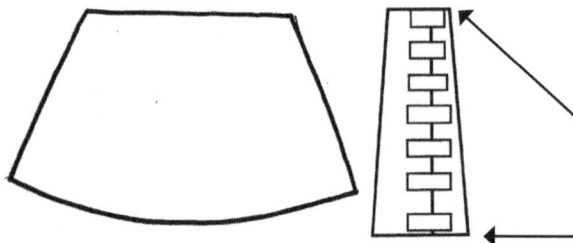

Cut **2** cardboard forms (one form for each finger of the puppeteer).

The top of the tube will fit the hand of the puppet.

The bottom of the tube will fit your thumb and/or little finger.

Puppets, Puppetry and Gogmagog

 **4**

Choose a design for your puppet hands.

Cut **4** hands from cardboard or foam material in proportion to your puppet head.

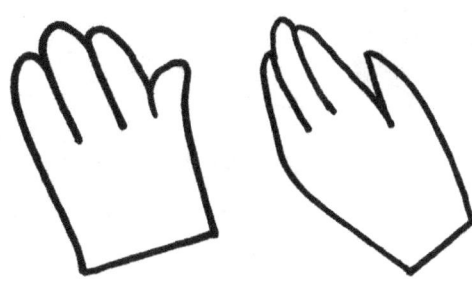

 **5**

Apply glue around the edge of **1** hand.

Glue it to the other half of the hand. Leave the wrist open.

Repeat for the other hand.

 **6**

Push a little *polyfill* or scrunched up newspaper into the hands if you want them to have more body.

 **7**

Insert the hand into the tube.

Repeat for the other hand.

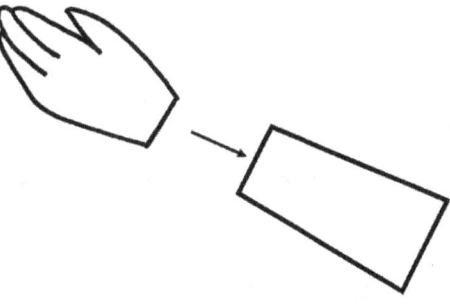

 **8**

Tape the hand and cuff firmly together.

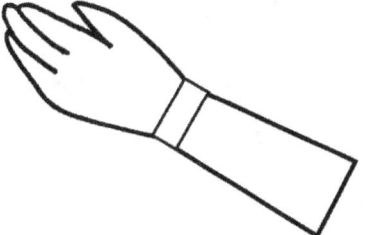

Puppets, Puppetry and Gogmagog   Glove Puppets

Catalan Style Puppet

9 Apply **1** good layer of paper mache over the whole arm.

As this is a small object to mache, use the paper from a small brown paper bag which is much thinner and easier to use.

Make sure the join is well covered.

10 Paint the head and arms of the puppet.

Paint a white undercoat first.

Let dry.

Now you are ready to create the basic glove or costume.

11 The Catalan glove puppet usually has an under dress with inset sleeves to accommodate the unusual position of the hands.

Here I have drawn a simple version of a pattern for a costume.

Note: the inside part of the sleeve runs from the shoulder to what would be the waist of the puppet.

Create a pattern in paper of the design illustrated.

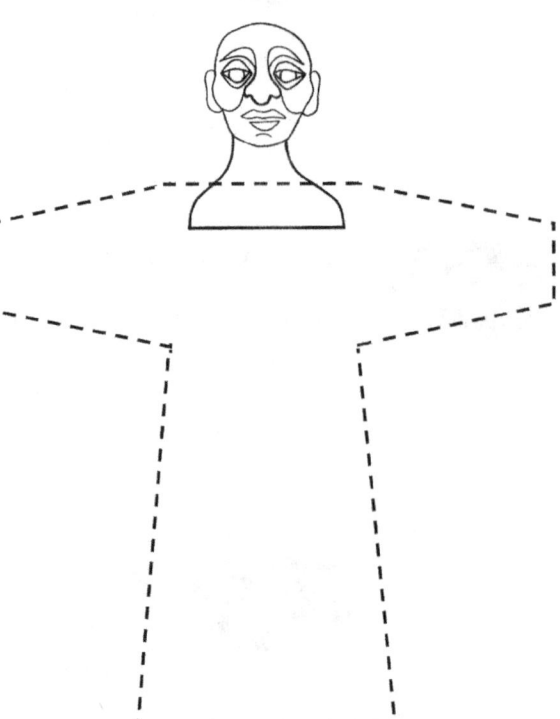

Make sure your pattern is long enough; that it reaches your elbow.

Cut the pattern **2** times (a front and a back) on the cloth of your choice.

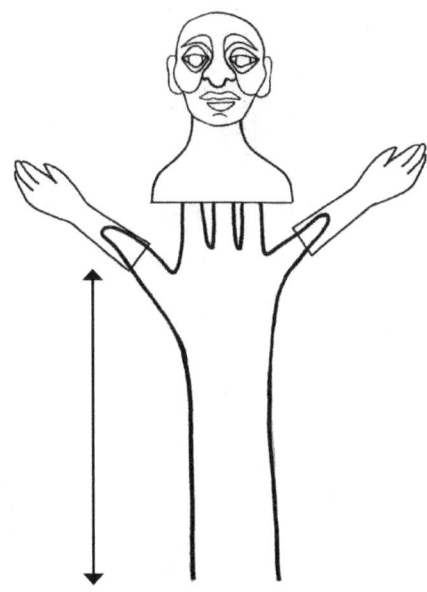

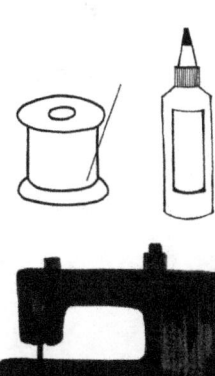

Sew the front and back right sides together. Leave the neck sleeve and bottom holes open.

14

Turn the glove right side out and sew a small hem around the bottom of the glove.

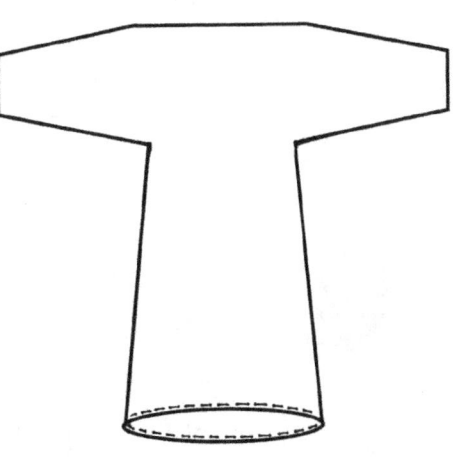

Catalan Style Puppet

Puppets, Puppetry and Gogmagog   Glove Puppets

Apply white glue around the bottom of the neck and the shoulders of the puppet head.

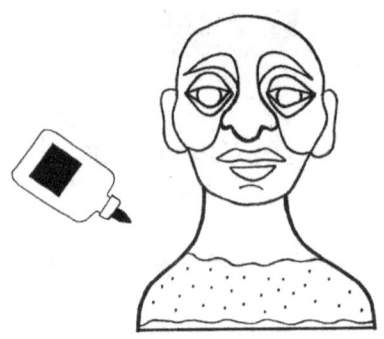

Carefully insert the neck of the puppet into the neck opening of the glove.

Press the cloth firmly around the neck and shoulders of the head.

Let dry.

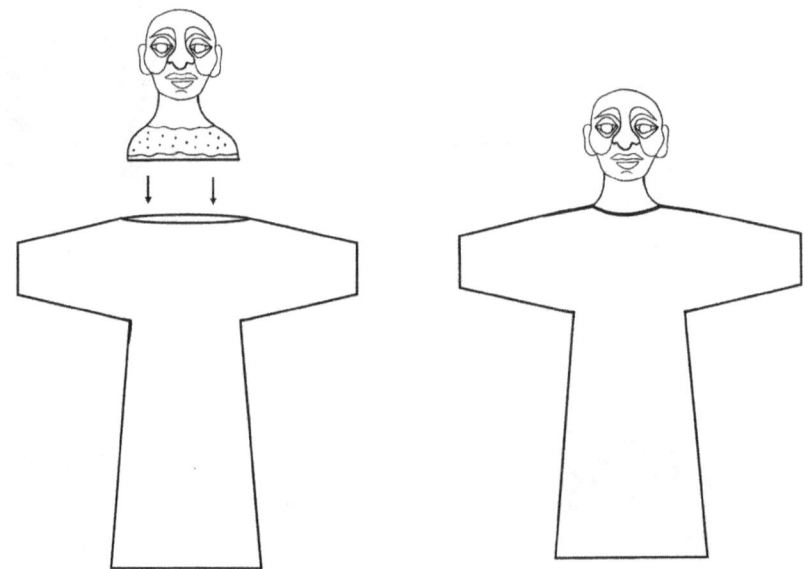

Apply white glue around the wrists/ forearms of the puppet.

If you want more of the forearm to show, apply the glue a little lower down.

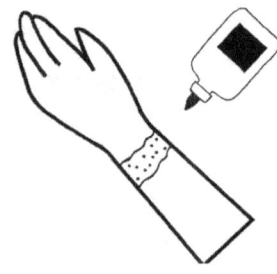

Puppets, Puppetry and Gogmagog

Carefully insert each hand/forearm (thumbs up) into the sleeve openings.

To give a neater finish copy step **33** on page **71** of the **Basic Glove Puppet** before you insert the arms.

Press the cloth firmly around each hand/forearm.

Let dry.

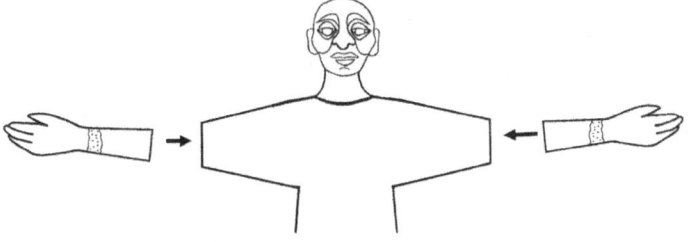

You may have extra cloth around the hand area.

Accommodate it around the forearm as you please.

Add hair or a hat or other details to your puppet.

You can add other elements of costume over the basic glove.

Be careful never to limit the movement of the puppet with very bulky costumes.

For puppet costume patterns and accessories I refer you to a free pdf so generously created and shared by Christy Graunke.

Here is a link to the pdf.
http://www.puppetpub.com/costumes.html

The beauty of the mouth puppet is that its mouth moves as it talks. Mouth puppets have a movable lower jaw operated by the puppeteer's thumb. The other 4 fingers of the puppeteer's hand enter the top part of the head. The mouth of the puppet moves as the puppeteer's hand open and closes, in synchronization with the words of the puppeteer.

Mouth Puppets

Here are instructions for a bird mouth puppet; a raucous, loony character.

1

Inflate a small water balloon.

Tie a knot.

This will form the base of your puppet head.

Materials:

water balloons, *vaseline*, newspaper, brown paper, paper mache glue, cardboard for beak y crest, pencil, masking tape, objects to make eyes with: polystyrene balls, disposable drinking cups, empty cotton reels, foam material or felt for the inside of the mouth, white glue, hot glue sticks, acrylic paint, cloth for the sleeve to cover the arm of the puppeteer.

Tools:

utility knife, stapler, hot glue gun, paint brushes.

2

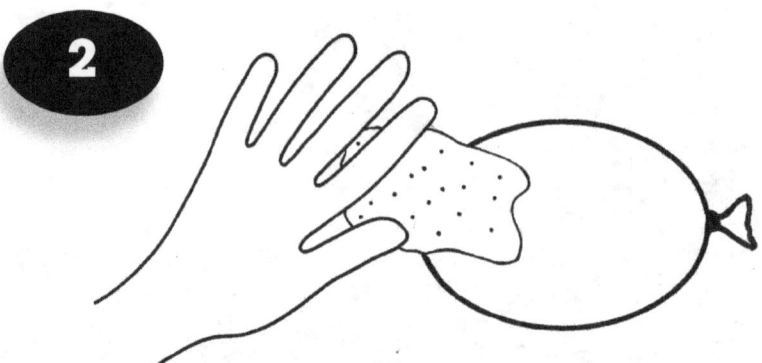

Apply a thin layer of *vaseline* over the balloon.

3

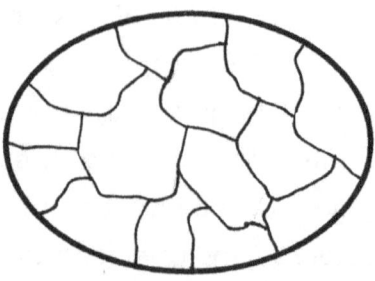

Apply **4** layers of paper mache (newspaper, brown, newspaper, brown).

Let dry.

Puppets, Puppetry and Gogmagog

4

When dry, draw a line around the centre of the balloon and cut with a utility knife.

You now have **2** halves, open at the bottom.

These **2** halves form the bases for the upper head and beak and the lower head and beak.

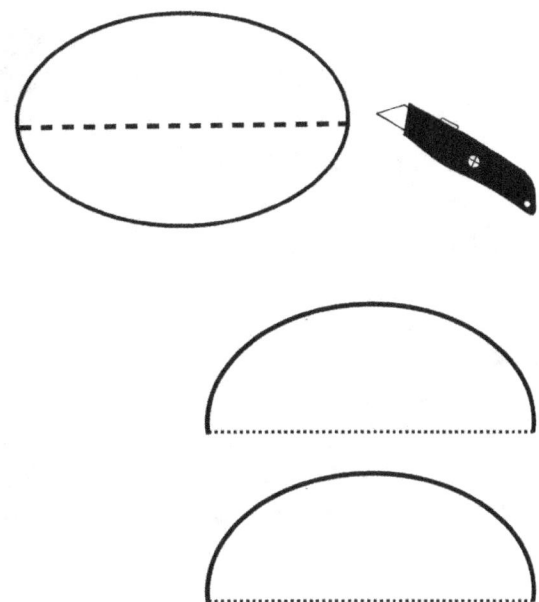

5

Draw and cut out a tall triangle to make the upper beak.

Bend along the dotted line to form a beak shape.

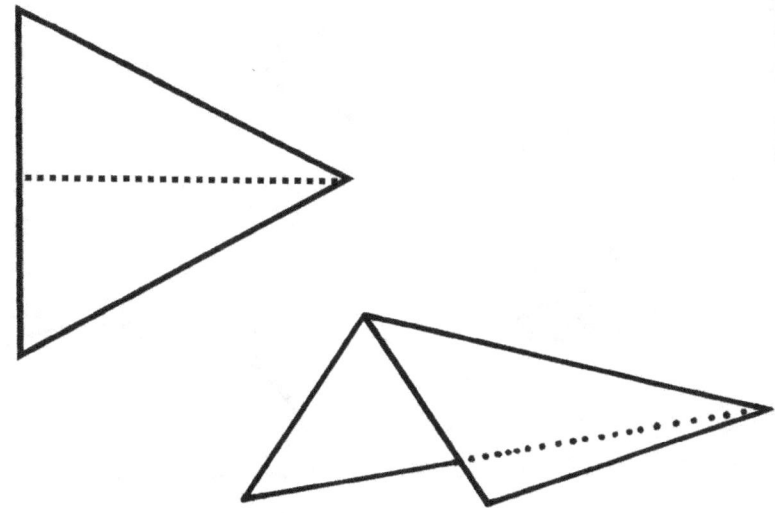

6

With the half balloon face down, fit the beak to one of the ends.

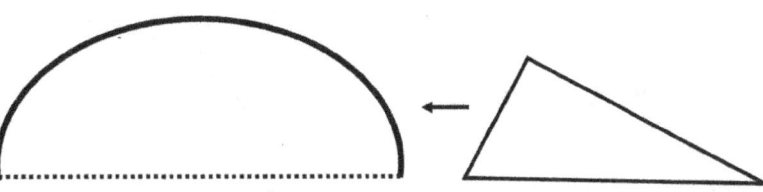

Mouth Puppet Made with a Ballon and Cardboard

7

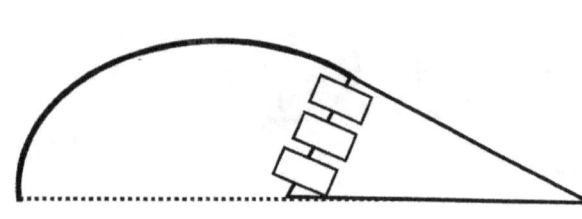

Once you have a good fit, tape the beak in place.

8

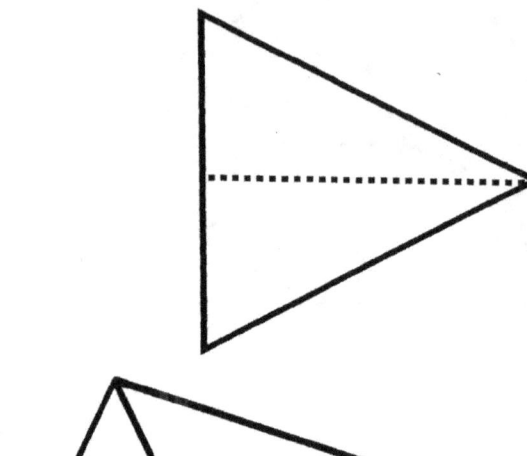

To make the lower beak, repeat the same steps as you followed for the upper beak.

Make the lower triangle shorter.

9

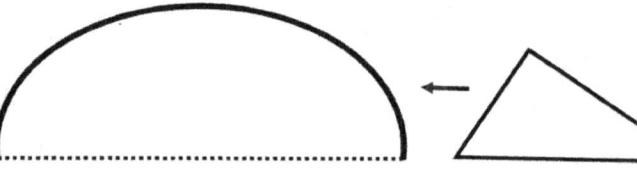

With the other half balloon face down, fit the beak to one of the longer ends.

10

Once you have a good fit, tape the lower beak in place.

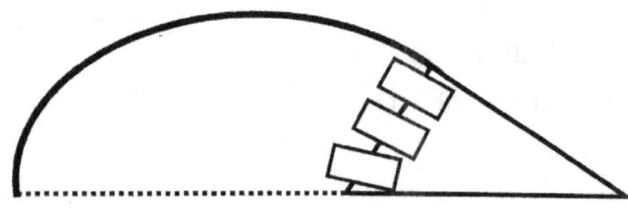

Puppets, Puppetry and Gogmagog

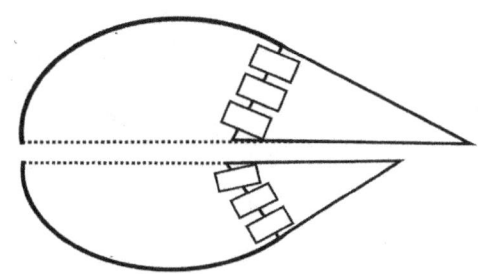

Now you have an upper and lower head and beak.

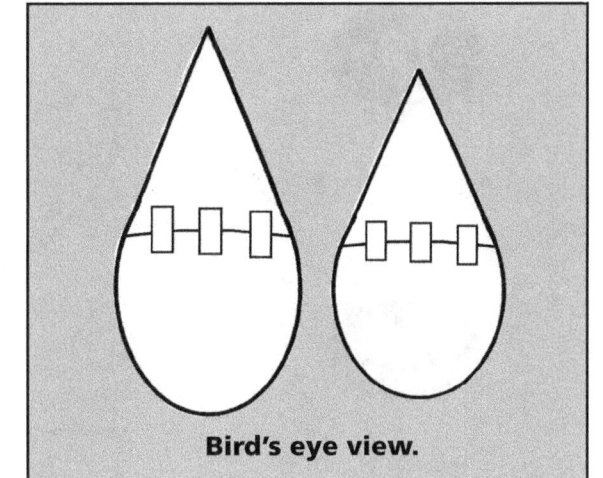

Bird's eye view.

The Palate for the Lower Beak

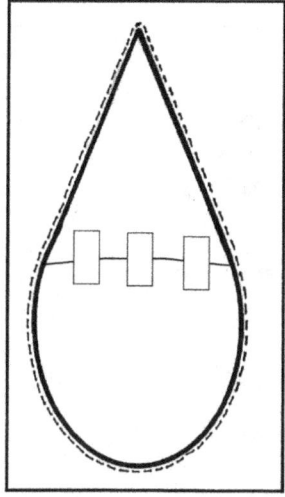
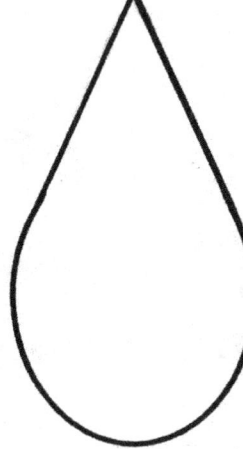

11

Place the lower head and beak face down on a piece of cardboard.

Trace around the head and cut out the shape.

This forms the lower palate of the lower head and beak.

12

Place the palate on to the lower head and beak.

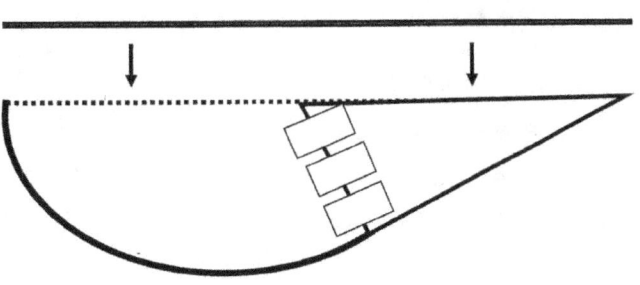

Mouth Puppet Made with a Ballon and Cardboard

13

Tape it in place.

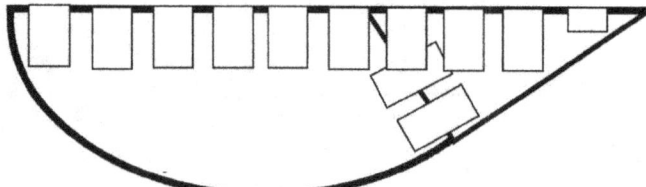

14

Apply **2** layers of paper mache (**1** newspaper, **1** brown) over the whole lower head and beak.

Let dry.

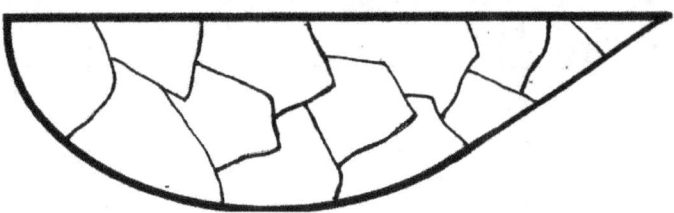

The Palate and Grip for the Upper Head and Beak

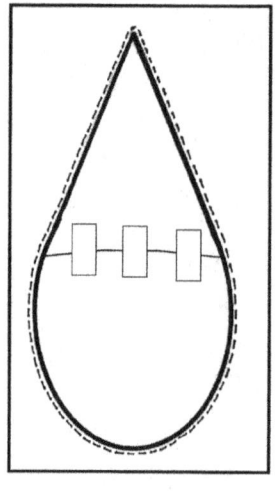

15

Place the upper head and beak on a piece of cardboard.

Trace around the form and cut it out.

You now have the palate of the upper head and beak.

16

Cut a strip of cardboard as shown. There should be about 3 inches/7.6cm on either side of the **4** fingers.

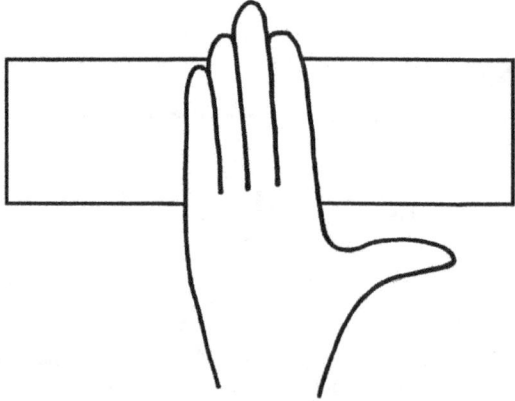

Puppets, Puppetry and Gogmagog

Score a vertical line as shown on the outside of both sides of the hand.

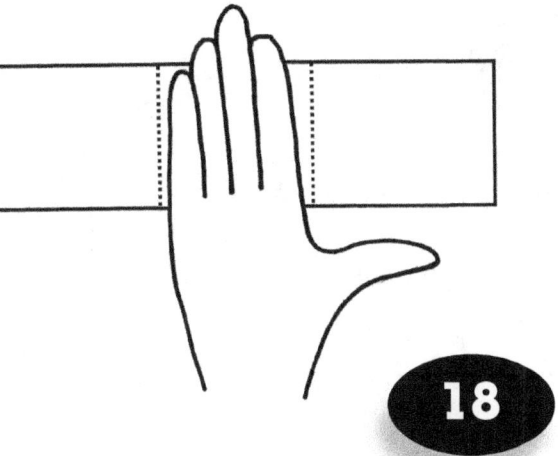

Turn the cardboard strip over and score **2** more vertical lines; this time dividing the space between the previous scores and the outer edges of the cardboard strip.

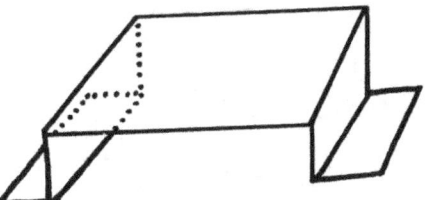

Bend along the scored lines, creating a shape as illustrated.

Staple the shape on to the lower part of the cardboard palate.

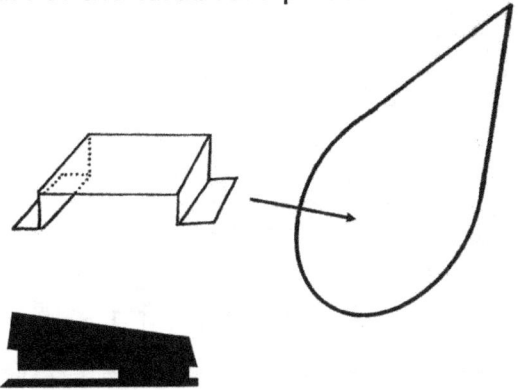

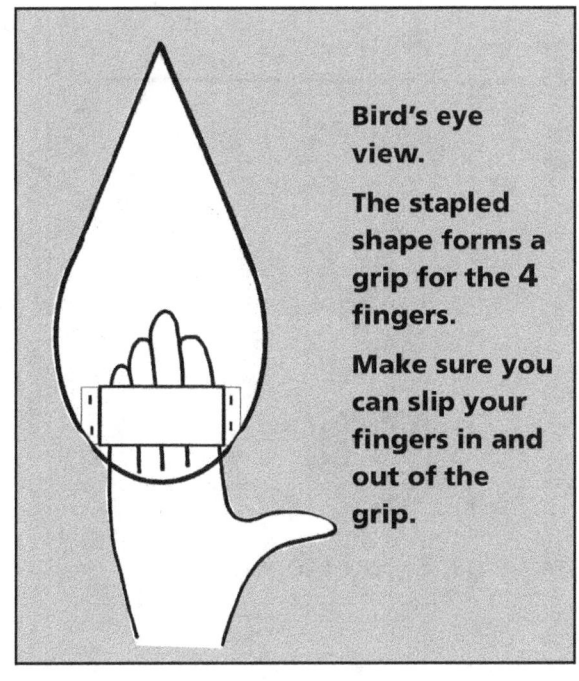

Bird's eye view.

The stapled shape forms a grip for the 4 fingers.

Make sure you can slip your fingers in and out of the grip.

Mouth Puppet Made with a Balloon and Cardboard

Draw and cut an opening on the rounded end of the upper head (opposite end to the beak).

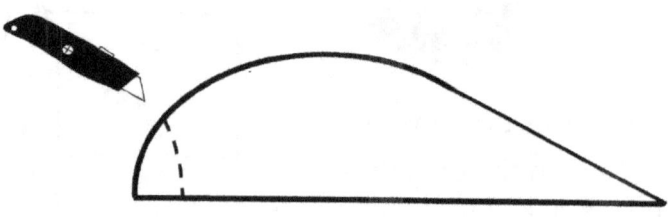

There should be enough room to fit your **4** fingers as shown.

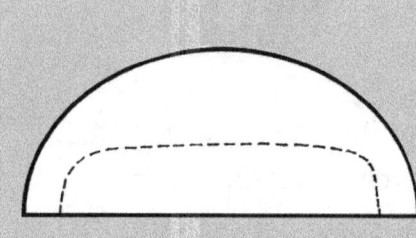

From the back it should look like this.

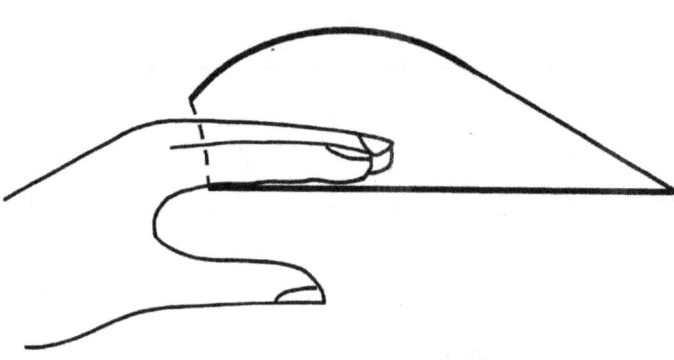

Place the mached upper beak on top of the palate and grip.

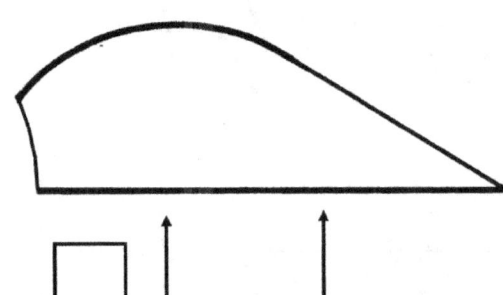

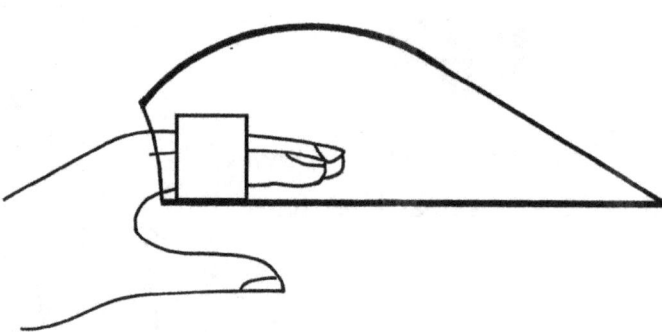

Tape the **2** pieces together.

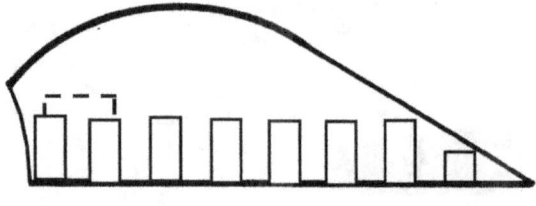

Apply **2** layers of paper mache (**1** newspaper, **1** brown) over the whole upper head and beak.

Let dry.

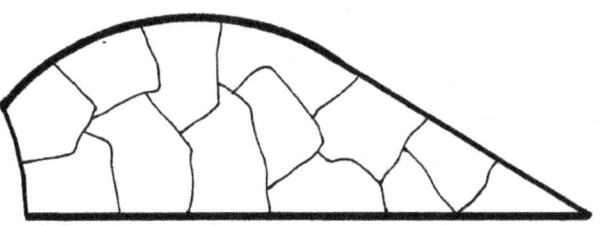

Adding Eyes and Other Details to the Upper Head and Beak

You can use any number of objects for eyes.

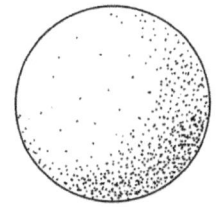   

| **Polystyrene Ball** | **Paper or Plastic Disposable Glass** | **Empty Cotton Reel** | **Scrunched Up Ball of Newspaper** |

Choose your eye objects and tape them in place on to the upper head and beak.

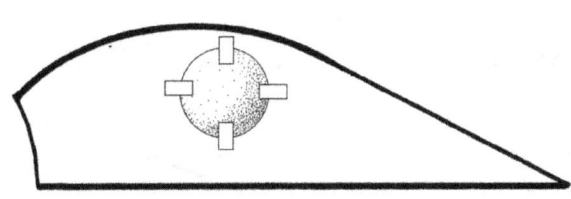

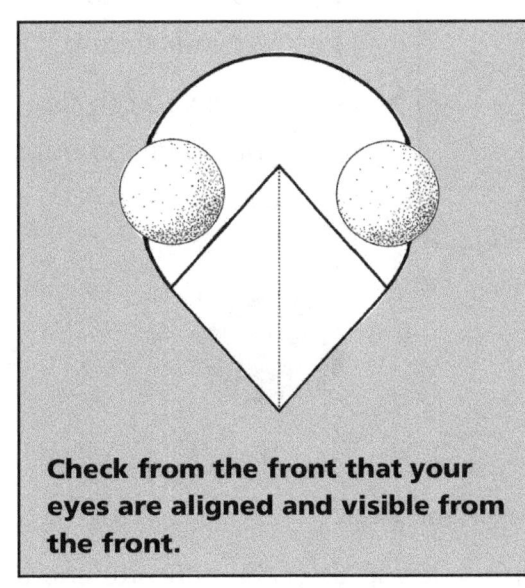

Check from the front that your eyes are aligned and visible from the front.

Puppets, Puppetry and Gogmagog

Mouth Puppets

Mouth Puppet Made with a Ballon and Cardboard

 Add a cock's comb made of cardboard.

Tape it securely in place.

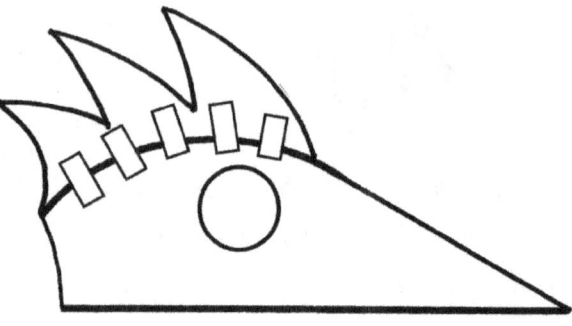

 Apply **2** layers of paper mache (**1** newspaper, **1** brown) over the eyes and comb.

Make sure you completely cover all the tape.

Let dry.

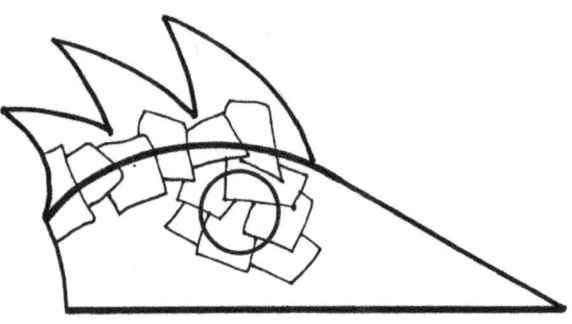

The Grip for the Lower Beak

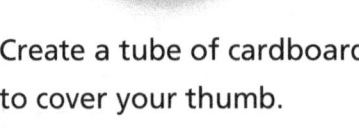 Create a tube of cardboard to cover your thumb.

Make sure you can slip your thumb in and out of the tube easily.

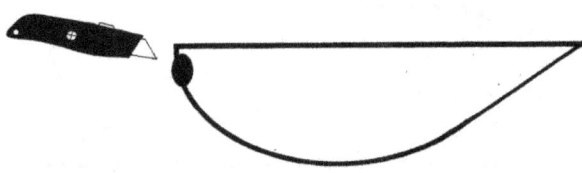

Draw and cut out a hole in the lower head and beak.

This hole will be at the opposite end to the beak.

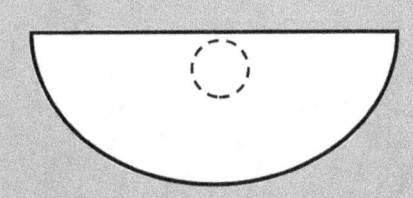

From the back it should look like this.

It should be big enough to insert the cardboard tube.

Apply white glue on the cardboard tube and insert it into the hole in the lower head and beak.

Let dry.

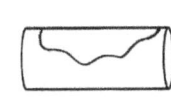

Cut of any part of the tube that overhangs the lower head and beak as shown.

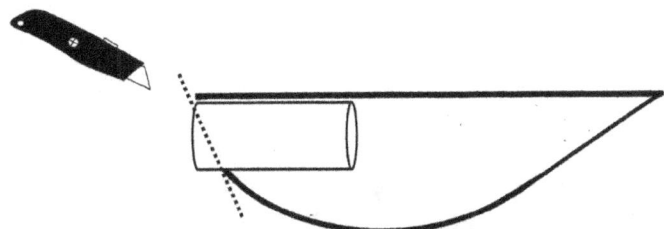

Here you can see the upper and lower head and beak in position on the hand.

Paint the two parts of the head of the puppet.

Apply an undercoat of white first.

Let dry.

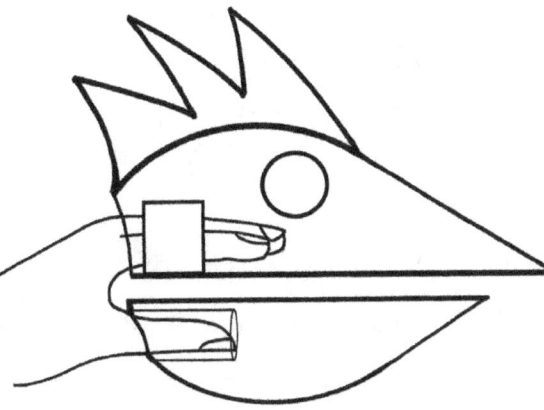

Joining the Upper and Lower Parts of the Head

Place the **2** parts of the head with the palates facing you.

There should be la little gap between the **2** parts.

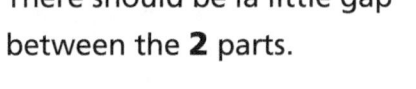
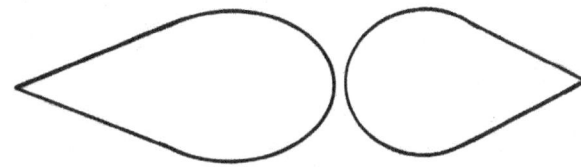

Puppets, Puppetry and Gogmagog

Mouth Puppets

91

34

Create a connecting palate as shown out of a contrasting cloth or felt or foam material.

Glue it into place; connecting the **2** parts of the mouth.

Let dry.

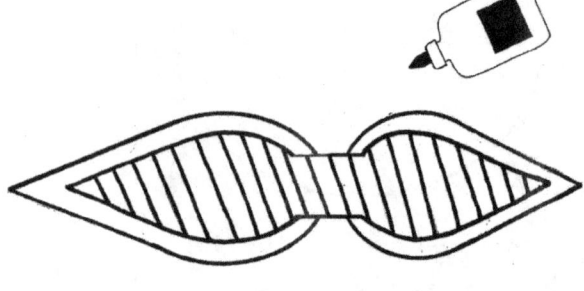

Here you can get a better view of the connecting palate.

35

Sew a cloth tube of material of your choice a little larger that the circumference of the back of the puppet head.

Glue it into place.

You can also use hot glue to do this.

Be careful. Hot glue can cause burns.

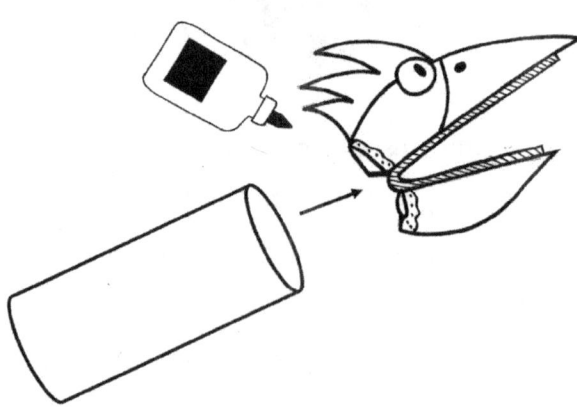

36

Finish decorating the puppet as you wish.

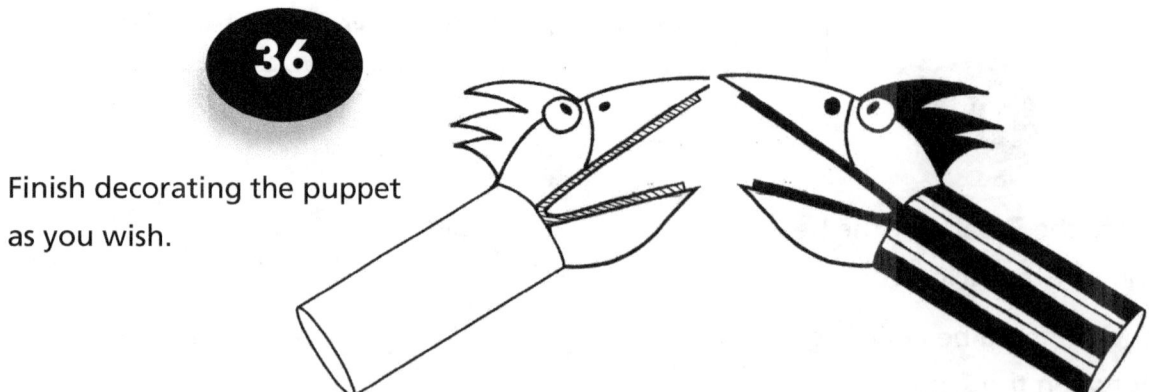

92

Puppets, Puppetry and Gogmagog

Mouth Puppet over Clay Mold

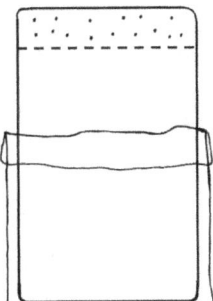
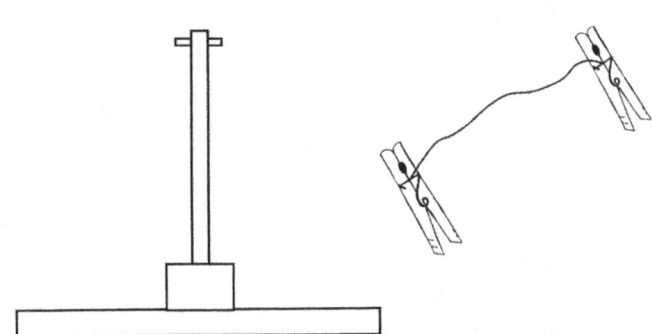

Materials:

clay, *vaseline*, newspaper, brown paper, paper mache glue, cardboard, duct tape, masking tape, foam material or felt for inside of mouth, paint.

Tools:

sculpting stand, clay cutters, utility knife, brushes.

1

Create the head following the steps of the **Basic Glove Puppet** on pages **57-64**.

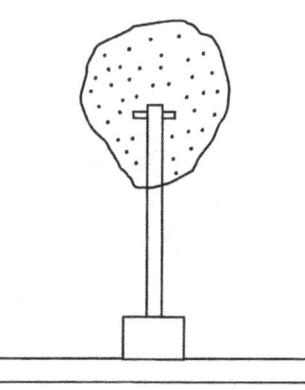

2

Add clay to make the facial features; smoothing and refining as you go.

Important:

a. Be aware of the mouth line. Later on this is the line you will cut horizontally through the head. A mouth with a level horizontal line is easier to manipulate later.

b. Do not make a neck.

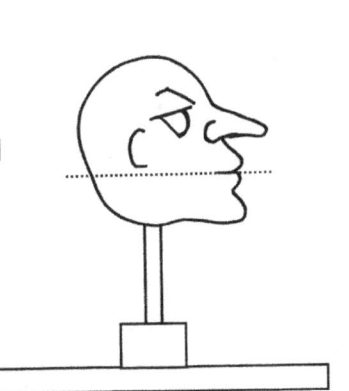

3

Apply a thin layer of *vaseline* over the clay mold.

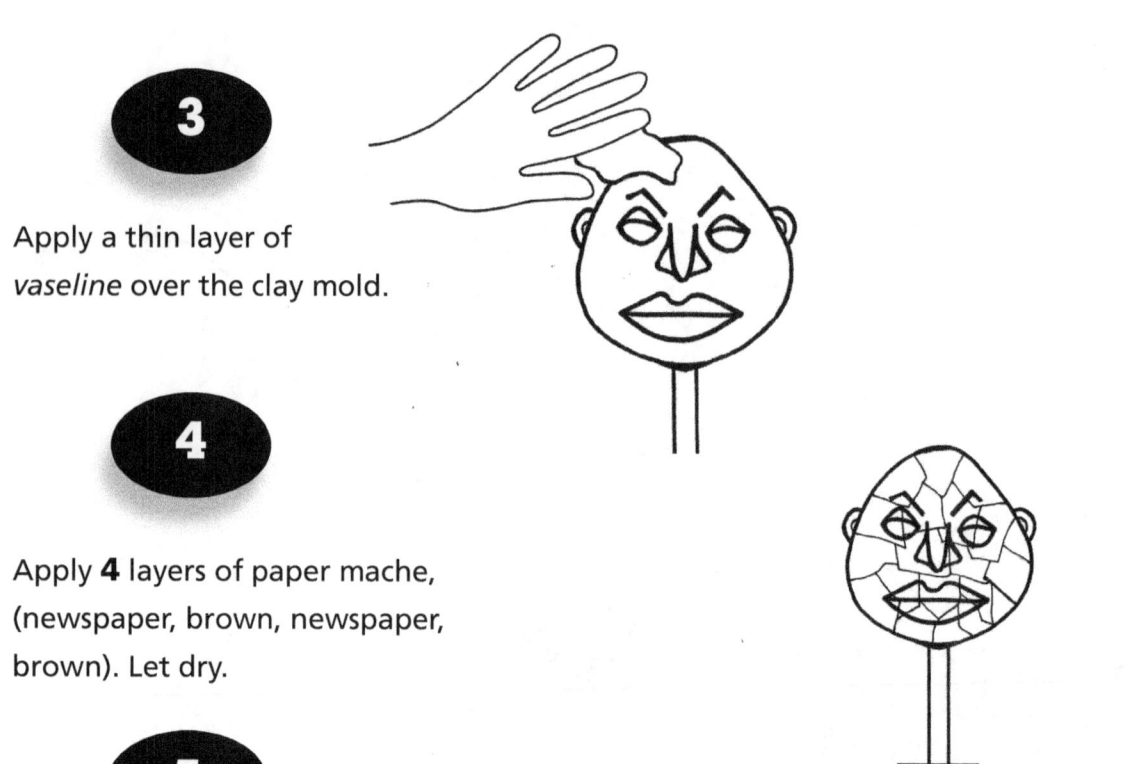

4

Apply **4** layers of paper mache, (newspaper, brown, newspaper, brown). Let dry.

5

Follow steps on pages **62-64** of the **Basic Glove Puppet** to take the mached head off the mold.

Tape and mache together again. Let dry.

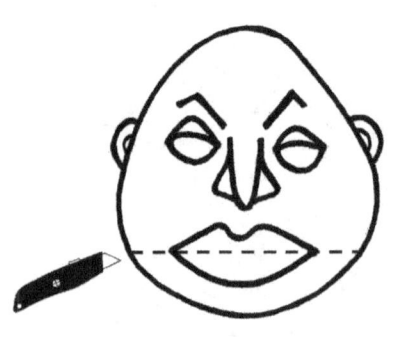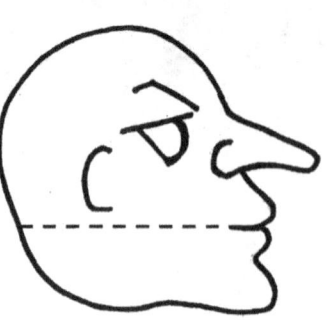

6

Carefully draw and cut a horizontal line around the head as shown.

The line goes horizontally through the middle of the mouth.

It is important that the line be as level as possible.

Puppets, Puppetry and Gogmagog

7 Follow steps **11-14** on pages **85-86** to create the palate for the lower jaw. Tape and mache into place.

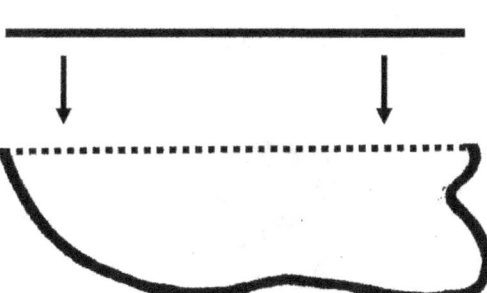

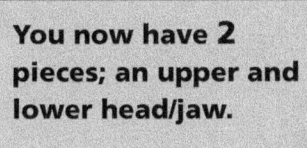

You now have 2 pieces; an upper and lower head/jaw.

8 Follow steps **28-31** on pages **90-91** to create the thumb tube for the lower jaw. Glue into place.

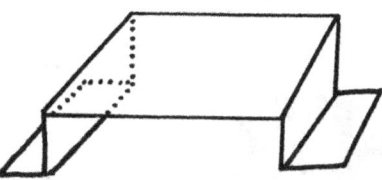

9 Follow steps **16-20** on pages **86-87** to create the palate and finger grip for the upper jaw.

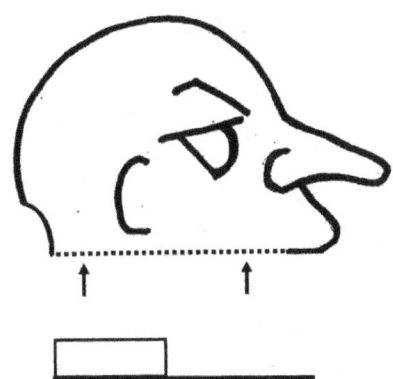

10 Tape and mache in place.

Mouth Puppet over Clay Mold

11

You now have **2** parts of the puppet that can fit on your hand.

Test that your hand fits well inside the puppet.

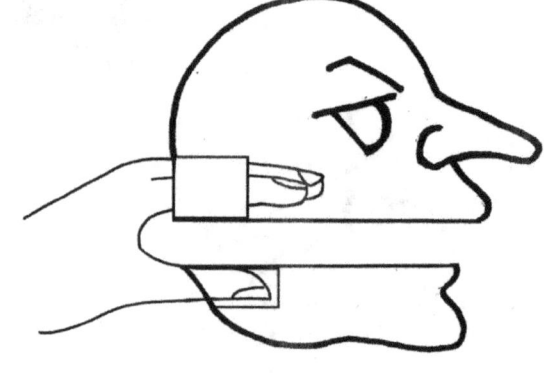

12

Paint the **2** parts of the puppet.

Apply a basecoat of white first.

Let dry.

13

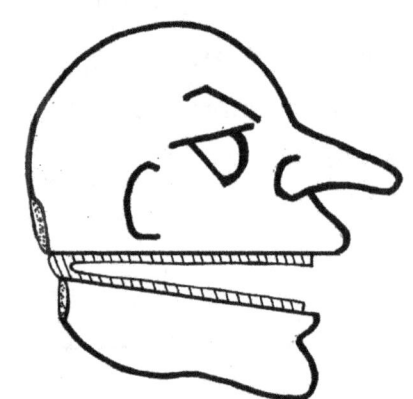

Follow steps **33-35** on pages **91-92** to create a connecting palate as shown out of a contrasting cloth or felt or foam material.

Glue it into place; connecting the **2** parts of the mouth.

Let dry.

14

Attach the sleeve following step **35** on page **92**.

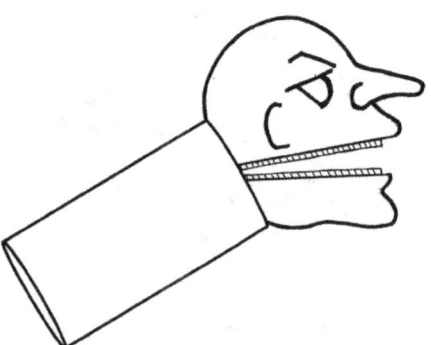

15

Finish decorating your mouth puppet.

Puppets, Puppetry and Gogmagog

A central rod is the back bone of this puppet. Its arms are often attached to 2 thinner rods of wood or metal. A rod puppet may be manipulated by one or two puppeteers. There are many kinds of rod puppets and combinations with other kinds of puppets. Sometimes the rods come from the top of the head and are manipulated from above. At other times they are operated from below with the central rod coming from the bottom of the head.

Rod Puppets

A marotte is a puppet with a head on a single stick. It has no arms or legs. It was originally a jester's stick that often looked like the jester himself. It can be made with very simple materials.

Different Ways of Making the Heads and Attaching Them to the Sticks

Materials:
a dowel stick about 18-24inches/ 45-60cm long, ½-¾ inch/ 13-16mm width, newspaper, brown paper, paper mache glue, masking tape, duct tape, different objects to form the base of the head: old tennis balls, polystyrene balls, old dolls head, empty liter water container, objects for eyes: polystyrene balls, ping pong balls, cardboard, disposable drinking cups, hot glue sticks, paint.

Tools:
hot glue gun, paint brushes.

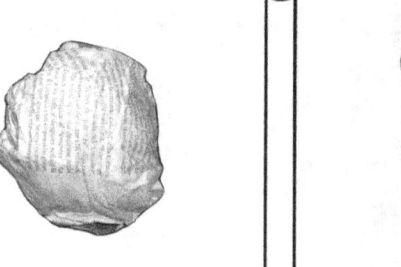

A scrunched up ball of newspaper is taped over the stick. Apply **4** layers of paper mache, alternating newspaper and brown paper. Let dry.

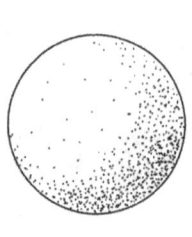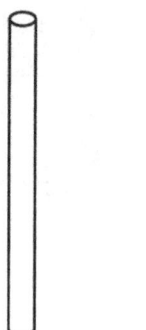

A polystyrene ball is attached to the stick. I use hot glue although it melts the foam also. Be careful; hot glue can cause burns. Apply **2** layers of paper mache, (**1** newspaper, **1** brown). Let dry.

Marotte

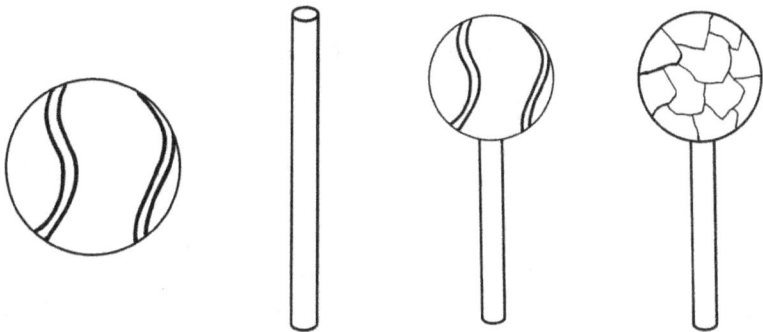

Try cutting a small hole in an old tennis ball. Glue it on to the stick with hot glue. Be careful. Hot glue can cause burns. Apply **4** layers of paper mache, (**1** newspaper, **1** brown). Let dry.

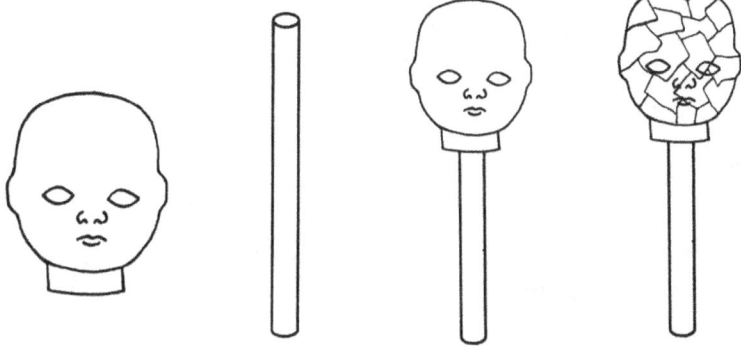

An old doll's head can be transformed into a marrotte head. Hot glue it on to the stick. Be careful. Hot glue can cause burns. Tape around the neck opening with duct tape. Apply **2** layers of paper mache, (**1** newspaper, **1** brown). Let dry.

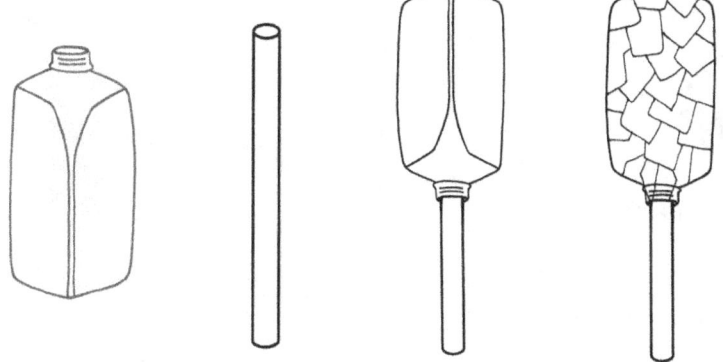

An empty liter water container can also become a marotte head. Tape it to the stick as shown. Apply **2** layers of paper mache, (**1** newspaper, **1** brown). Let dry.

Puppets, Puppetry and Gogmagog

The Facial Features

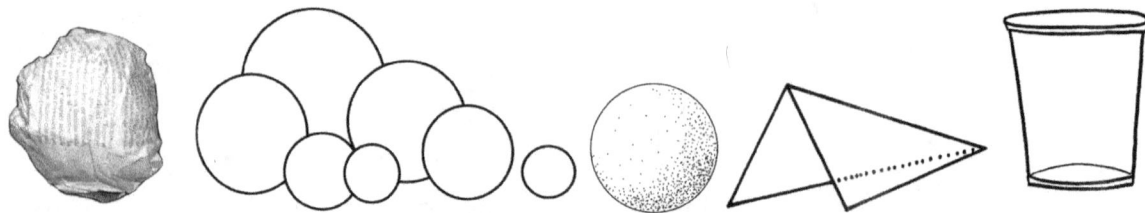

To make eyes, noses, mouths and ears you can use many kinds of objects: balls of newspaper, polystyrene or wooden balls, geometric cardboard forms and disposable cups are just a few.

1

I have decided to use the water container as a base for the head of the marotte.

Glue or tape on **2** polystyrene balls for eyes.

2

Create a beak from a triangle of cardboard.

Glue or tape it on to the head.

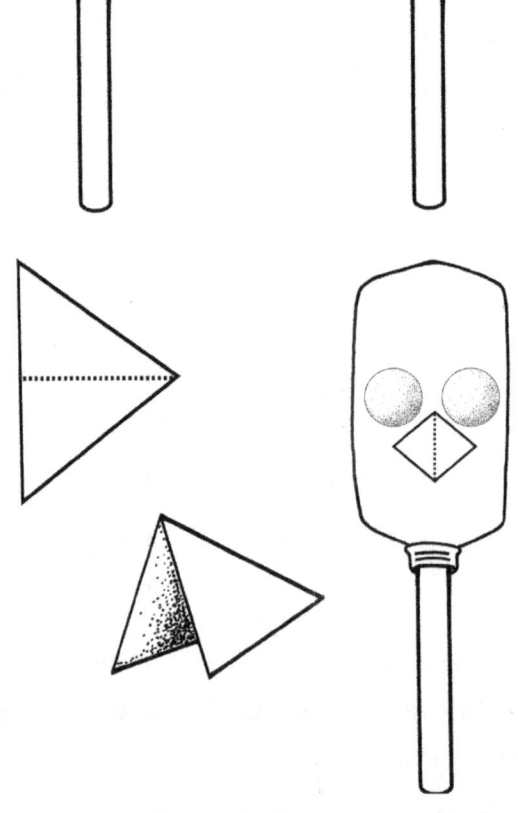

Puppets, Puppetry and Gogmagog

Cut off the top of a disposable glass as shown.

Glue or tape it on to the head to form the mouth.

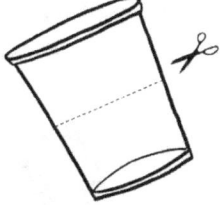
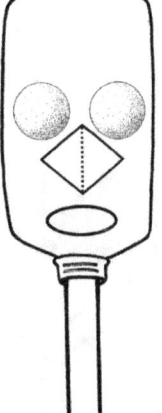

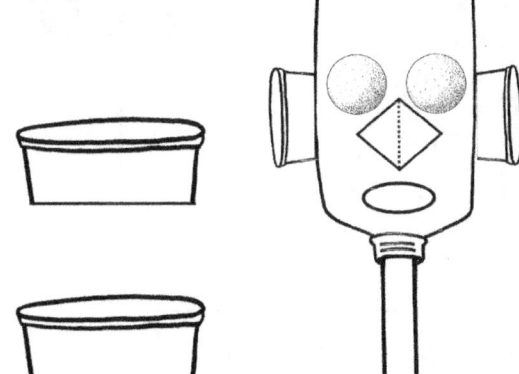

Cut off **2** more tops of disposable glasses to use for ears.

Glue or tape them into place.

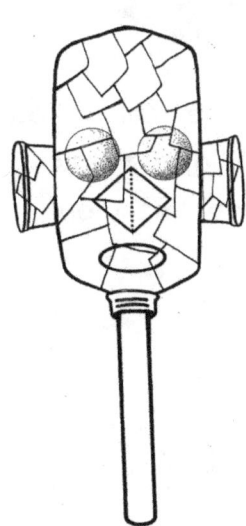

Apply **2** more layers of paper mache (**1** newspaper, **1** brown) over the features and head, completely covering the tape.

Let dry.

Paint and decorate your marotte.

Apply a basecoat of white first.

Marotte

Puppets, Puppetry and Gogmagog   Rod Puppets   **101**

Gallery of Possibilities

You can create a detailed head sculpting all the features in clay.

Variation: Marotte Made Over a Clay Mold

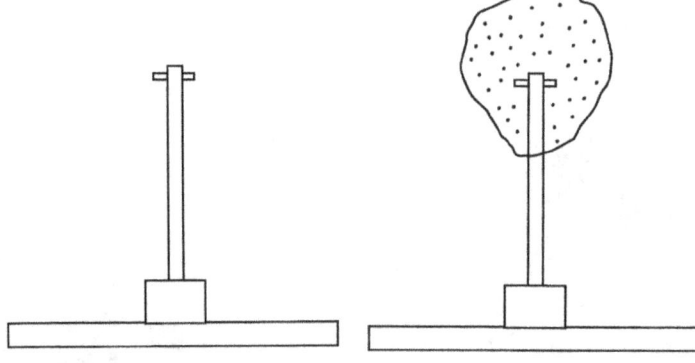

To create the head, follow steps **1-17** of the **Basic Glove Puppet** head on pages **57-64**.

Materials and tools: the same as the **Basic Glove Puppet** head on page **56**.

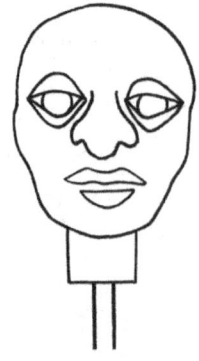 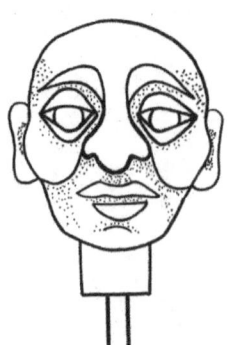 

Puppets, Puppetry and Gogmagog

Glue the head on the stick with hot glue. Be careful; hot glue can cause burns.

If the neck is wider than the stick, tape it on securely with duct tape.

Paint and decorate your marotte.

Apply a basecoat of white first.

Apply **2** layers of paper mache (**1** newspaper, **1** brown) over the duct tape. Let dry.

Marotte

The marotte is held in one hand and the other hand of the puppeteer becomes the hand of the puppet character.

Variation: Marotte with the Puppeteer's Hand

Create your head using any of the methods previously mentioned.

Cut a large circle of cloth. The diameter will depend on how long you want the costume to hang.

Additional materials: large piece of cloth to make a full circle costume for the marotte and puppeteer.

3

Fold the circle in half.

4

Find the midpoint along the folded edge and cut a small semi circle. This is the opening for the neck of the puppet. Don't make it too big.

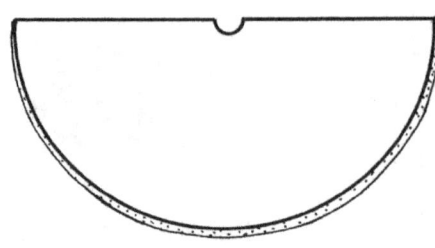

5

Glue the neck of the puppet inside the neckline of the costume.

Let dry.

6

Cut a small hole in the costume as shown. This hole is for your hand to come through.

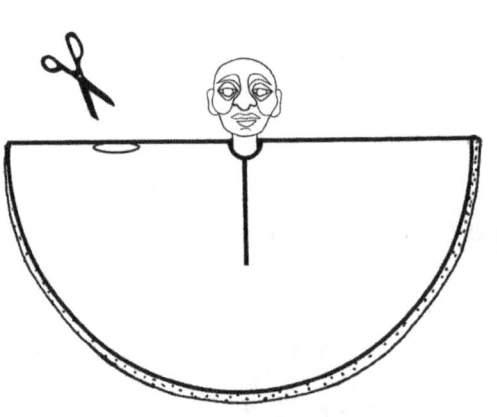

Now you can operate the marotte with one hand on the stick (unseen) and your own hand appearing as the puppet's hand.

104

Puppets, Puppetry and Gogmagog

The pop-up puppet is an extension of the marotte. The head and arms are attached to a cloth body and appear out of and disappear into a cone. The action is controlled by a stick that passes through the cone and is attached to the head.

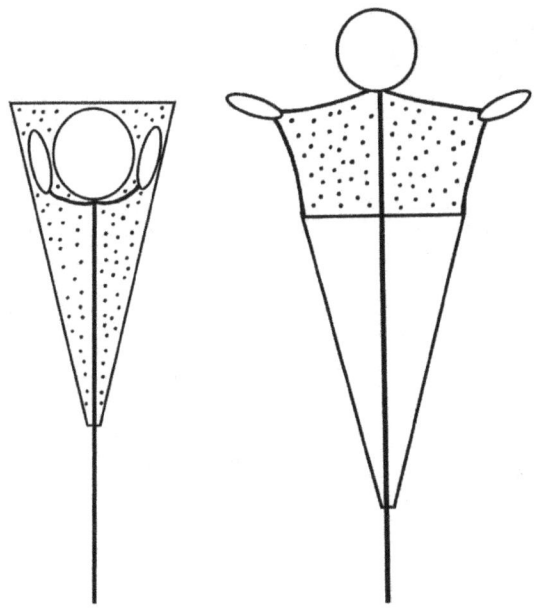

Pop-up

Materials:
cardboard for the cone, pencil or marker, masking tape, newspaper, brown paper, long thin dowel, **1** plastic egg or small polystyrene ball, white glue, hot glue sticks, fabric glue, air dry clay, acrylic paints, hot glue sticks, cloth for costume, sewing thread, foam material or felt for hands.

Tools:
scissors, hot glue gun, sewing machine, paint brushes.

The first thing to think about is the size of the cone in relation to the head and hands.

The head, hands and cloth body all have to fit inside the cone when the stick is pulled down.

The Cone

Cut a circle from cardboard. The diameter will depend on how tall you want the cone to be. It will also depend on how wide you want the mouth of the cone. For example the height can be **2½** times the diameter (4 inches/10cm diameter, 10 inches/25.5cm height).

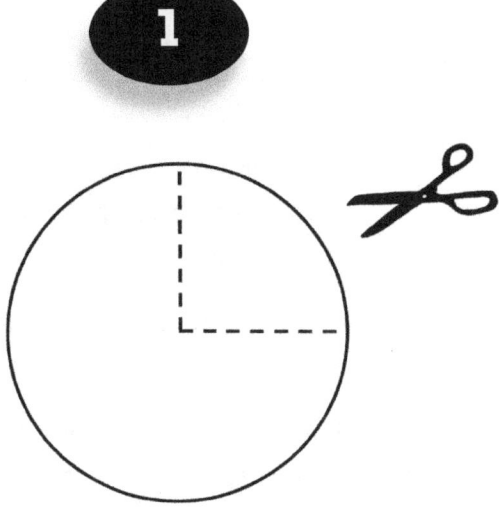

Puppets, Puppetry and Gogmagog   Rod Puppets **105**

2

Form the cone and tape it together with masking tape.

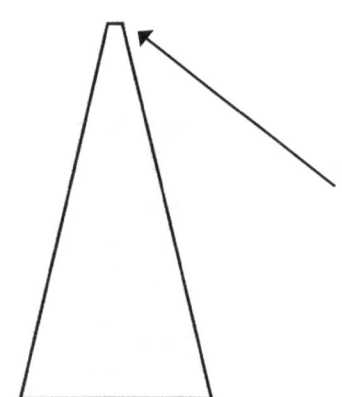

3

Cut off the very tip of the cone so that your stick can easily pass through.

4

Apply **2-4** layers of paper mache, alternating newspaper and brown paper.

The number of layers depends on how thick the cardboard is. If you have doubts, apply **4** layers.

Let dry.

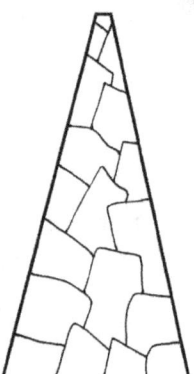

5

Test that your stick can still move easily up and down inside the cone.

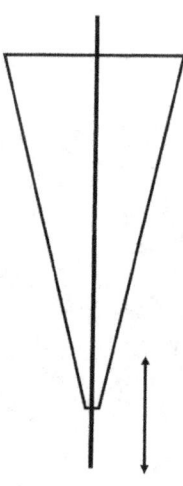

The Head

I have at hand different sizes of polystyrene balls, ping pong balls and plastic eggs.

For the following instructions I will use a plastic egg.

Remember the finished head must be able to fit into the cone (allowing for hands as well) so don't make it too big.

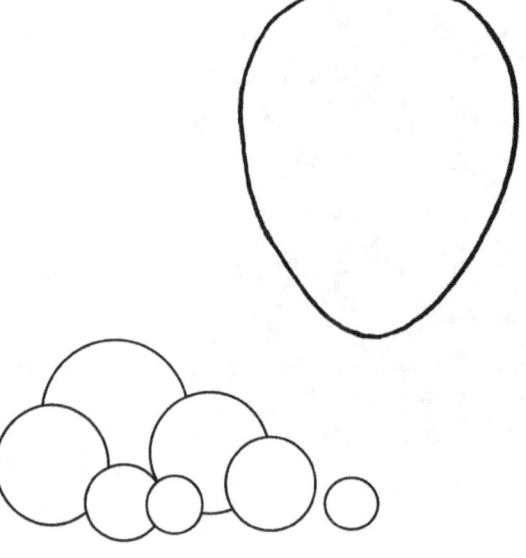

106

Puppets, Puppetry and Gogmagog

Apply **2** layers of paper mache (**1** newspaper, **1** brown paper) over the plastic egg.

Let dry.

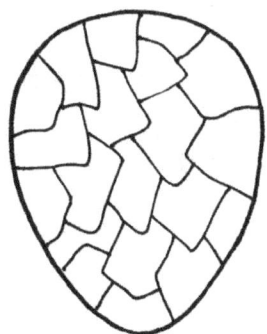

Knead a small quantity of air dry clay and form the facial features on the mached egg. See page **132** for more information about air dry clay.

Let dry.

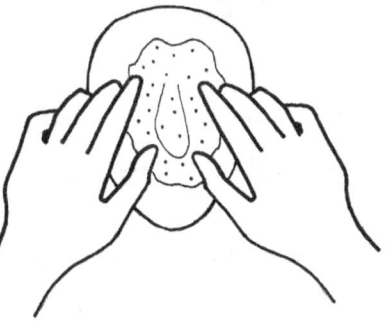

Paint and decorate the head once the air dry clay is really dry.

Apply a basecoat of white first.

Remember that the head must fit (along with the hands) inside the cone.

Make a small hole at the bottom of the head and attach the stick to the head with hot glue.

Be careful; hot glue can cause burns.

Puppets, Puppetry and Gogmagog

The Costume

Choose your cloth to make the costume. It is better if the cloth is not too bulky.

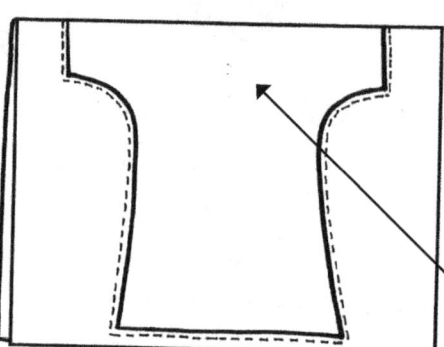

Create a pattern on a large piece of paper, copying the form shown. Make sure the bottom edge will fit around the mouth of the cone.

Pin it on to the cloth and cut it out. Remember to leave an additional space for seam allowance.

Do not cut along the folded edge.

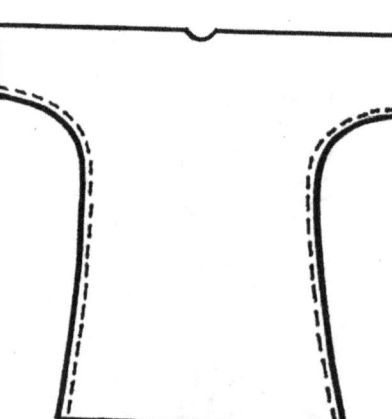

With right sides together, sew by machine, by hand or glue the front and back as shown.

Don't sew the sleeve openings shut.

Turn the costume inside out and proceed to the creation of the hands.

The Hands

14

The hands for a pop-up are generally quite small.

Choose your hand design.

15

If you make the hands from foam material cut **2** thicknesses out for each hand and glue them together with fabric glue.

You can also make the hands from sturdy cardboard.

Make sure they will fit into the openings of the sleeves.

16

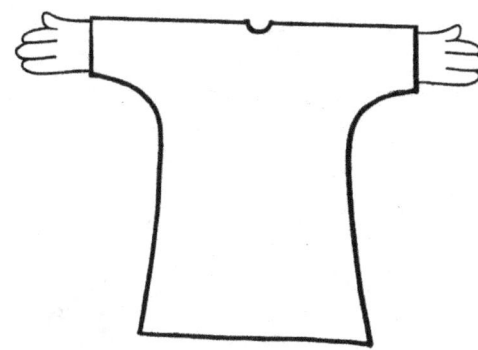

Glue each hand to the sleeves (thumbs up).

Let dry.

17

Insert the head and stick through the neck opening in the costume.

18

Glue the neck of the costume to the stick.

Pop-up

Puppets, Puppetry and Gogmagog Rod Puppets **109**

19

Apply glue around the top of the outside edge of the mouth of the cone.

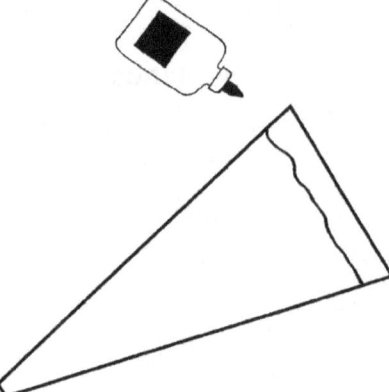

20

Carefully insert the cone into the hem of the costume.

Let the hem overlap 1 inch/2.5cm outside of the cone.

Fix in place and let dry.

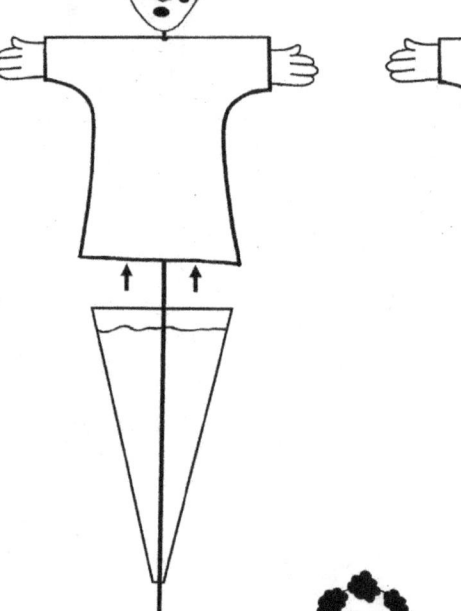

21

Finish decorating the pop-up as you please.

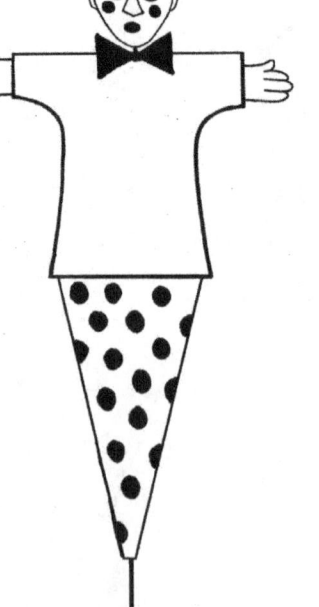

Rod Puppet Manipulated from Below

Materials:

for materials required for making the paper mache head see page **56**, different sized dowels: ¾ inch/19mm for central control and for the handles of the hand controls, ¼inch/6mm for hand controls, small wood screws and washers, thin plywood or thick corrugated cardboard for shoulders and hands, sand paper, hot glue sticks, small piece of foam rubber, carpenter's glue, epoxy, white or fabric glue, cardboard for hand alternative, newspaper, brown paper, paper mache glue, flexible aluminium wire (thick and thin), duct tape, air dry clay (hand alternative), umbrella spokes (hand alternative), string, cloth for costume, sewing thread, paint.

Tools:

drill and drill bits, scissors, hot glue gun, sewing machine, sewing needles, upholstery needle, paint brushes.

The rod puppet that is manipulated from below is basically an extension of the marotte.

The simplest rod puppet is a head on a stick with a cloth attached to the neck that covers the puppeteer's hand.

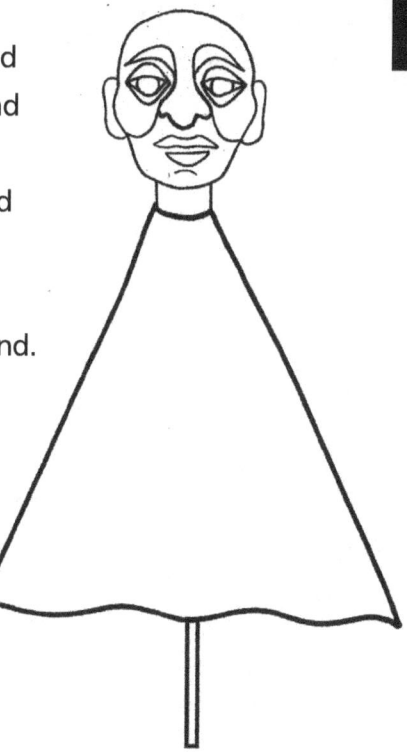

Consider this:

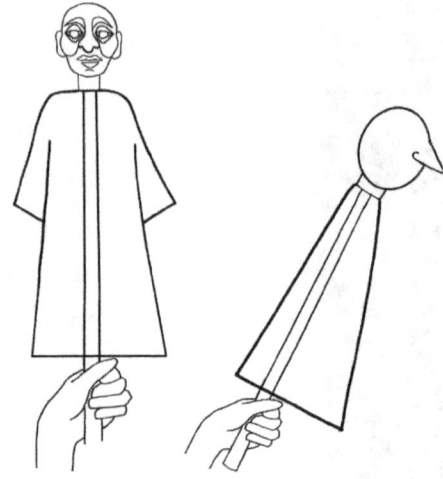

Short Central Rod

A short central rod gives great flexibility to the puppet. It can bend forwards, backwards and side to side with the movement of the wrist.

The wrist of the puppeteer is at the height (more or less) of the waist of the puppet.

Long Central Rod

The long central rod allows the puppeteer to manipulate the rod puppet higher over the head.

However the puppet cannot bend from the waist without additional mechanisms.

The long central rod is essential if you want to add legs and feet to the puppet.

Rod Puppet with Fixed Head

This puppet has hands that are manipulated with thin rods and the head is fixed to the central rod.

Create the head of the puppet following steps **1-17** for the **Basic Glove Puppet** on pages **57-64**.

Decide whether you want a long or short rod and attach it to the head according to the following instructions.

112

Puppets, Puppetry and Gogmagog

Rod Puppet Manipulated from Below

2

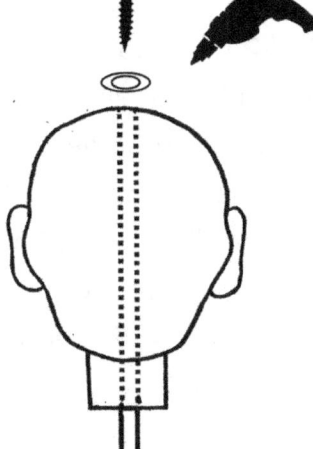
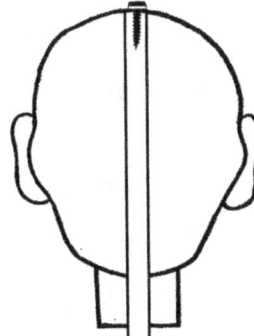

Drill a small hole in the top of the head.

Join the head and the central rod with a wood screw, separated by a small washer.

The Shoulders

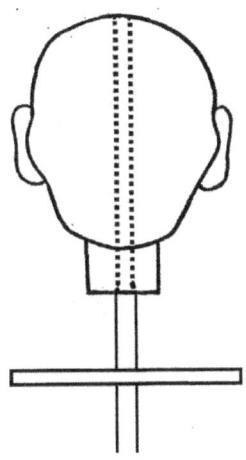

In this next step you will create a shoulder plate of thin plywood or very thick cardboard.

The width of the shoulder plate should be in proportion to the head. It may be a little narrower to allow for extra bulk of the costume later on.

3

Cut a piece of plywood the desired length of the shoulders. The depth should be about **3** thickness of the central rod.

4

Drill a hole in the middle of the shoulder plate to accommodate the central rod. It should be a tight fit; so don't make the hole too big.

5

Drill **2** small holes in the middle of either end of the shoulder plate. Later on the hands will be joined to the shoulder plate by strong strings through these holes.

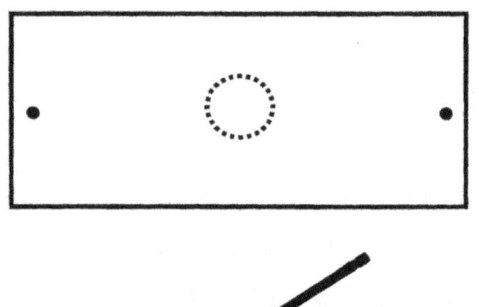

I use a spade bit to make the central hole.

6

Round off the edges of the plate as shown. Sand the edges of the plate smooth.

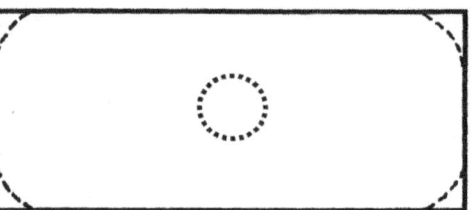

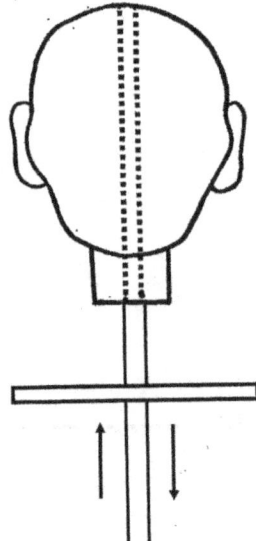

> **Test that you can slide the shoulder plate on to the central rod.**
> **It should be a tight fit.**

Puppets, Puppetry and Gogmagog

The padding for the shoulder plate will be created from foam rubber.

I generally use foam rubber that is about 2 inches/ 5cm thick.

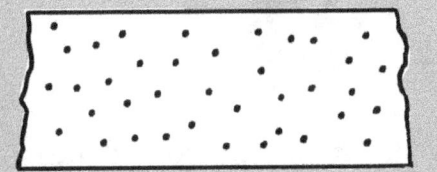

7

Trim the foam rubber to the shoulder shape you desire.

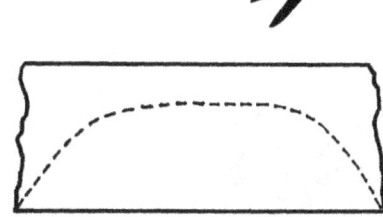

8

Glue the foam shoulder on to the shoulder plate with hot glue.

Be careful; hot glue can cause burns.

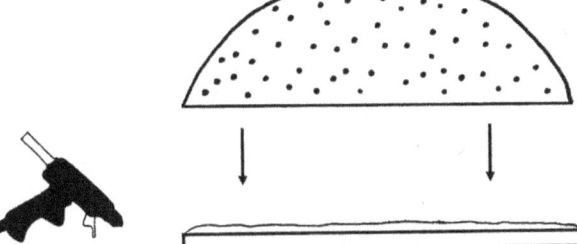

9

Trim away a hole in the middle of the foam to meet the hole in the wooden shoulder plate.

10

Apply wood glue to the hole in the wooden shoulder plate and to the borders of the hole in the foam.

You can also use hot glue for the borders of the foam hole. Be careful; hot glue can cause burns.

Rod Puppet Manipulated from Below

Puppets, Puppetry and Gogmagog

Accommodate the central rod into the shoulder.

Let dry.

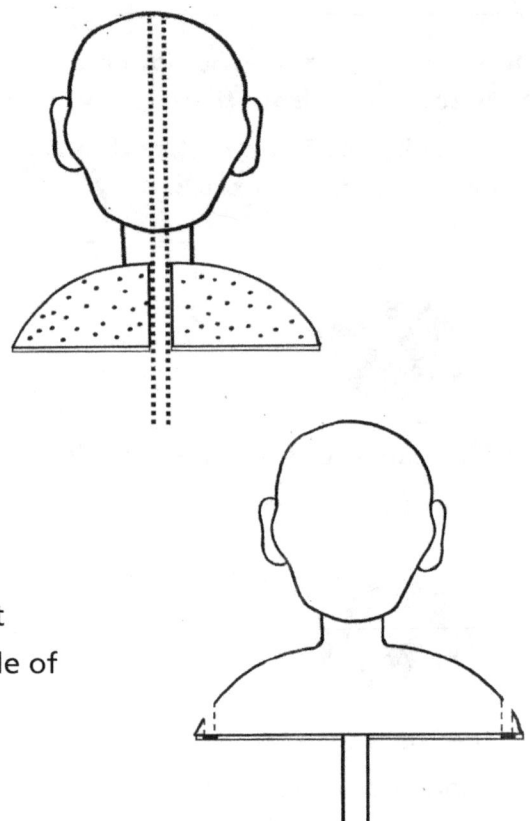

Make sure you can access the small holes at either end of the shoulder. I cut away a little of the foam for this.

The Hands

The rods that control the hands of the rod puppet are directly attached to the hands themselves; so the hands must be thick enough for a rod to attach to and strong enough to take all the movement.

Version 1

1. Cut a hand shape in proportion to the head. You can use thick corrugated cardboard for this.

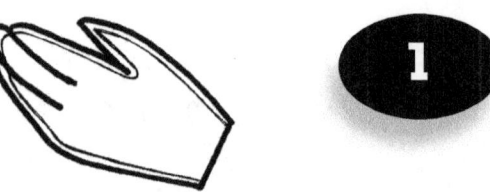

Create a copy of the shape and glue the together. Repeat for the second hand.

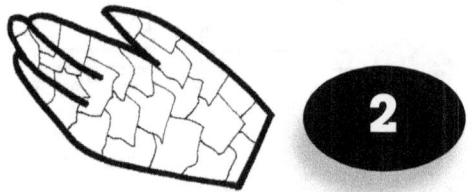

2. Apply **1** layer of brown paper mache to both hands.

Let dry.

Puppets, Puppetry and Gogmagog

Rod Puppet Manipulated from Below

Version 2

1 With this method you can bend the fingers into the shape you want.

Cut **2** shapes as shown out of thin plywood or thick corrugated cardboard.

These form wrist and hand plates.

2 Cut lengths of thick aluminium wire and bend them into the finger shapes as shown.

Lay them onto the hand plate.

The thumb will be attached to the other side of the hand plate.

3 Hot glue the aluminium finger wires in place.

The thumb wire will be glued onto the other side of the hand plate.

Be careful; hot glue can cause burns.

4 Tape over the glued finger and thumb wires.

Puppets, Puppetry and Gogmagog

 Flesh out the fingers, thumbs and palms with rolls and balls of scrunched up newspaper and tape them into place.

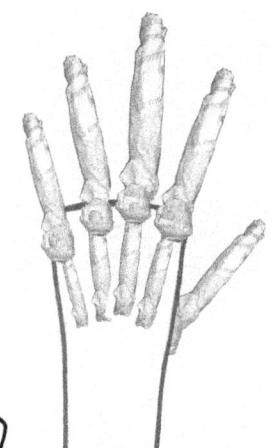

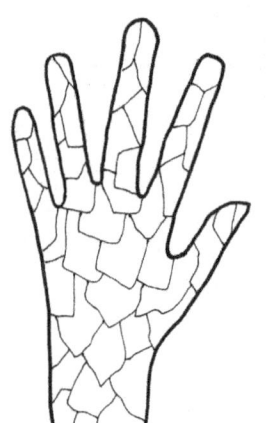

 Apply **2** layers of paper mache (**1** newspaper, **1** brown) over the whole hand and wrist.

Let dry.

Version 3

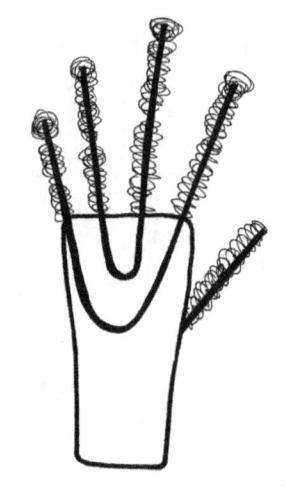

 Create the hand and wrist plate as shown in **Version 2**.

Create the finger wires and glue them into place as shown in **Version 2**.

Twist thinner aluminum wire around the finger wires to give them shape.

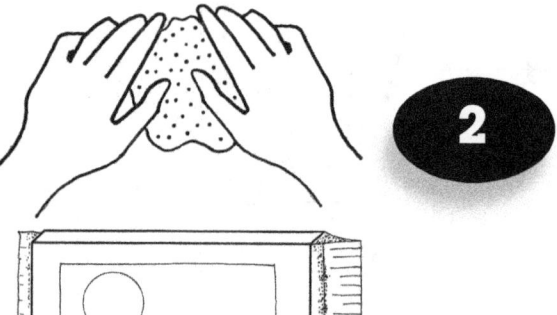

 Take a small amount of air dry clay and knead it a little for use in the next step. Go to page **132** for more information about air dry clay.

Remember to close the air dry clay package tightly when not in use.

Puppets, Puppetry and Gogmagog

Rod Puppet Manipulated from Below

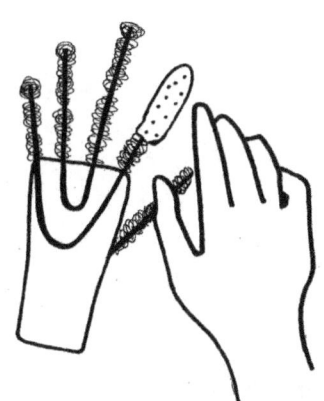

Flesh out the fingers with small amounts of the air dry clay.

Add form to the palms and wrists.

Let dry thoroughly.

We now continue with the process on page 116.

Drill a small hole through the middle of the end of each wrist.

This will accommodate the string that will be used to attach each hand to the shoulder plate later on.

Paint head and hands.

Apply a white base coat fist.

Let dry.

Tie a long string to each hole at the end of the shoulders.

Tie a hand to the end of each string. The hands may be loosely tied until you can ascertain the exact length of string in proportion to the sleeve later on.

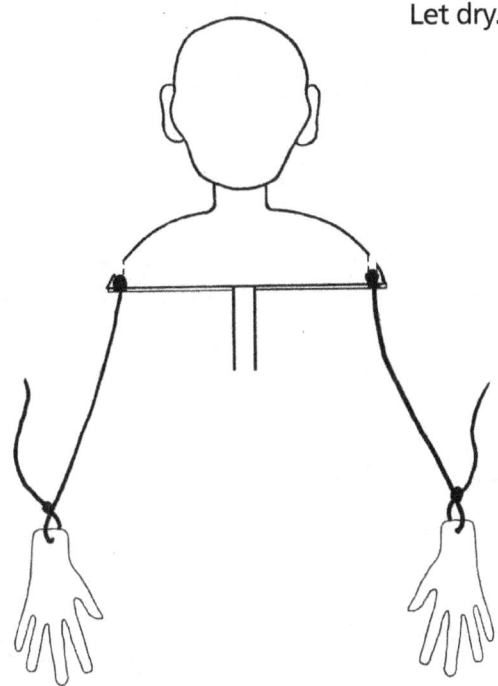

Puppets, Puppetry and Gogmagog

The Basic Costume

The length of the costume should cover the central rod if the rod is long. If the central rod is short, the costume should cover the arm of the puppeteer beyond the elbow.

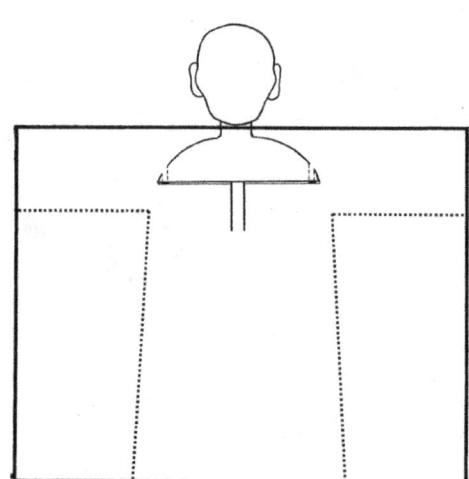

Create a pattern in paper as shown.

Lay the puppet on top of a large piece of paper. Draw a line around the neck and shoulders.

Extend the line to create the length of the costume. It is always better to have too much than too little.

Create a small margin for seam allowance.

Cut out the pattern.

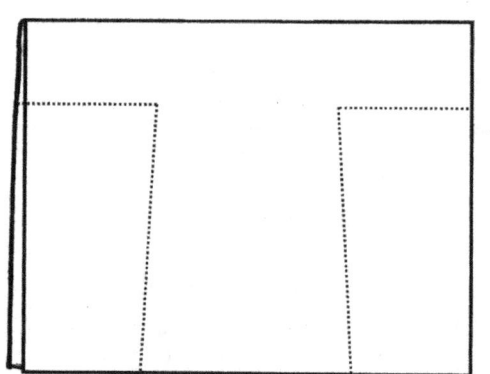

Fold the cloth you have chosen in **2**.

Pin the pattern on the cloth; the neck and shoulder line lies on the fold.

Cut around the pattern. **Do not cut along the fold.**

120

Puppets, Puppetry and Gogmagog

Sew the edges of the costume right sides together as shown.

Do not sew the ends of the sleeves or the bottom of the costume closed.

Cut a **small** half circle for the neck opening.

Do not make this too big. It should be only just big enough for the neck of the puppet.

Passing through **1** thickness of the cloth only, cut a small vertical line about 1.5 inches/38mm from the middle of the neck opening down towards the bottom of the costume.

This vertical opening will be on the back side of the costume. This opening will allow the head of the puppet to pass through later on.

Turn the costume right side out.

Sew a small hem around the bottom of the costume.

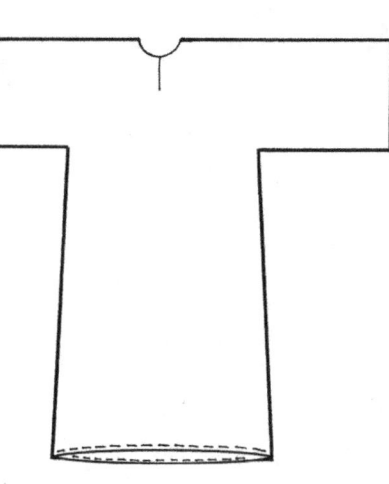

Rod Puppet Manipulated from Below

Puppets, Puppetry and Gogmagog — Rod Puppets **121**

Accommodate the head and shoulders inside the costume as shown.

Glue the neck of the costume to the neck of the puppet.

Close the vertical slit at the back of the costume with needle and thread.

Check the length of the hand strings and tie securely.

Apply glue to the wrist ends of the hands.

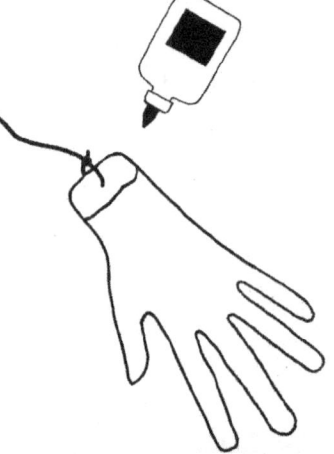

Glue the sleeves to the hands.

The Control Rods for the Hands

The control for hands can be made of wooden dowels (if the puppet is small), thin metal rods or umbrella spokes.

I generally paint the rods black.

Here are **4** alternatives for rods and how to attach them to the hands.

Version 1

Drill a small hole in a thin dowel.

Attach the rod to the hand with a small wood screw and epoxy as shown.

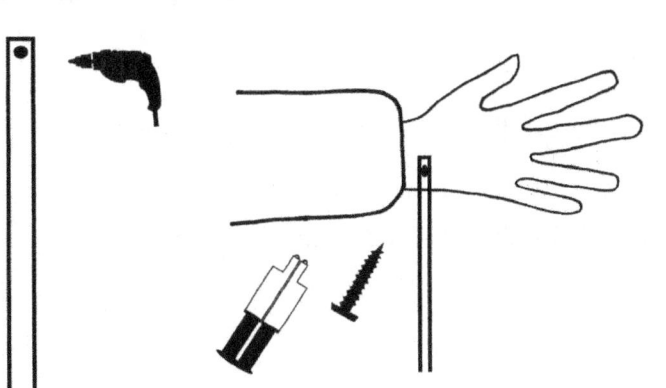

Version 2

Drill a small hole in a thin dowel.

Thread an upholstery needle with string and tie a big knot at one end.

Pass the needle through the dowel and then horizontally through the wrist to the other side.

Tie the string off tightly with another big knot.

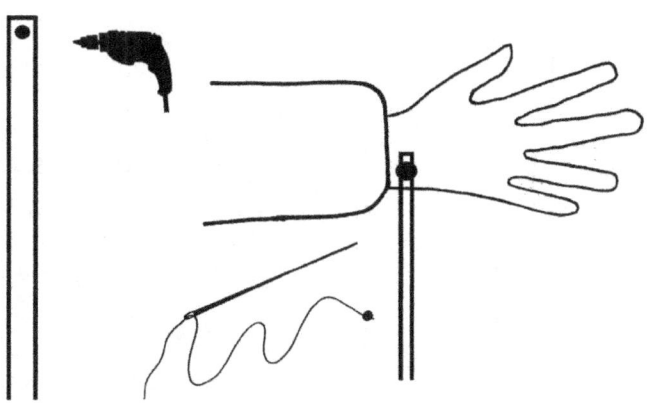

Rod Puppet Manipulated from Below

Version 3

Use an umbrella spoke and attach it as shown with a screw and epoxy.

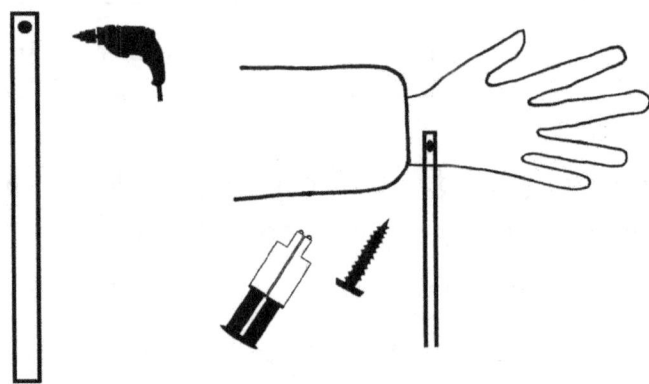

Version 4

Drill a small hole in the wrist as shown.

Insert a wooden dowel or metal rod as far as it will enter into the hand and glue into place with epoxy.

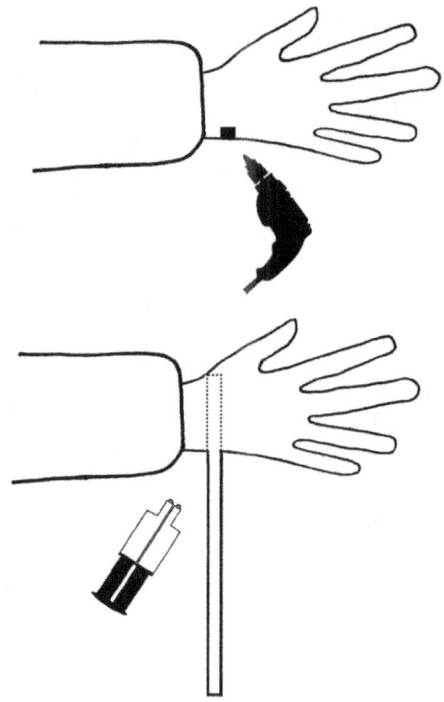

Attaching Grips to the Rods

Once you have ascertained the length of the rods, you can create the grips. These will make manipulation easier.

Cut a thicker piece of dowel for the grip. It should be longer enough to fit into the palm of your hand.

Drill a hole the width of your control rod into one end of the wooden grip as shown.

Glue the control rod into the grip.

Rod Puppet Manipulated from Below

29

With you rod puppet assembled, finish painting and add further elements of costume.

Additional materials for turning head: small wood collar (see illustration), strip of cardboard, small piece of rope (clothesline).

The Turning Head Mechanism

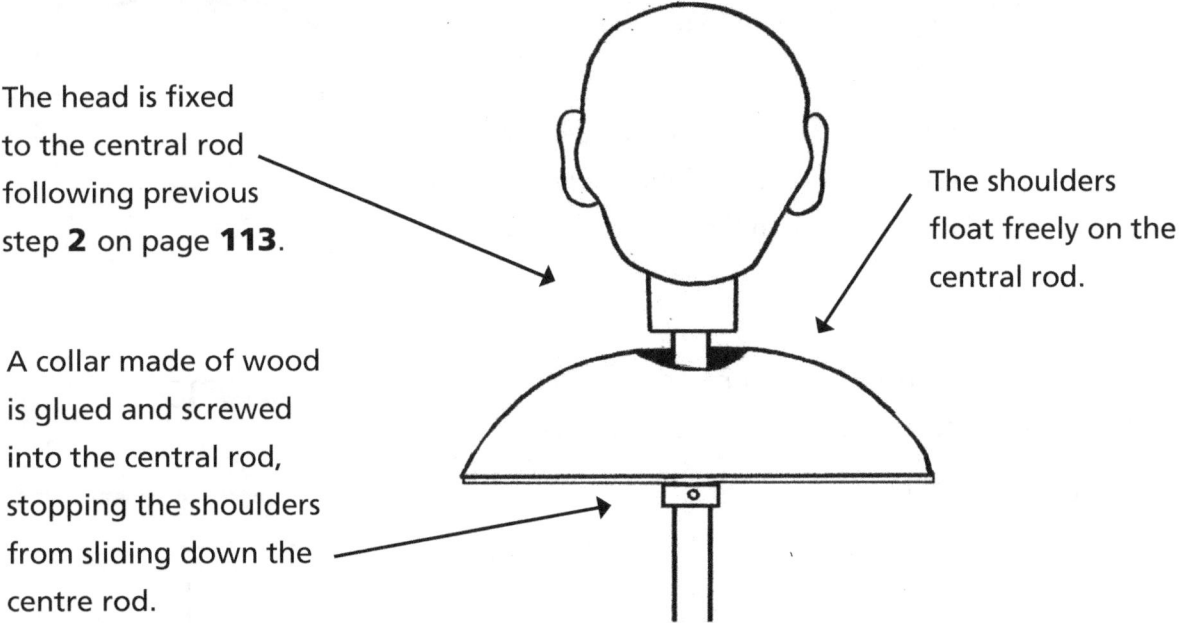

The head is fixed to the central rod following previous step **2** on page **113**.

A collar made of wood is glued and screwed into the central rod, stopping the shoulders from sliding down the centre rod.

The shoulders float freely on the central rod.

Puppets, Puppetry and Gogmagog

 Make the shoulder plate following the previous steps **3-12** on pages **113-116**.

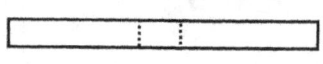

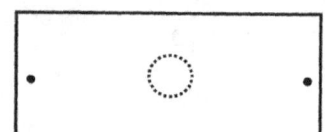

Make sure the hole in shoulder plate is a little bigger than the width of the central rod. The rod must move freely in the shoulder plate.

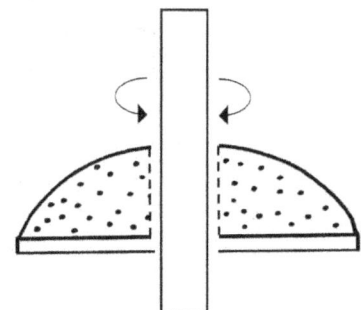

2 Attach the collar to the central rod, using one of the alternatives below.

Version 1

Screw a round wooden collar to the central rod below the shoulders at the level you wish.

This wooden collar can be made of plywood. It must fit tightly around the central rod.

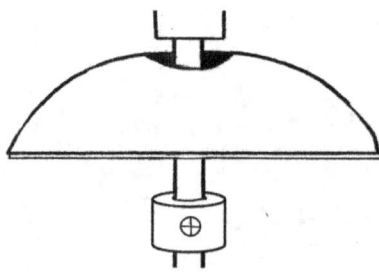

Version 2

Cut a long strip of cardboard.

Apply white glue to one side of the cardboard.

Wrap the cardboard round and round the central rod at the height you desire until it is thicker than the hole in the shoulder plate. Let dry.

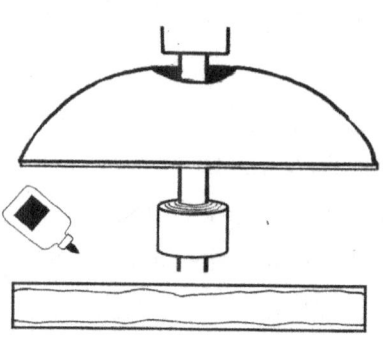

Version 3

Glue and wrap rope around the central rod at the level you desire. Let dry.

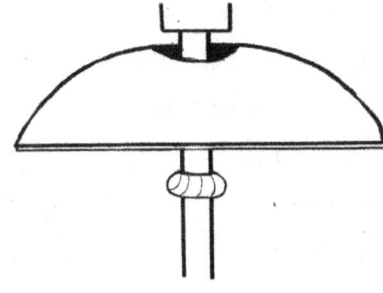

Rod Puppet Manipulated from Above

Materials:
the materials needed to create the paper mache head are the same that appear on page **56** for the **Basic Glove Puppet** head. Different sized dowels: ¾ inch/19mm for central control and for the handles of the hand controls, ¼inch/6mm, small wood screws and washers, thin plywood or thick corrugated cardboard for shoulders and hands, sand paper, hot glue sticks, small piece of foam rubber, carpenter's glue, epoxy, white or fabric glue, cardboard, newspaper, brown paper, paper mache glue, duct tape, air dry clay, umbrella spokes, string, cloth for costume, sewing thread, paints.

Tools:
drill and drill bits, scissors, hot glue gun, sewing machine, sewing needles, upholstery needle, paint brushes.

You can make simple rod puppets with the central rod coming from the top of the head.

These puppets are useful as minor characters in a show with rod and string puppets or to perform on the ground in front of you.

1

Create the head using any of the processes for the **Marotte** on pages **100-103** or for the **Basic Glove Puppet** head on pages **57-64**.

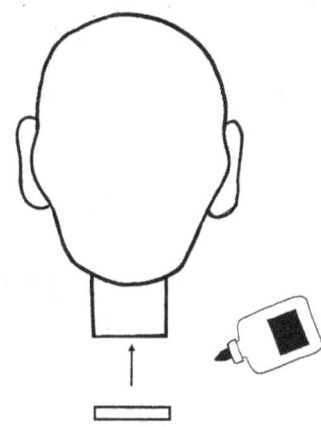

2

If the puppet has a neck, cover the opening with strong cardboard or thin plywood. Glue and/or tape it into place. If you have used tape, cover the tape with **2** layers of paper mache (**1** newspaper, **1** brown).

Let dry.

Puppets, Puppetry and Gogmagog   Rod Puppets **127**

Drill a hole in the top of the head the size of the width of your wooden rod.

  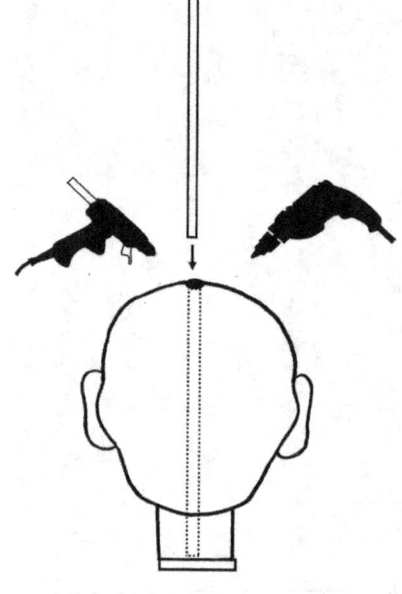

Pass the rod through the hole until it reaches the bottom of the neck.

Glue it into place on top of the head. I use hot glue for this. Be careful; hot glue can cause burns.

If you are worried that the rod will come loose, drill a hole through the base of the neck.

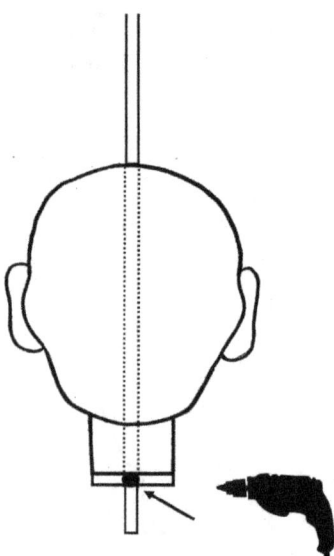

Pass the stick though this hole.

Drill a smaller hole laterally. It should be the size of a smaller stick that you will pass through the central rod at the bottom of the neck.

Position the small stick and glue it into place. Now your central rod will not come out.

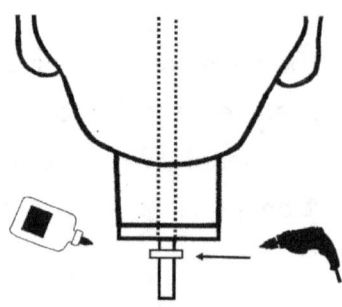

Attach cloth around the neck for a costume.

Follow steps **10-18** on page **108** of the marotte to create a full circle costume if you so desire.

You now have a very simple rod puppet operated from above.

If you want to add shoulders, follow steps **3-6** on pages **113-114**.

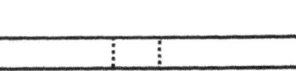

Fix the central rod in place using the same procedure in steps **8** and **9** on page **128**.

If you want padding on the top of the shoulders, follow steps **7-12** on pages **115-116**.

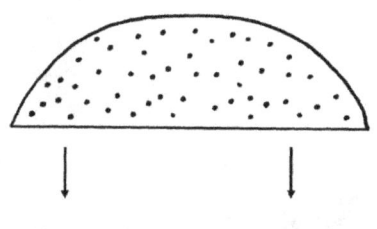

> **Make sure you can pass the central rod through the shoulder plate and padding.**

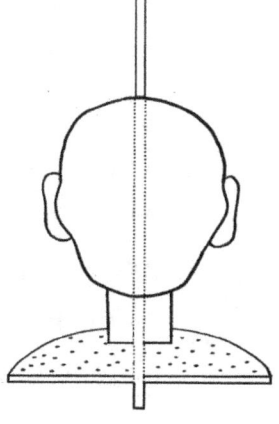

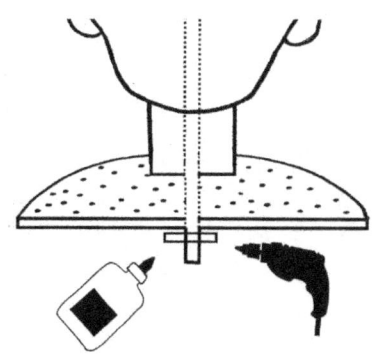

Rod Puppet Manipulated from Above

Puppets, Puppetry and Gogmagog

Rod Puppets **129**

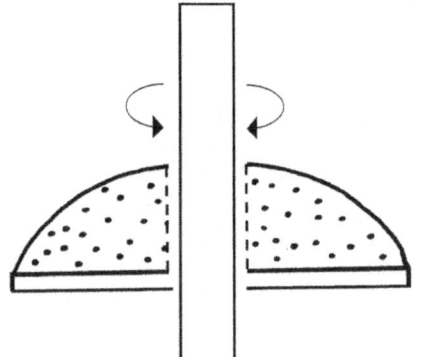

You can also make a turning head mechanism for this puppet.

Follow the instructions on page **126**.

Just remember the rod is now above the head and not below.

Fix the turning central rod following the same instruction in step **13** of this puppet.

The shoulder plate (especially if it is wooden) is also good to suspend daggling legs from.

I use thick string and attach each piece to screw eyes attached to the wooden plate.

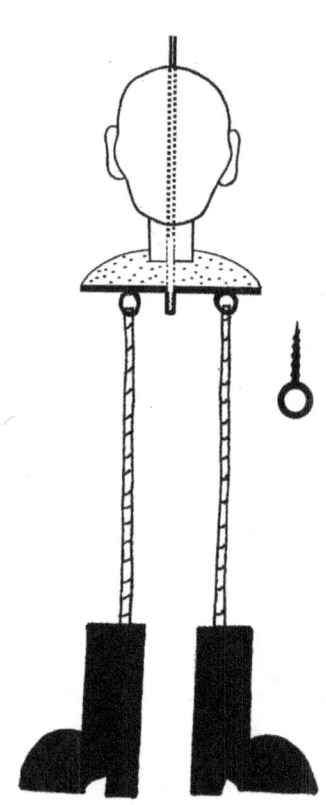

The Feet, Boots and Shoes

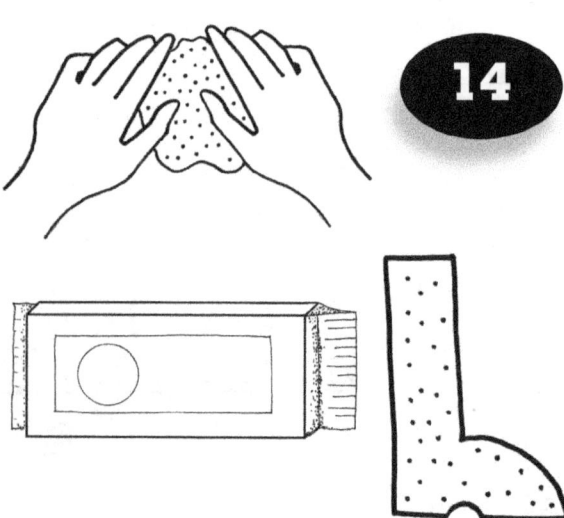

14

I use air dry clay for modeling boots, shoes and sometimes hands.

Knead the clay and create the shapes you want. Go to page **132** for more information about air dry clay.

Remember to keep the packet closed when not in use.

When you are happy with your design, let the boots dry. These can take a day or more to dry thoroughly.

Puppets, Puppetry and Gogmagog

Rod Puppet Manipulated from Above

15 Drill a hole in the top of the boot as shown.

The width of the hole should be the width of the heavy string you are going to use to hang the legs from the shoulder plate of the puppet.

16 Mix up a small quantity of epoxy.

Poke it into the drilled hole and then force the string into the hole. I use a kebab stick to help me with this.

Let dry thoroughly.

Attach the boots to the screw eyes at bottom of the shoulder plate of the puppet as previously illustrated.

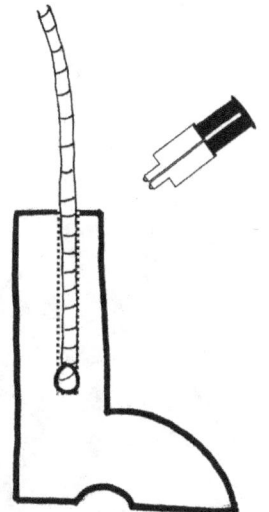

17 Make a costume for your puppet, following the instructions on pages **120-121**.

Attach hands if you desire following the instructions on page **122**.

18 Finish painting and adding details to the costume.

Puppets, Puppetry and Gogmagog   Rod Puppets **131**

One of my favorite puppets to create and manipulate, the rod string puppet is in a way the precursor of the string puppet or marionette. I began to make these puppets after seeing a set of simple puppets made for children that had been constructed in the Czech Republic.

The puppet has a central wire rod that runs from the top of the head to a simple control. The arms are controlled by strings that run from the hands to the control.

Materials:
1 plastic egg, a package of air dry clay, wire coat hanger, news paper, brown paper, paper mache glue, a small block of wood, small eye screws, small thin dowels, acrylic paint, hot glue sticks, **3** small wooden balls; **2** the same size and **1** even smaller (all the wooden balls should be able to slide on to the coat hanger wire) black string to string the puppet hands to the control, acrylic paints.

Tools:
wire cutters, drill and small drill bits, paint brushes, pliers, long nose pliers, hammer, tapestry needle, hot glue gun.

Construct the head following step **3** on page **44** of the **Jiggler Puppet**.

Use air dry clay to mold the facials features directly onto the mached egg.

Air dry clay is an extremely useful material. I use it to make the features on small heads and for hands, feet and shoes.

The clays generally come in white or terracotta colours. Different products have their pro and cons. Some clays are easier to work with. Some clays weigh more than others when dry.

Moisten the clay to work better with it.

The clay takes a while to dry. I leave the pieces I am working on overnight to dry thoroughly.

Keep the package securely closed when you are not working with it.

Mold the facial features with air dry clay.

Let dry.

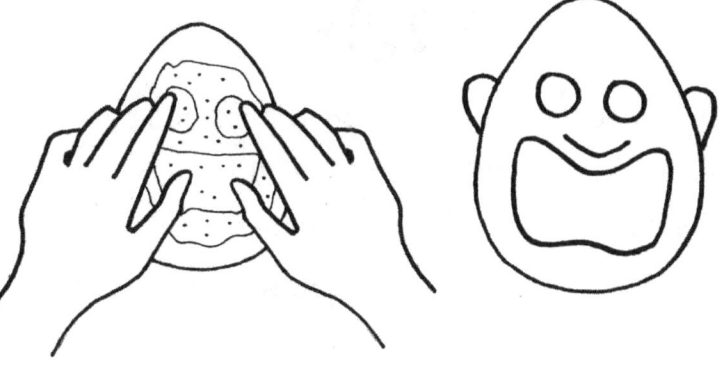

The Central Rod

Using wire cutters, cut the hook off a wire coat hanger at the points illustrated.

Straighten it out. I use pliers for this.

Drill a small hole in the top and bottom of the head for the wire to pass through.

Pass the wire through the head.

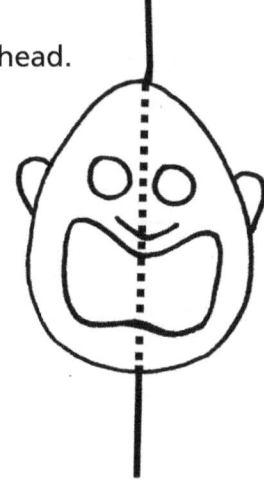

Create a long loop at the bottom of the head by bending the wire with pliers as shown.

This loop forms the neck of the puppet.

It is also the means by which the head is attached to the torso.

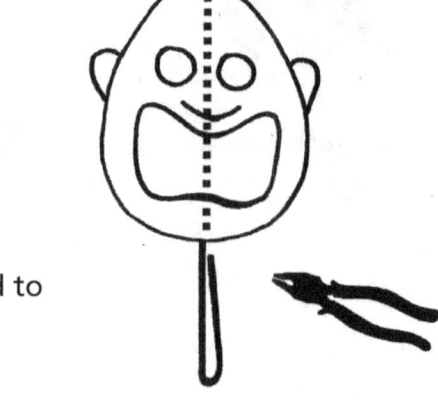

7

Have at hand a small block of wood which measures 2x2x1 inches/ 5x5x2cm. This is good for a puppet whose total height is approximately 8 inches/20cm tall.

Drill a hole in the middle of one end of the wooden block. The hole should be bigger than the bent wire neck created in step **6**.

Check the illustration for the position of the hole.

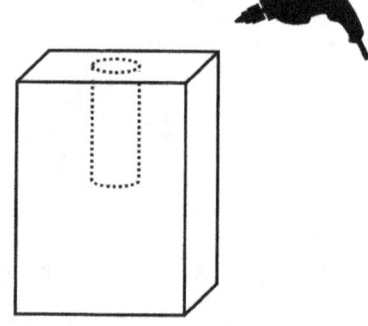

Drill a smaller lateral hole at the point shown in the illustration. The hole should go right through to the other side.

This hole will be for the shoulder strings later on.

Check that the neck wire fits easily into the vertical hole.

It should be able to turn freely. This will allow the head to turn from side to side.

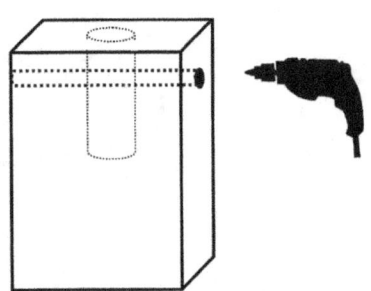

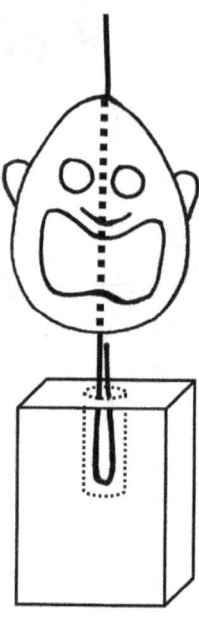

Puppets, Puppetry and Gogmagog

Hammer a small nail from the front of the block, through the loop and into the other side of the wood.

The nail should not be so long as to pierce through to the outside of the other side of the wood.

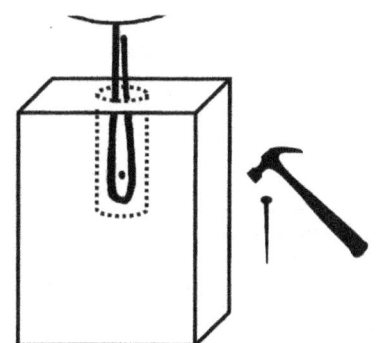

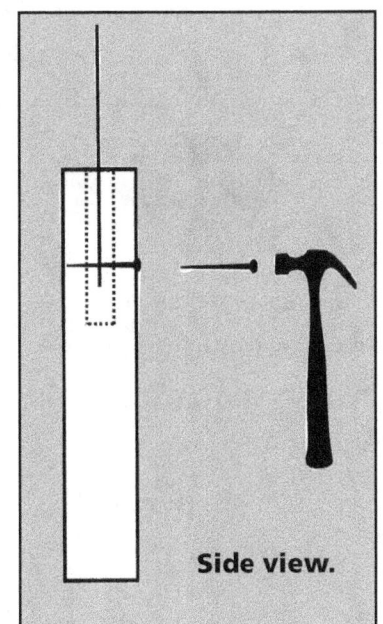

Side view.

Force the head down over the wire neck loop a little way.

Check that there is a little space between the bottom of the head and the top of the torso block.

Check that the head can still turn sideways.

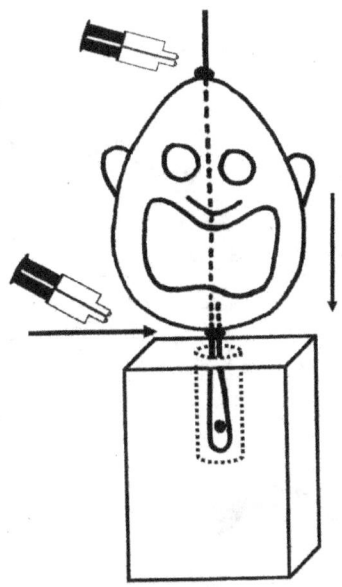

The turning head.

Add a spot of epoxy to the point where there neck wire joins the head.

Add epoxy to the point where the wire meets the top of the head.

Let the epoxy dry thoroughly.

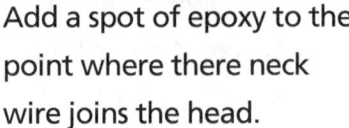

Rod and String Puppet

The Hands and Feet or Shoes

14

From air dry clay create the hands and feet/shoes in proportion to the head and body.

Let them dry thoroughly.

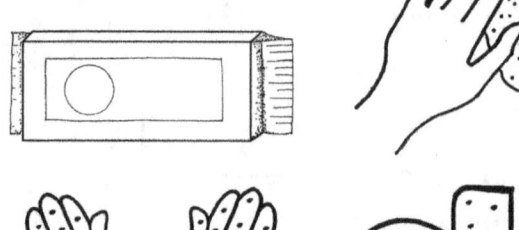
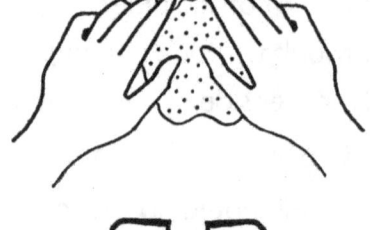

15

Carefully drill a small hole in the hands as shown. The hole should be big enough for the arm dowel to enter.

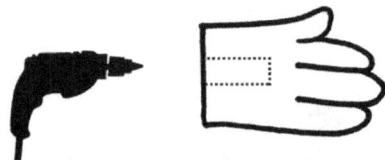

16

Apply epoxy to a short piece of dowel (you can crop the arm dowels later to size) and push the dowel into the hole in the hand.

17

Carefully drill a small hole in the top of each shoe as shown. The hole should be big enough for the leg dowel to enter.

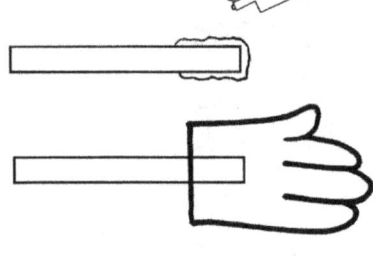

18

Apply epoxy to a short piece of dowel (you can crop the leg dowels later to size) and push the dowel into the hole in the shoe.

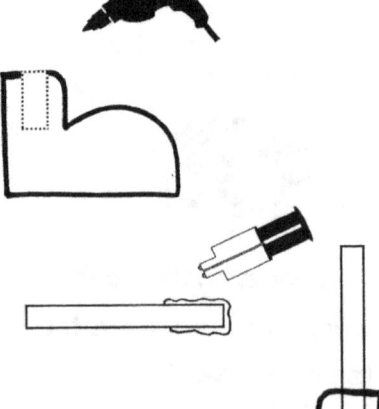
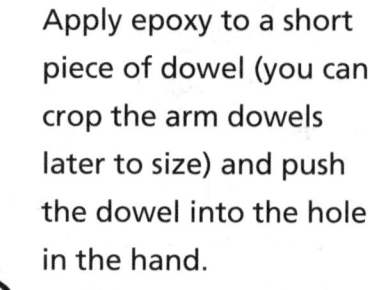

Puppets, Puppetry and Gogmagog

Have at hands **4** very small screw eyes.

Carefully screw a screw eye into the ends of the arm and leg dowels. You must have gauged how long you want the arms and legs before screwing in the screw eyes.

Screw **2** more screw eyes into the base of the wood torso at the point shown in the illustration. The legs will be suspended from these points.

The Body/Costume

I create the bodies out of thick brown paper and make them stronger with paper mache. I then paint the costumes directly onto the mached body.

You can of course make cloth costumes. See the pdf costume reference on page **72**.

Make a kind of cone body out of strong brown paper or light card and tape it directly on to the wooden torso.

You may have to do this in pieces.

Rod and String Puppet

Puppets, Puppetry and Gogmagog   Rod Puppets **137**

Apply **2** layers of paper mache (**1** newspaper, **1** brown) over the body shape.

Take care with the bottom border.

Let dry.

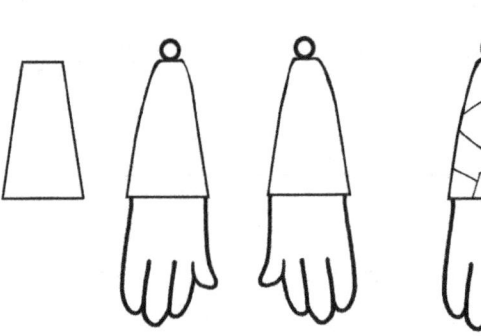

Create little cones of brown paper or light card to form the covering for the arms.

Don't cover the screw eyes.

Apply **2** layers of paper mache (**1** newspaper, **1** brown) over the cones. Sometimes these cone arms are so small I just use brown paper.

Let dry.

Locate the lateral holes at the top of the sides of the block. I use an upholstery needle for this.

Pass the needle threaded with strong string through the hole to the other side.

Tie the arms to the body securely.

138

Puppets, Puppetry and Gogmagog

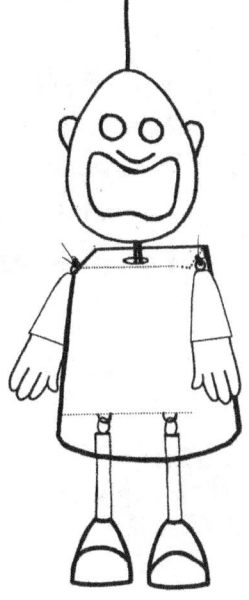

26

Attach the legs to the screws at the bottom of the body.

You can tie them together with string or you can open one screw eye with pliers; hook it through the other screw eye and then close it again with pliers.

I use needle nose pliers for this.

27

Paint the puppet.

Paint an undercoat of white paint first.

Rod and String Puppet

The Control

You should still have a long wire coming out of the head.

28

Determine the height of the head wire and bend the wire forward at a **90** degree angle as shown.

Puppets, Puppetry and Gogmagog

> **Have ready:**
> **2 medium wooden balls with holes about the same size as the coat hanger wire.**
> **1 smaller ball with the same sized hole.**
> **1 small dowel (¼inc/6mm wide and about 3½inches / 8cm long.)**

29

Drill a hole exactly at the half way point of the dowel. The hole should be big enough so the dowel can slide onto the coat hanger wire.

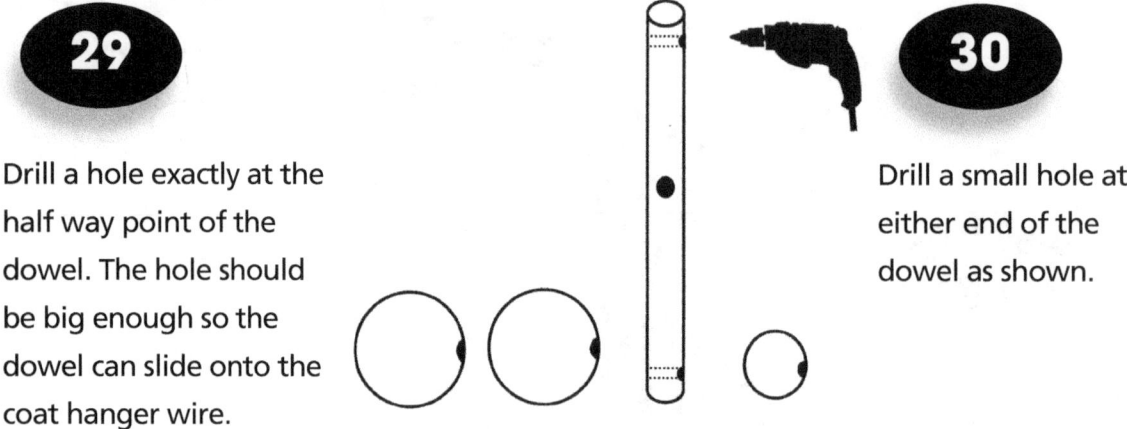

30

Drill a small hole at either end of the dowel as shown.

31

Hot glue **1** of the **2** medium balls on to the wire as shown. **This ball should not move.**

Note the position of the ball in relation to the bend in the wire. It is important to have some space here for your fingers to hold the control. I would say the gap could be about 1 inch/2.5cm.

Be careful; hot glue can cause burns.

Slide the dowel on to the wire. **The dowel should move around easily.**

Position the second of the **2** medium size balls on to the wire as shown. Hot glue it in place.

This ball should not move.

Be careful not to get hot glue on to the dowel.

Be careful; hot glue can cause burns.

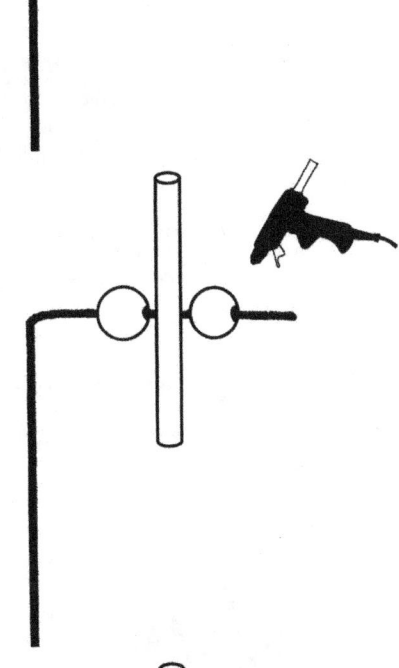

Bend the tip of the wire up as shown. If it is too long, trim it.

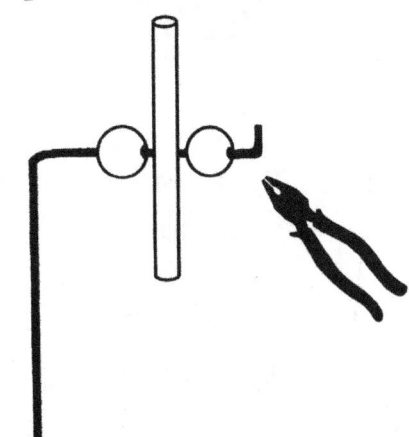

Hot glue the tiny ball on to the top of the bent wire as shown.

Be careful. Hot glue can cause burns.

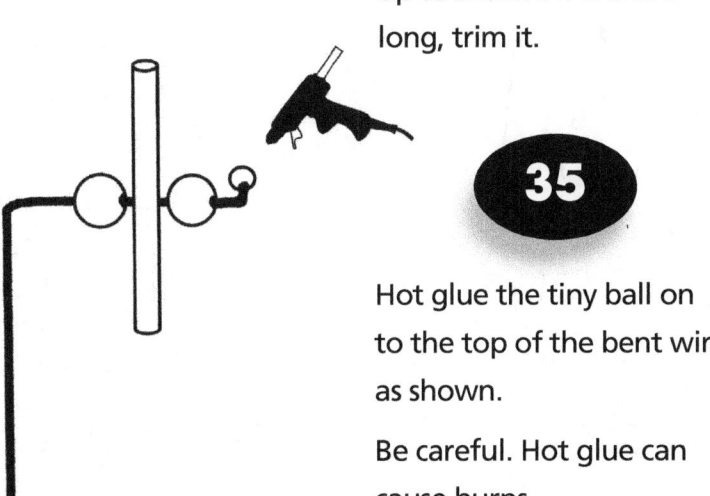

Rod and String Puppet

Puppets, Puppetry and Gogmagog

Rod Puppets

141

36

Drill a small hole through each hand as shown.

37

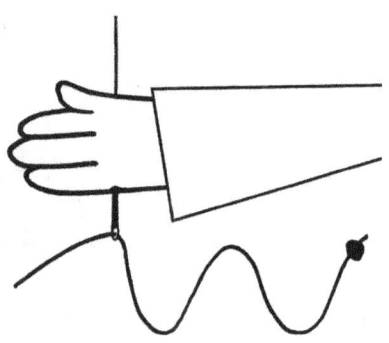

Thread an upholstery needle with long, strong black string and tie a large knot at the end.

Pass the needle from the bottom of the hand through to the top as illustrated.

38

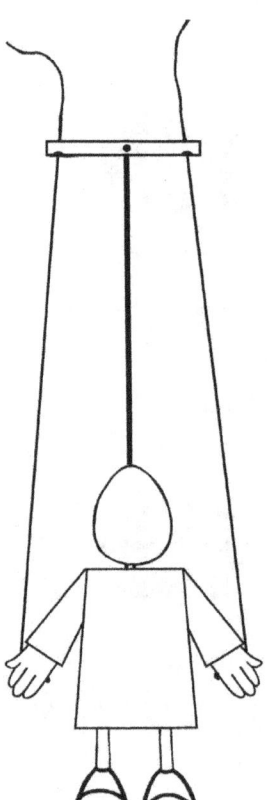

Tie each string to its respective hole in the dowel. The length of each string should be equal.

The hands should be "at rest" more or less when you tie off the string.

39

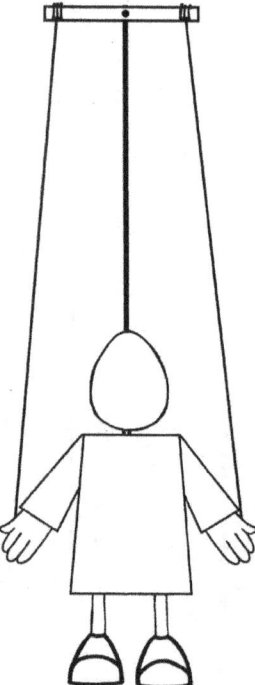

Trim the strings on the control.

A marionette is a puppet controlled from above by strings that connect different parts of its body to the control manipulated by the puppeteer. Traditionally the puppeteers are hidden and control the puppets from a bridge above the stage. However other puppeteers perform in full view of the public. The number of strings a marionette has depends on the complexity of its actions. Marionettes are often used to perform operas, or dramatic theatrical pieces.

Marionettes

The Kathputli marionettes are from Rajasthan, India. They are controlled by **2** or **3** strings. One string goes from the top of the head to the back of the waist and the other string goes from one hand to the other. Sometimes the hand strings are separated and attached by loops to **2** of the puppeteer's fingers.

The puppet itself is a head and torso, traditionally carved in wood, with a full circle skirt that covers the body from the waist down.

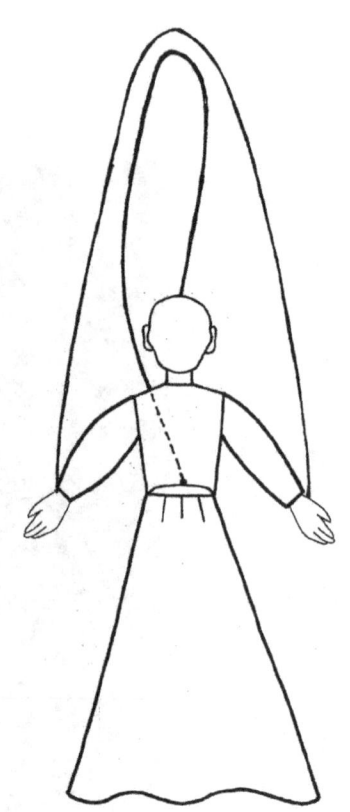

Materials:
clay, clay cutters, *vaseline*, paper mache glue, newspaper, brown paper, cloth for costume, cardboard, masking tape, duct tape, thick floristry wire, hot glue sticks, fabric glue, polyfill, black string /marionette string, sewing thread, acrylic paints.

Tools:
Scissors, hot glue gun, sewing needle, sewing machine, utility knife, paint brushes.

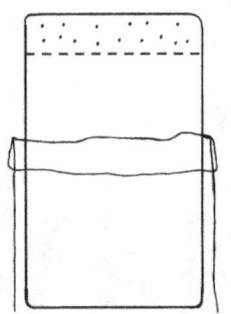 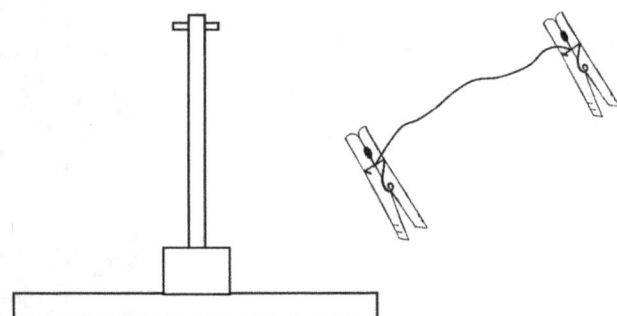

1

Create the head of the puppet following the instructions on pages **57-64** of the **Basic Glove Puppet**.

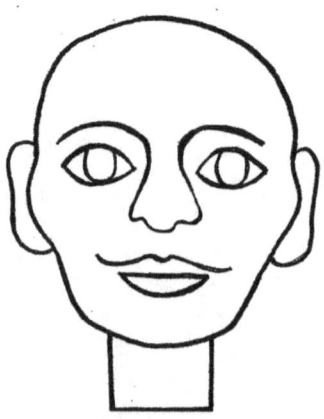

144

Puppets, Puppetry and Gogmagog

The Body

Shape the torso from clay. In this case it is from the neck down to the waistline.

Make sure it is in proportion to the finished head of the puppet.

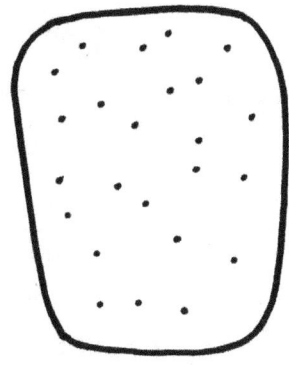

Work and refine the torso.

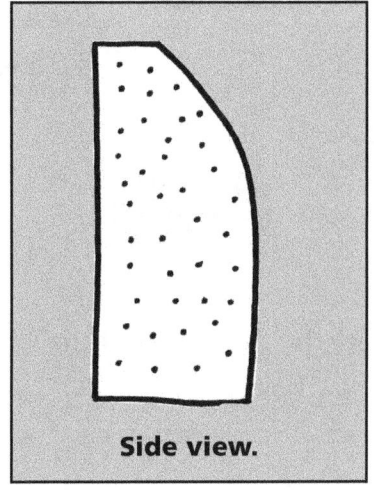

Side view.

Apply a thin layer of *vaseline* all over the torso, including the base.

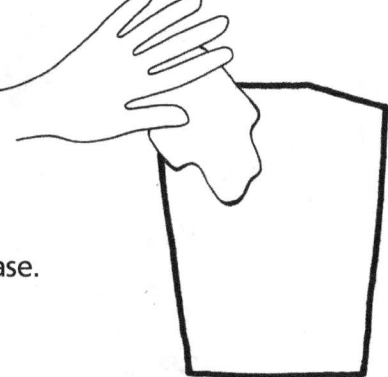

Apply **4** layers of paper mache, alternating newspaper and brown paper.

Include the base.

Let dry.

Kathputli Style Marionette

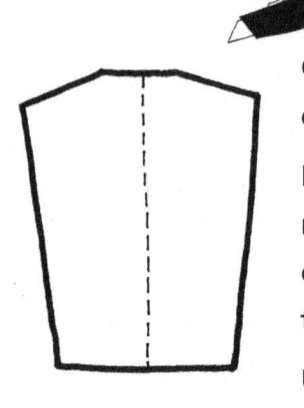

Cut the dry mached torso off the clay mold as shown.

Draw a pencil line first from the middle of the waist, over the top of the neck, down the middle of the back and through the base.

Use a utility knife to cut along the line.

Side view.

Pry the two halves of the clay mold.

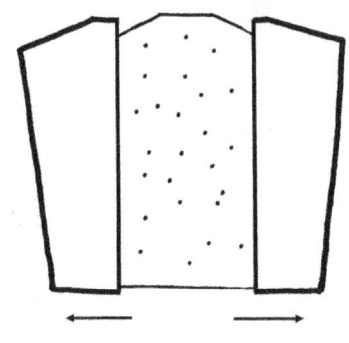

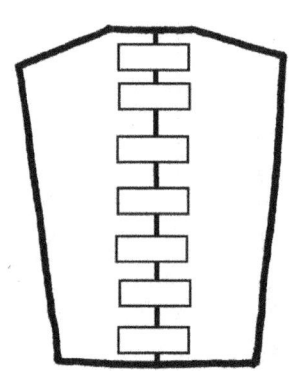

Carefully tape the **2** halves together again with duct tape.

Do this straight after cutting them off the mold so the edges won't warp.

Apply **2** layers of paper mache (**1** newspaper, **1** brown) over the tape.

Make sure you mache a little beyond the tape.

Let dry.

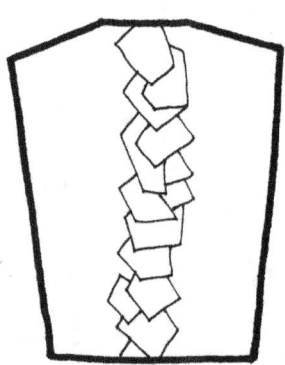

10 Hot glue the head to the torso.

Be careful; hot glue can cause burns.

11 Tape over the join with duct tape.

12 Apply **2** layers of paper mache (**1** newspaper, **1** brown) over the tape.

Let dry.

Kathputli Style Marionette

13 Create **4** small shapes as shown out of medium to heavy floristry wire. Total length is probably around 1½ inches/38mm. These are used in the next steps to attach the strings to the body.

I use needle nose pliers for this.

After attaching them to the puppet with glue and paper mache, only the eyes will remain exposed.

14 Hot glue **3** wires to the places indicated in the illustration; in the middle and at the top of each shoulder and at the centre top of the head.

Be careful. Hot glue can cause burns.

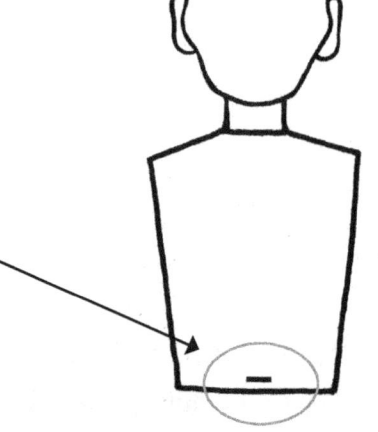

15 Hot glue the fourth wire to the back and centre of the bottom of the waist as illustrated.

16 Cover the ends of all **4** wires with tape and mache over the tape.

Let dry.

17 Paint the head and torso. The torso will be covered with cloth later on.

Apply a white undercoat first.

Puppets, Puppetry and Gogmagog

18

Choose your cloth to cover the torso.

Place the head and torso on top of the cloth and draw around the edge as shown. Leave a little extra cloth all the way around.

19

Using fabric glue, glue the cloth to the shoulders and to the sides of the torso.

Try not to get glue on the middle of the torso as this glue has a tendency to stain.

Glue the bottom of the cloth under the base of the torso.

Let dry.

20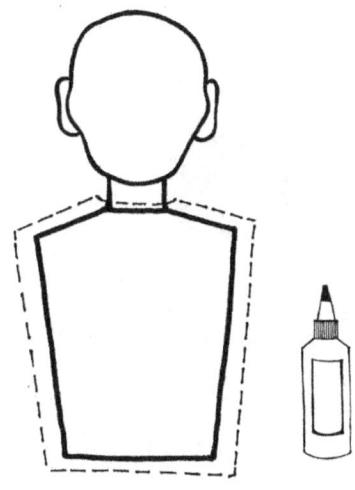

Repeat the same steps for the back.

Glue the bottom of the cloth under the base of the torso.

Let dry.

Make sure you still have access to the wire loops in the shoulders and at the back of the waist.

If you can't see them, carefully cut the cloth away at each point so that the loops are revealed.

Kathputli Style Marionette

The Arms

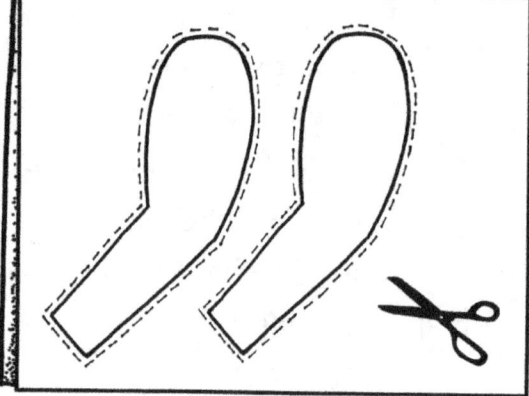

21

Create a pattern in paper for the sleeve. The puffy mutton leg sleeve in the illustration works well.

22

Place the pattern on a double thickness of cloth and cut the pattern out twice.

You will now have **4** sleeves.

23

Place **2** sleeves (right sides of the cloth together) together for each arm and sew around the edge.

Do not sew the part where the hand will be inserted.

Turn each completed sleeve inside out so that the right sides of the cloth are to the outside.

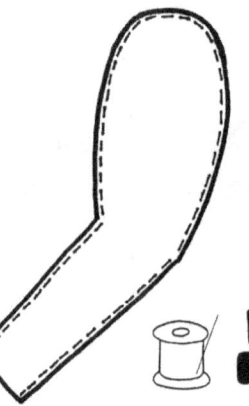

24

Fill each sleeve with *polyfill* giving the arms more body.

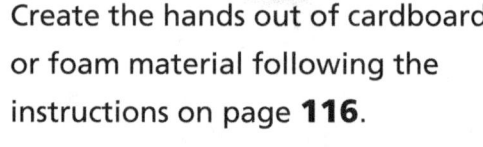

25

Create the hands out of cardboard or foam material following the instructions on page **116**.

Apply **1** layer of brown paper mache over the cardboard (if you have used cardboard).

Fill the hands with a little *polyfill* if you have used foam material.

Puppets, Puppetry and Gogmagog

26

Using hot glue or fabric glue, attach each hand inside each sleeve.

If you have thumbs, remember which way they go... upwards.

The Skirt

27

Cut a large full circle of cloth for the skirt of the puppet.

The radius should correspond to the length of the skirt you want.

The radius is the distance from the midpoint of a circle to its outer edge.

28

Fold the circle in half and cut out a small semi circle in the exact middle of the folded line. This forms the waist of the skirt.

Before you cut, check the waist of your puppet torso. Do not cut it too big.

29

Insert the head and torso in the hole and glue in place with hot glue or fabric glue.

Be careful; hot glue can cause burns.

Let dry.

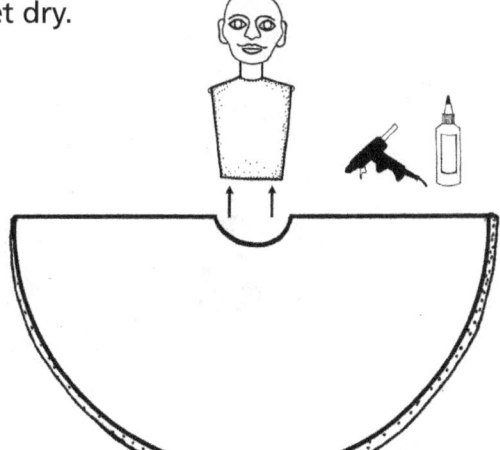

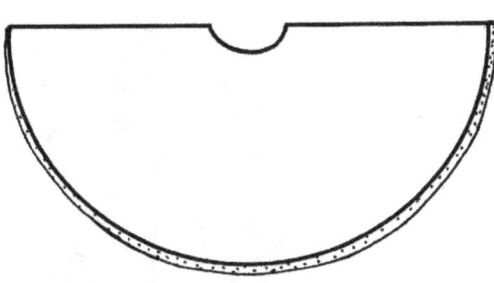

Kathputli Style Marionette

Puppets, Puppetry and Gogmagog   Marionettes **151**

30

Sew the tip of the top of the arms to the wire "eyes" in the shoulders.

31

Add any further costume detail, hair etc.

Do not impede the full circle movement and flow of the skirt.

Be careful not to cover the loop at the top of the head.

32

Tie one long string to the loop in the head. Tie the other end of the same string to the loop at the waist at the back of the puppet.

Start with long string and adjust to your height.

33 Sew one long string from one wrist to the other.

Puppets, Puppetry and Gogmagog

9 String Marionette

The marionette is a puppet operated entirely by strings connecting parts of the body to a control held above. There are many ways to make marionettes and many specialists in this field.

Here is the way I make a basic **9** string marionette. The head, torso, hips, hands and feet or shoes are made of paper mache. The arms and legs are made of dowel.

Materials:

the materials for making the basic paper mache head over a clay mold are found on page **57**.

Small amount of thin plywood or thick corrugated cardboard, duct tape, hot glue sticks, epoxy, newspaper, brown paper, paper mache glue, medium to thick floristry wire, small screw hooks, **2** cup hooks (one smaller than the other), clay and *vaseline* for the torso, hips and feet, dowels: ½ inch/13mm, ¾inch/19mm, a small quantity of semi transparent cloth to connect the torso to the hips, a small block of wood, wire coat hanger, rope to create a gallows to suspend the marionette while stringing it , acrylic paint, different materials to make the hands (see page **116**), a strip of thin plywood 12inches/30.48cm long for the central bar of the control, (lattice is quite good for this), black string for stringing the marionette.

Tools:

hot glue gun, utility knife, saw, drill and drill bits, wire cutters, pliers, tapestry needle, paint brushes.

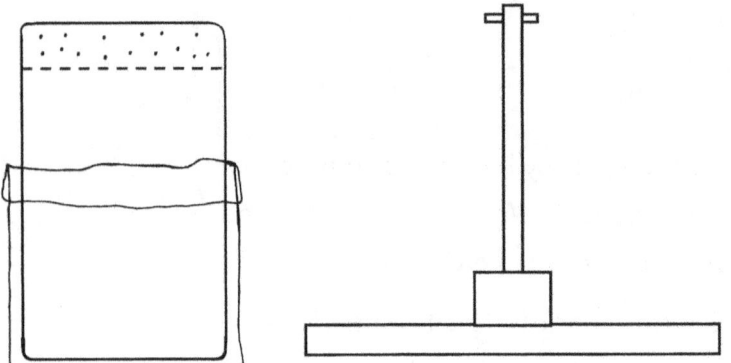
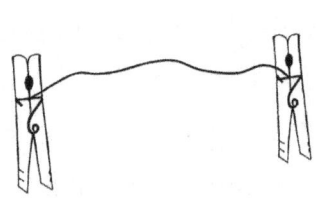

1

Create the head following the instructions on pages **57-64** for the **Basic Glove Puppet** head.

The neck should be narrower as it will later on have to fit comfortably into the shoulder opening of the torso.

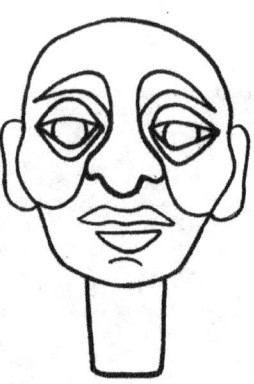

2

Make a small circle of plywood or corrugated cardboard to cover the bottom of the neck.

Glue, tape and mache into place.

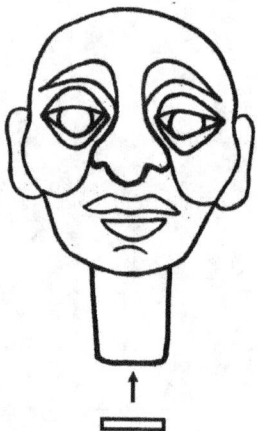

Fix the hook eyes on to the head. Instructions for making the hooks of floristry wire can be found on page **148** of the **Kathputli Style Marionette**. These serve the purpose of either connecting body part to body part or are used for the stringing the marionette later on.

The first is at the bottom of the neck.

If you have used cardboard to cover the bottom of the neck, make the "eye" from floristry wire as shown. Hot glue it, cover the ends with tape and the paper mache over the tape. Let dry.

Be careful. Hot glue can cause burns.

If you have used wood to cover the bottom of the neck, screw in a screw eye.

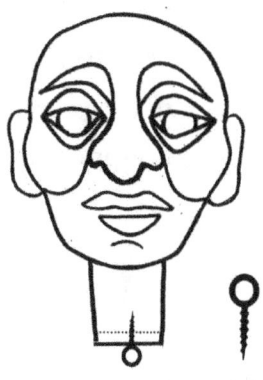

Attach **2** more wire "eyes" to the sides of the head just above and behind the ears.

Stick the ends with hot glue; tape over the glue and paper mache over the tape.

Be careful; hot glue can cause burns.

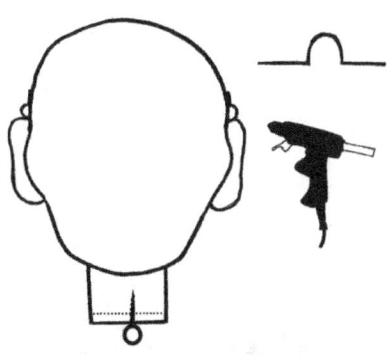

You can paint the head at this point if you like or further on when you have made the hands.

Apply a white undercoat first.

The Two Parts of the Body

The body of the marionette is divided into **2** parts; the upper torso (top of shoulders to the ribcage) and the hips below.

The broken line indicates where the waist of the puppet will be later on.

 Form the torso and hips from clay.

Each part should be in proportion to the head.

The shoulders should be a little wider than the head so that the shoulder strings will later run unimpeded to the control.

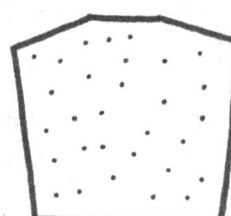
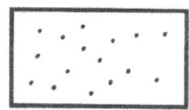

 Cover the torso and hips with a thin layer of *vaseline*.

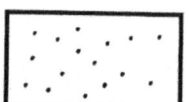

 Apply **4** layers of paper mache (alternating newspaper and brown paper).

Include the bottoms of the torso and hips.

Let dry.

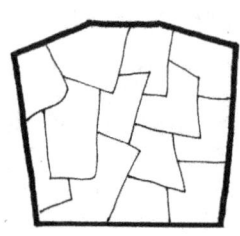
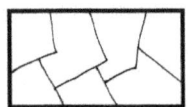

Puppets, Puppetry and Gogmagog

8

Cut off the dry mached pieces from the clay molds following the instructions on page **146**.

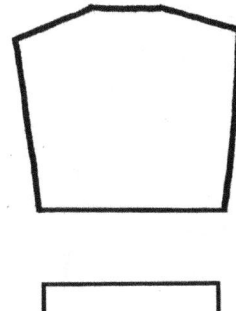

9

Stick the parts back together again with duct tape and paper mache.

Let dry.

10

Cut a hole in the upper part of the torso. This is to accommodate the neck of the marionette later on.

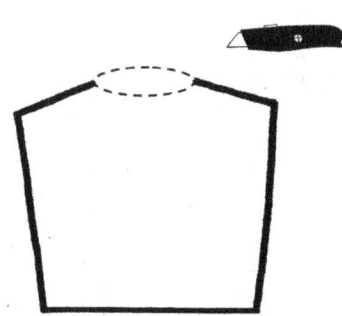

11

Apply a single layer of brown paper mache around the border of the hole to make it stronger and neater.

Let dry.

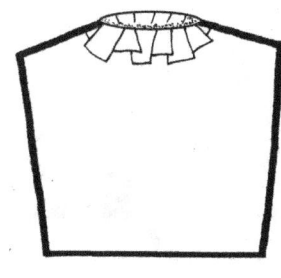

12

Cut **2** holes in the middle and top of either side of the upper torso. This is to accommodate an internal dowel that marks the shoulders.

Don't make the holes larger than the width of the dowel.

13

Push a dowel laterally through the through the holes and hot glue into place.

Be careful; hot glue can cause burns.

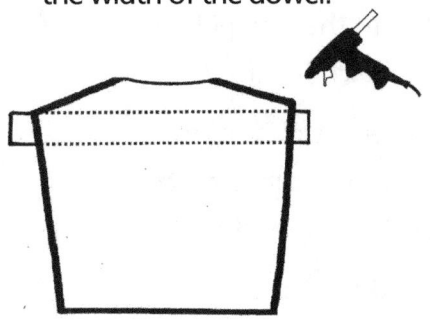

Puppets, Puppetry and Gogmagog

14

Cut off any extra overhanging dowel with a coping saw.

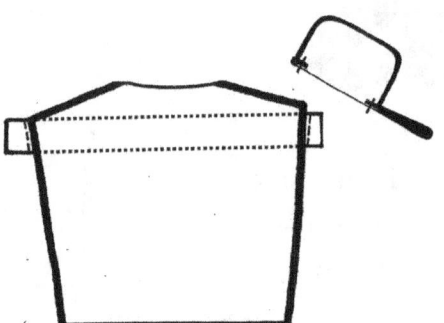

15

Screw **3** screw eyes into the places illustrated.

1 in the middle of either end of the horizontal dowel.

1 in the exact middle of the dowel. Gain access through the neck hole.

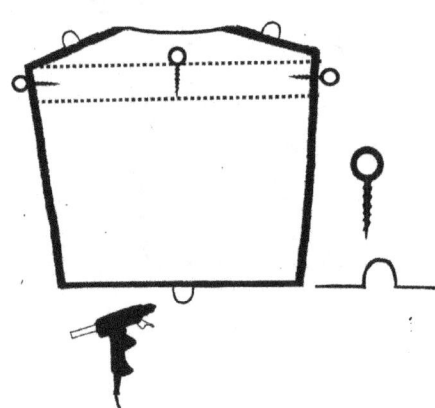

16

Glue **3** floristry wire hook eyes where indicated in the illustration.

1 in the top and middle of either shoulder.

1 in the middle of the base of the torso.

Glue, tape and mache over the ends of the wire hook eyes.

Be careful; hot glue can cause burns.

17

Glue **1** floristry wire hook eye to the top middle point of the hips.

Cover the ends of the wire hook eye with tape and paper mache.

Let dry.

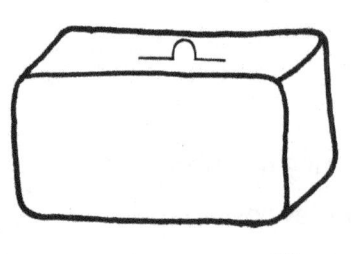

158

Puppets, Puppetry and Gogmagog

Join the torso and hips together with string.

Estimate the gap, imagining the waistline.

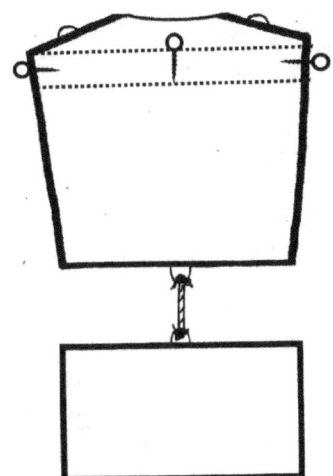

Glue a thin material or mesh around the gap.

Try to keep the **2** parts of the body as level as possible.

Be careful; hot glue burns.

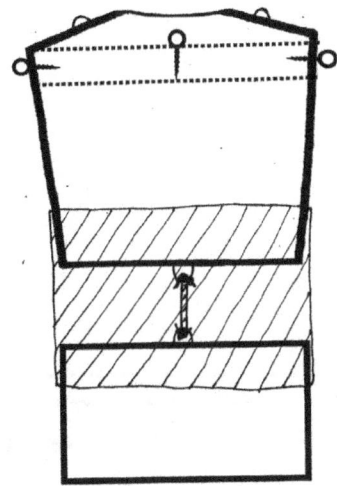

Join the head and torso together with string through the screw eyes.

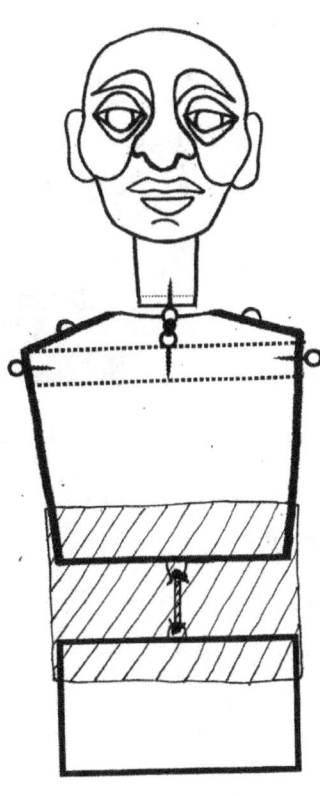

9 String Marionette

Puppets, Puppetry and Gogmagog   Marionettes **159**

21

Cut a thin plywood rectangle the size of the base of the hips. Trace around the hips and then cut the wood.

22

Cut a rectangular prism of wood. I use a wood that measures 1x1inch by the depth of the hips/ 2.5x2.5cm by the depth of the hips.

This prism goes from the front to the back of the wooden plate, exactly in the middle. It acts as a separator for the legs.

Glue into place with epoxy.

23

Drill a horizontal hole through the leg separator as shown.

This hole should be below the midpoint of the block.

The coat hanger wire should be able to pass through the hole.

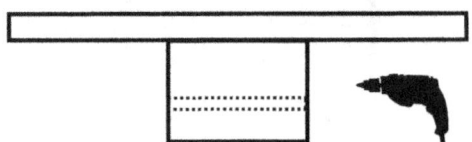

24

Drill **2** holes at either end (in the middle point of each end of the plate) of the hip plate as shown.

Coat hanger wire should be able to pass through the holes.

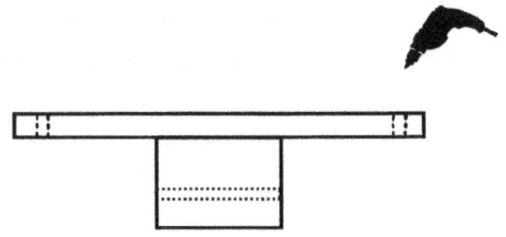

Puppets, Puppetry and Gogmagog

Cut **4** equal lengths of dowel for the upper and lower parts of the legs.

If the marionette is tall I use ½inch/13mm dowel for this.

Drill horizontal holes in the tops of all **4** dowels as shown.

27

Drill horizontal holes in the bottoms of **2** dowels as shown.

Coat hanger wire should be able to pass through the holes.

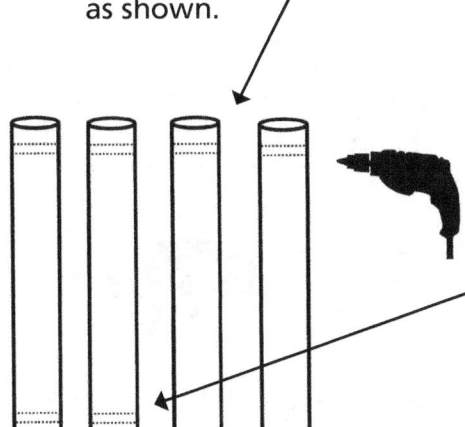

9 String Marionette

Take a long piece of coat hanger wire and join the upper leg pieces to the hip plate as shown.

You will need to use pliers to bend the wire where necessary.

Be as precise as possible. Have patience.

The upper legs will now swing freely on the horizontal wire.

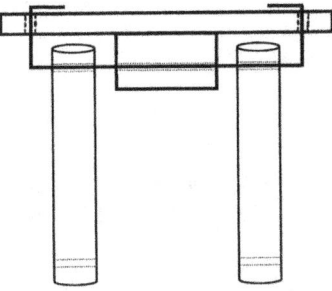

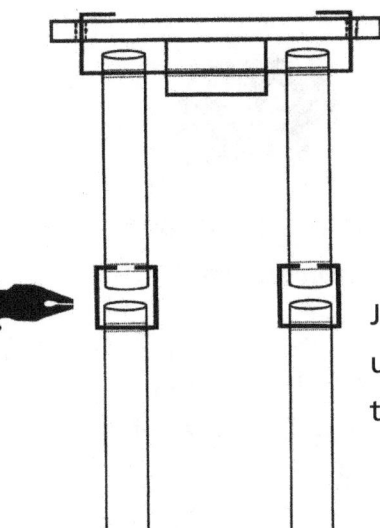

Join the lower legs to the upper legs as shown with the coat hanger wire.

Puppets, Puppetry and Gogmagog   Marionettes

The Shoes

30

Create the feet or shoes you want out of clay.

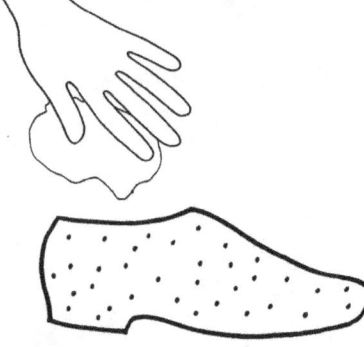

31

Cover the clay mold with a fine layer of *vaseline*.

32

Apply **4** layers of paper mache alternating newspaper and brown paper.

Let dry.

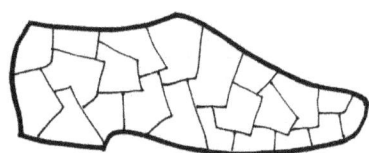

33

Cut the dry mached shoes off the clay molds following the instruction for cutting off the torso on page **146**.

34

Tape and mache the paper mache pieces together again following the instructions on page **146**.

Let dry.

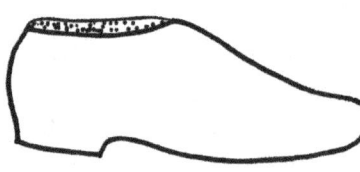

35

Cut a hole in the top of each shoe leaving an opening as shown above.

Apply **1** layer of brown paper mache around the border of the opening.

Let dry.

> You can paint the shoes now or later on when you have the costume made. Apply a white base coat first.

Puppets, Puppetry and Gogmagog

Have a few sticks of hot glue at hand. Squeeze a lot of hot glue into the shoe, especially at the heel.

Place the bottom part of the legs (at a right angle) into the hole as shown. Make sure the shoes are not set into place with the toes pointing inwards.

Hold it in place until set.

Add more hot glue around the stick where it meets the heel.

Let dry.

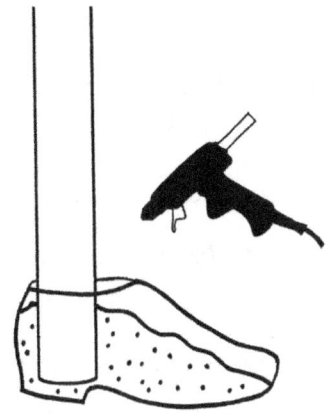

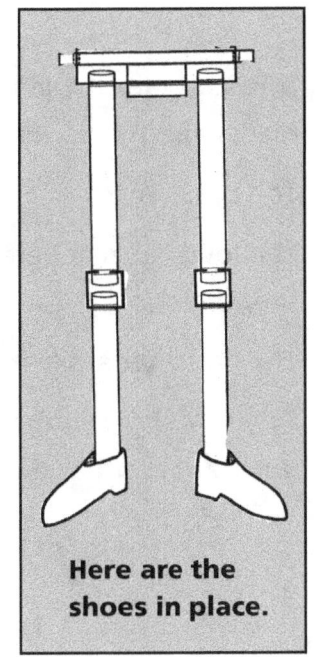

Here are the shoes in place.

9 String Marionette

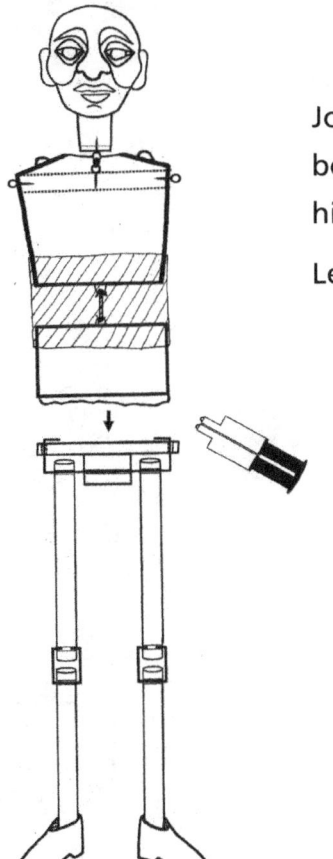

Join the hip plate to the bottom of the mached hips with epoxy.

Let dry.

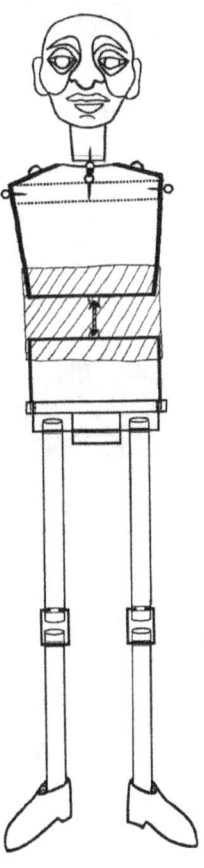

Puppets, Puppetry and Gogmagog   Marionettes

The Arms

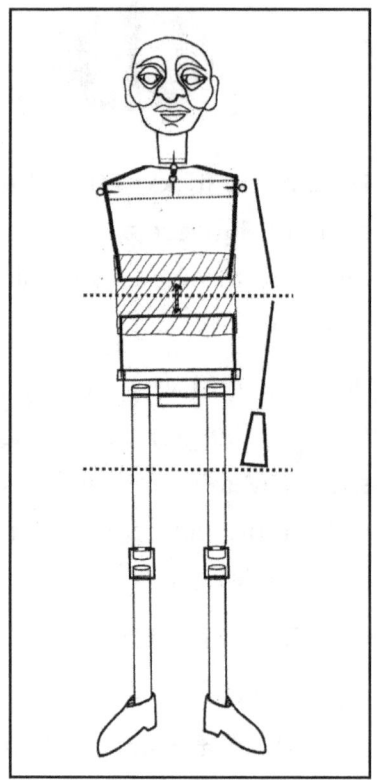

Now consider the length and position of the **2** arm pieces and the hands.

The upper arm generally reaches to the waistline.

The lower arm generally reaches to the bottom of the torso.

The hand generally reaches to the middle of the thigh.

So you will cut your arm pieces accordingly, allowing for the space that the screw eye will take up later on.

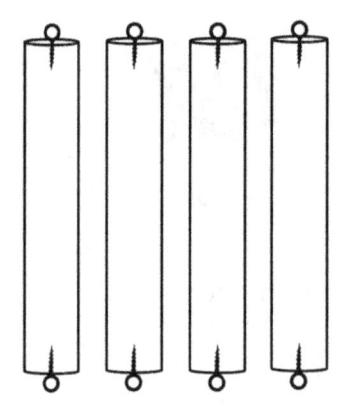

Cut **4** dowels the same length (**2** arms, **2** forearms).

Attach screw eyes to the middle of each end.

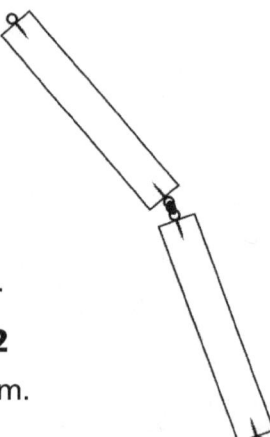

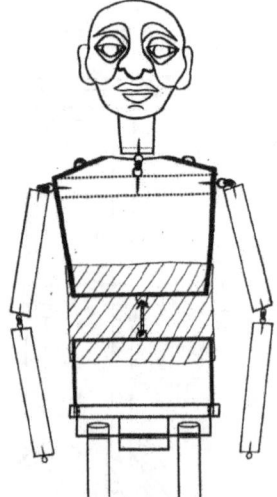

Join **2** of the dowels together with string through the screw eyes.

Repeat with the other **2** dowels for the other arm.

Join the arms to the shoulders with string through the screw eyes.

Puppets, Puppetry and Gogmagog

The Hands

Consider the size of the hands in relation to the head (see page **21**).

Consider the position of the hands on the arms. Where will they reach to?

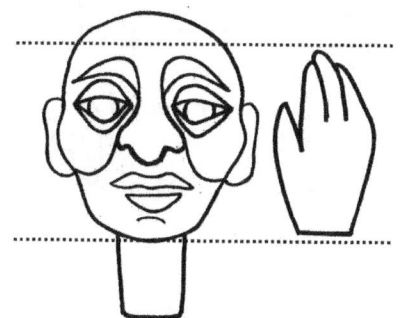
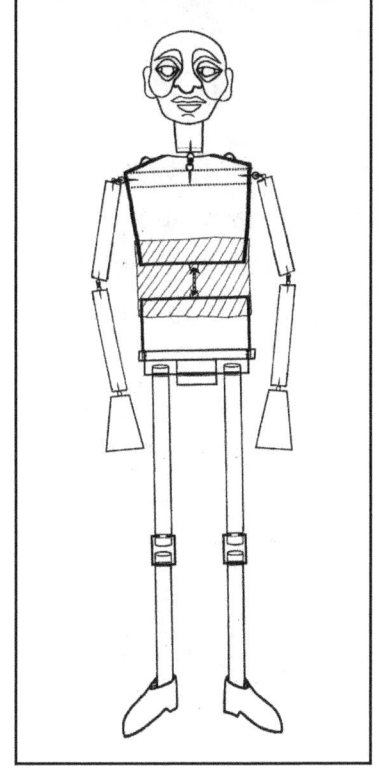

 **42**

Create the hands using one of the methods on pages **116-119**.

It is important that they have some sort of depth at the wrists and that the wrists are closed at the base.

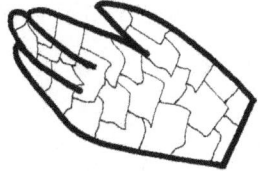 **43** Glue a floristry wire hook eye to the middle of the base of each wrist.

Be careful; hot glue can cause burns.

Tape over the glue and mache over the tape.

Let dry.

 **44** Paint the hands. Apply a white base coat first.

45

Join the hands to the forearms with string through the screw eyes and floristry wire hook eyes as shown.

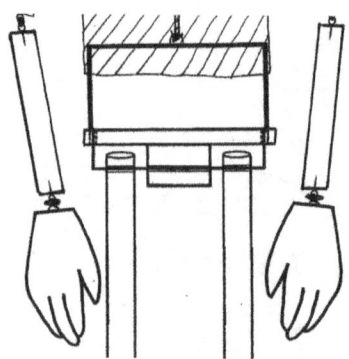

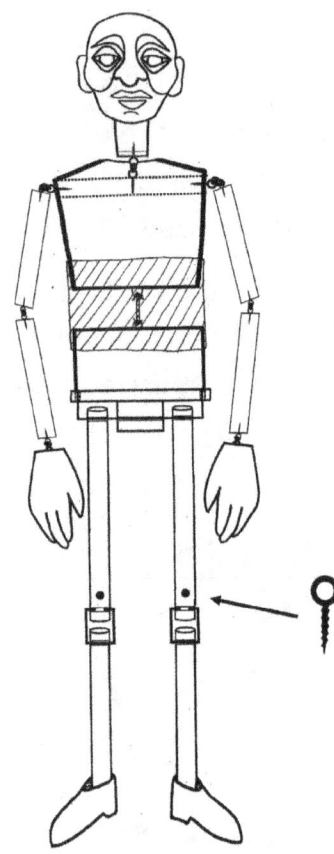

46

Attach **1** screw eye to the **2** points indicated in the illustration.

The Control

> The shoulder and head bars float below the main control.
>
> They are attached by a strong string which is knotted below the floating bar.
>
> This string passes through a wooden ball. The ball has a knot on top of it which holds it in place.
>
> The string then passes through the central bar and is knotted in place.

In the marionette world there are many kinds of controls but they are basically divided into horizontal (airplane control) and vertical controls. I use a horizontal control. There are many little steps. Be patient.

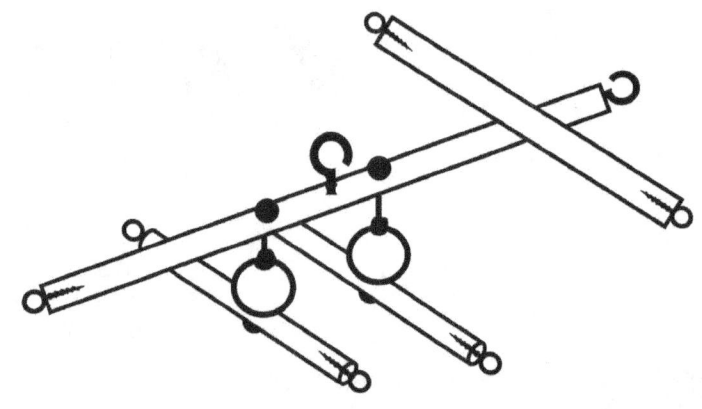

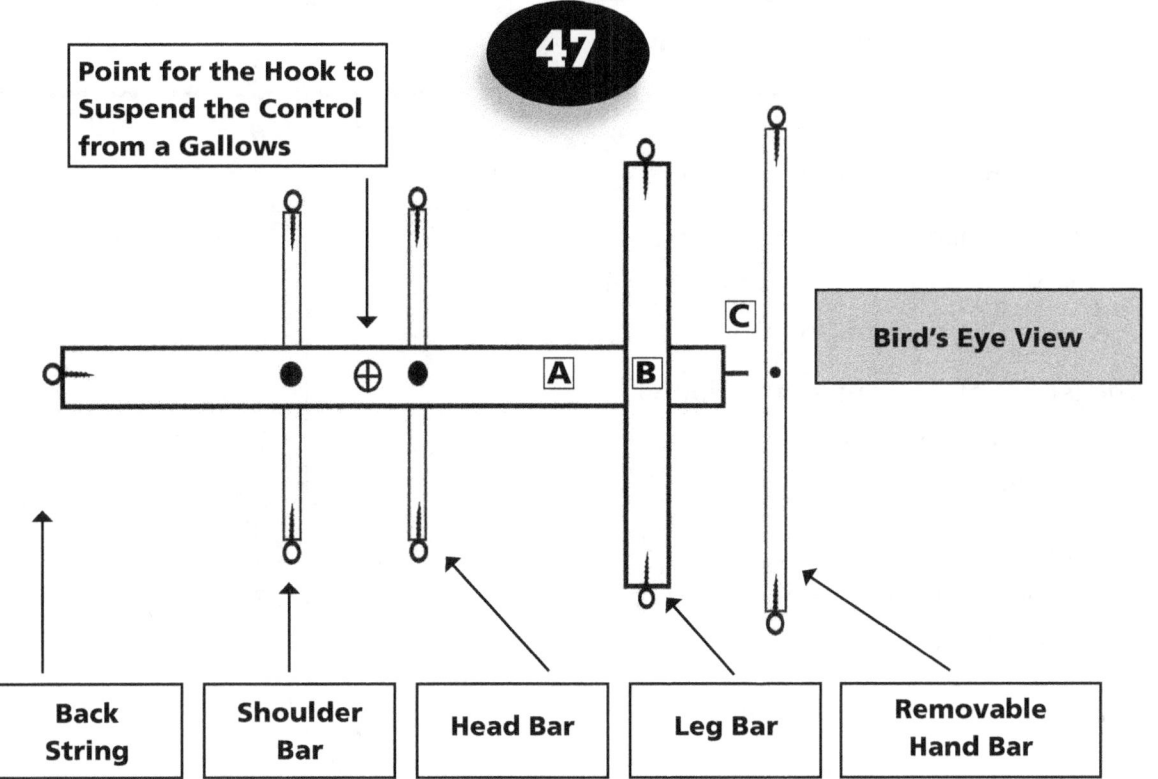

A is a flat thin piece of wood about 12inches/30.5cm long x ¼ inch/6mm wide. This forms the central bar of the control.

B is another flat thin piece of wood about 8 inches/20.32cm long. The length will depend on the size of the puppet. Attach it on top of and in the middle of the central bar with wood glue and a small screw.

C Attach a screw hook to the front of the central control bar.

This removable hand bar is made of a thinner dowel. Drill a hole in the exact middle big enough to fit loosely over the screw hook at point **C**. Attach a screw hook into each end.

Drill **2** hole at the positions indicated ● for the strings that attach the floating shoulder and head bars.

Attach a bigger hook at point ⊕ . This is to hang the control and marionette to a "gallows".

The shoulder and head bars are made of thinners dowels the same size as the removable hand bar.

Drill a hole in the exact middle of each bar. Attach screw eyes to each end of the bars.

Attach a screw eye to the end of the central bar. This is for the back string.

Puppets, Puppetry and Gogmagog   Marionettes **167**

Stringing the Marionette

This drawing illustrates the gallows.

The control hangs by its central hook to a rope that hangs from another hook in the ceiling (in my workshop).

The length of the rope should allow the marionette to stand on a surface without bending at the knees.

The gallows is essential for stringing the marionette and getting the right tension in the strings.

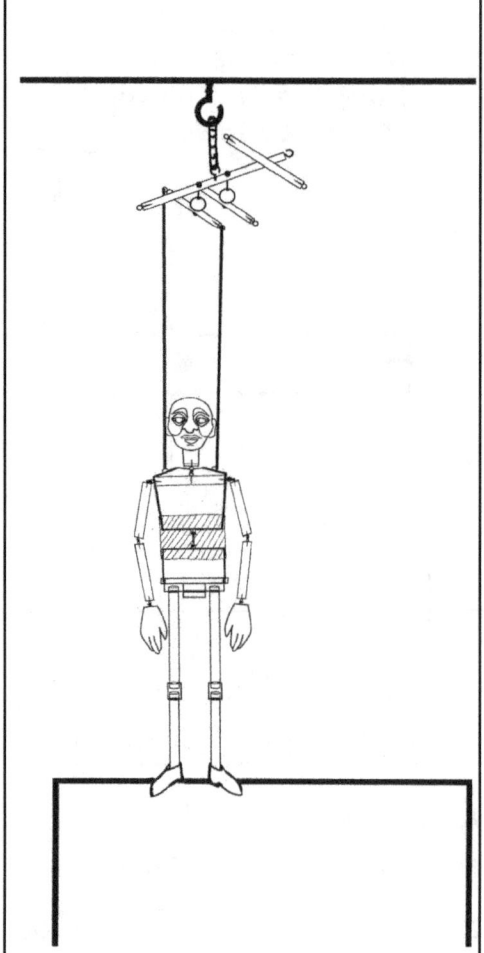

The following illustrations describe the order of stringing the marionette. Each bar has been drawn on top of the previous bar. This is so the string to bar relationship is clear. In actual fact the bars are placed at intervals along the horizontal central bar of the control. The stringing is done after the costume has been made. However I have kept the following illustrations without costume so as to see the stringing steps better.

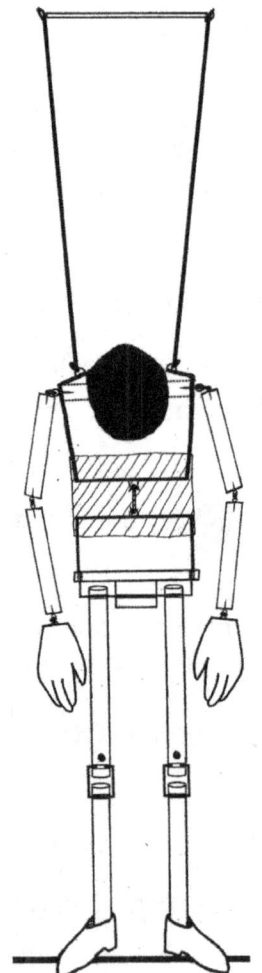

48

First attach the shoulder strings to the shoulder bar.

The whole weight of the marionette is held by these strings.

The head will fall forward at this point.

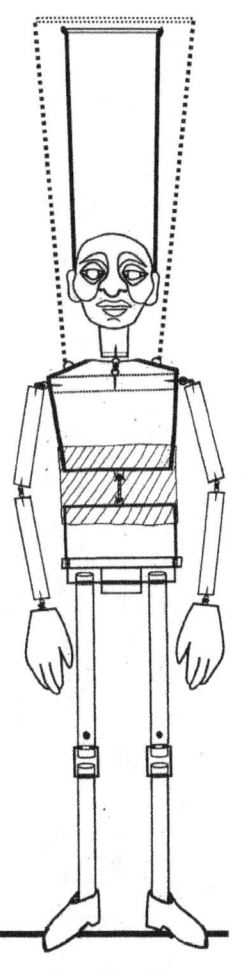

Next attach the head strings to the head bar through the floristry wire hook eye behind the ears.

These strings should not have too much tension.

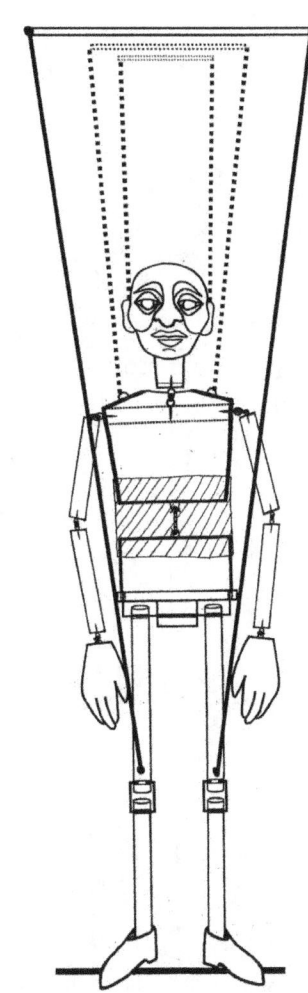

Next tie the legs strings from the screw eyes just above the knees to the leg bar.

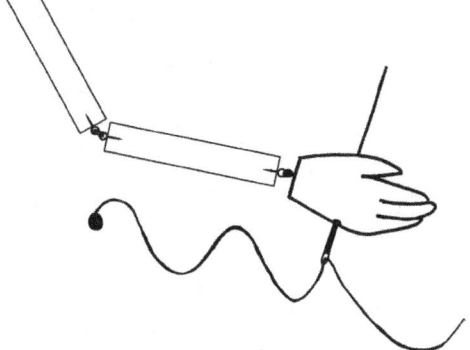

Use a threaded upholstery needle to pass the string through the bottom of the hand to just in front of the thumb on the top and other side of the hand.

Tie a very large knot in the string.

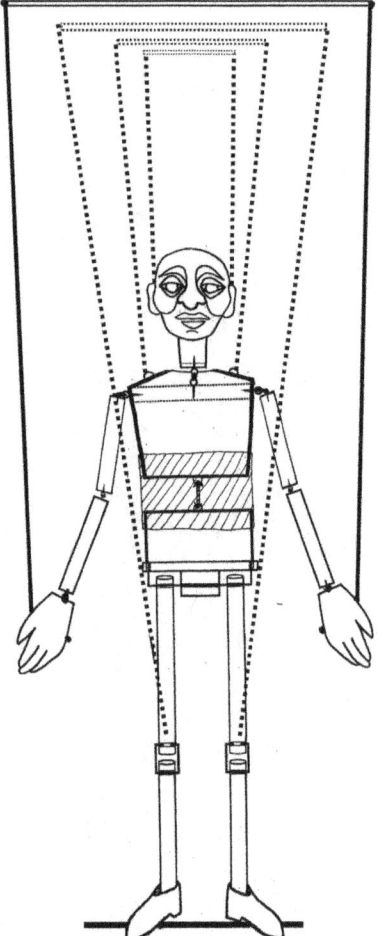

Tie the hands strings to the removable hand bar.

The hands should be strung at a rest position but not dangling loosely at the sides.

Lastly, tie the back string to the screw eye at the end of the control.

This string can be a little loose.

Sometimes you can glue lead weights to certain points of the marionette so it will move better.

Often these points are: behind the elbows, in the feet and sometimes in the hip.

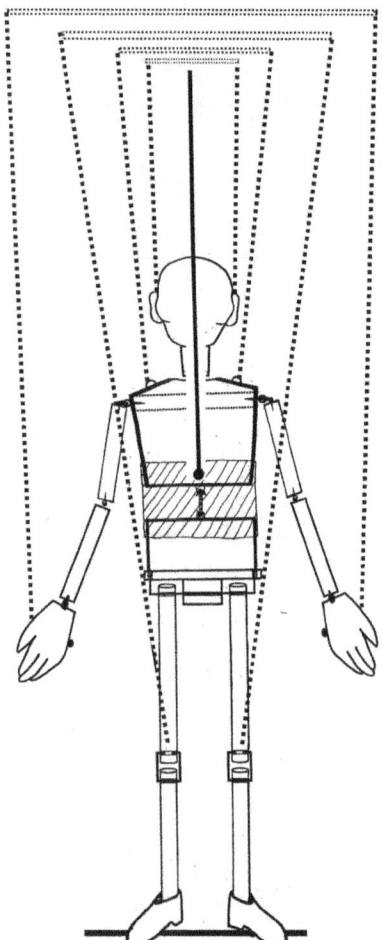

The strings have to pass through the costume.

Sew the costume before you string the marionette.

Make sure the costume is not too tight so that it does not impede movement.

The pdf on page **72** has basic costume patterns.

Puppets, Puppetry and Gogmagog

A table top puppet is a puppet usually operated by rods or by the hands of the puppeteer from behind; the rods tending to be horizontal rather than vertical. The puppets are manipulated on a flat surface of table. The puppeteers are seen by the public.

Table Top Puppets

Materials:
1 plastic egg, newspaper, paper mache glue, air dry clay, hot glue sticks, ¼inch/6mm dowel for the control, acrylic paint, cloth for the body and for the internal bag, sand or a similar filling, *polyfill*, sewing thread, small washer that fits over the dowel, a few small lead fishing weights, acrylic paints.

Tools:
drill and drill bits, hot glue gun, scissors, sewing machine or sewing needles, stapler and staples, paint brushes.

This wonderful comical puppet was invented by the French company **Garin Trousseboeuf.** http://www.garin-trousseboeuf.com

It consists of a small cloth bag inside of which is a smaller cloth bag filled with sand or a heavy filling. The rest has polyfill. A small head is attached by a stick to the bag.

172

The Head

I like to use plastic eggs or modify the containers of lemon extract as a base for these heads. They are quite small. I create the facial features with air dry clay.

Take a plastic egg and cover it with **2** layers of paper mache (**1** newspaper, **1** brown).

Let dry.

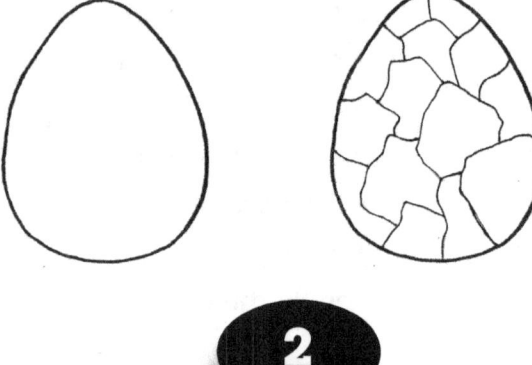

Knead some air dry clay. See page **132** for more information about air dry clay.

Remember to keep the bag closed when not in use.

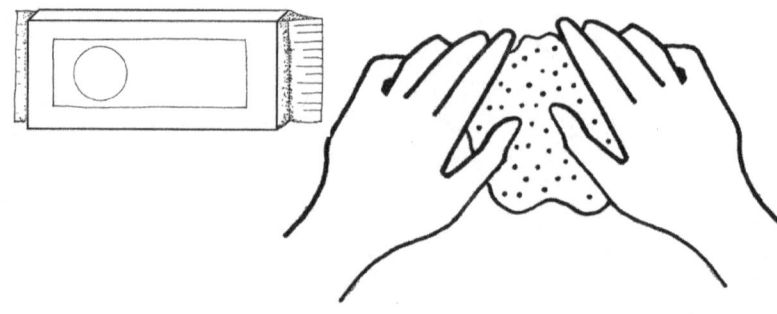

Puppets, Puppetry and Gogmagog

Mold the facial features of your puppet.

Let dry.

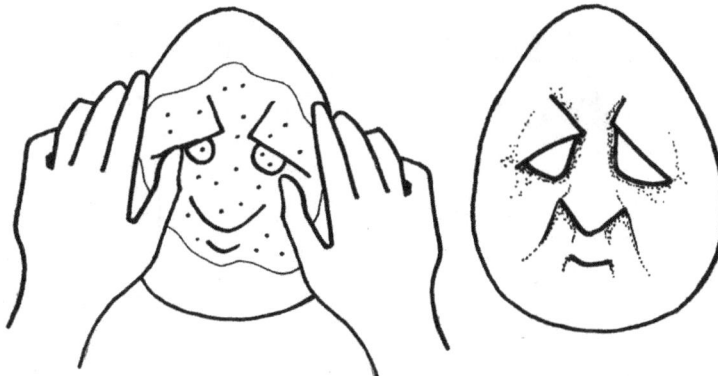

Drill a small hole in the back of the head in the position shown.

The hole should be no wider than the width of the dowel you use for a control.

Insert the dowel into the head and hot glue into place as shown.

Be careful; hot glue can cause burns.

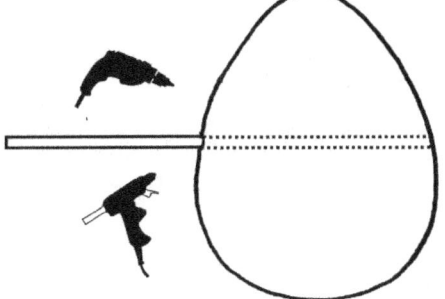

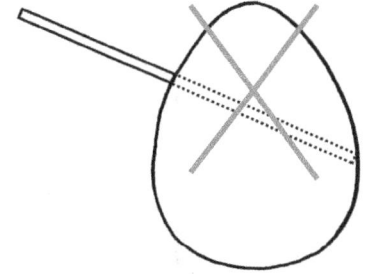

Do not insert the control stick at this angle. It reveals too much of the puppeteer's hand during manipulation.

Paint the head.

Paint a white undercoat first.

Let dry.

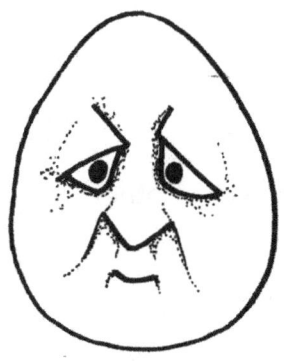

Sand Bag Puppet

6

The Body

Fold a piece of cloth in **2**.

Create a paper pattern for **2** rectangles, one smaller than the other.

The tall rectangle is the body of the puppet; measuring 8 inches/20.32cm high and 5 inches/12.7cm wide.

The short rectangle is the sand bag; measuring approximately 4 inches/10cm high and 5inches/ 12.7cm wide.

Place the pattern on the fold and cut out.

Do not cut along the fold.

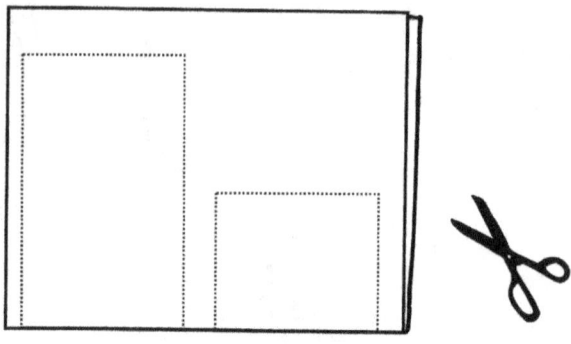

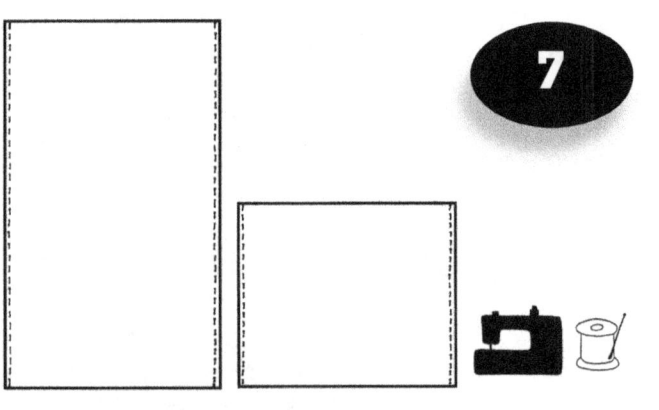

7

With right sides together, sew down the sides of each bag as shown.

8

Turn the small bag inside out.

Fill to about ¾ the small bag with sand or other heavy filler as shown.

The sand creates the weight of the puppet.

You can experiment with the quantity of sand.

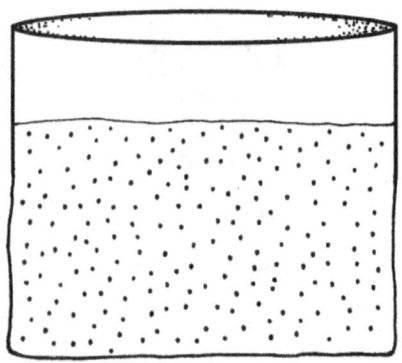

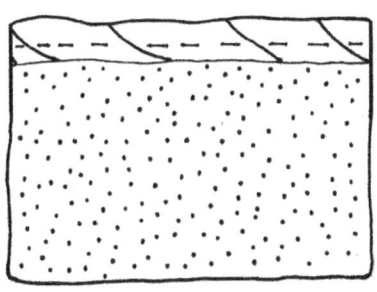

9

Fold the top down and staple it shut. This is a temporary measure.

Later when you place this sandbag inside the large bag, you can judge for yourself if you need to add or subtract sand.

When you are satisfied with the quantity of sand, sew the bag shut.

Sand Bag Puppet

10

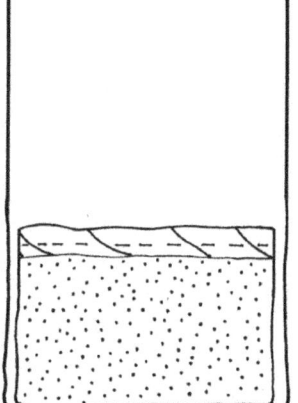

Turn the big bag inside out.

Place the sand bag inside the big bag.

11

Fill the big bag with *polyfill*.

Experiment with the quantity.

12

Pierce a small hole as shown from one side of the bag to the other.

I use the sharp point of the scissors for this.

13

Pass the stick and head through the holes as shown.

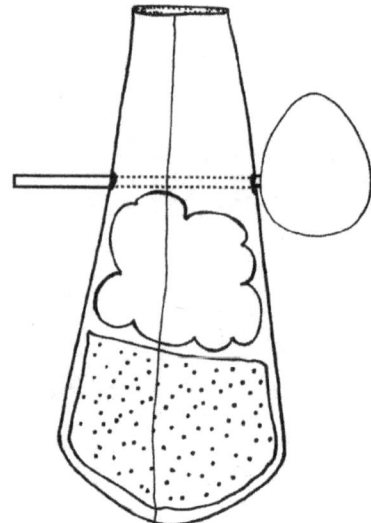

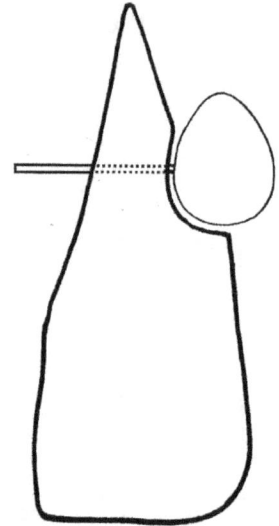

14

Push the cloth further towards the head, squeezing the bag a little more closed.

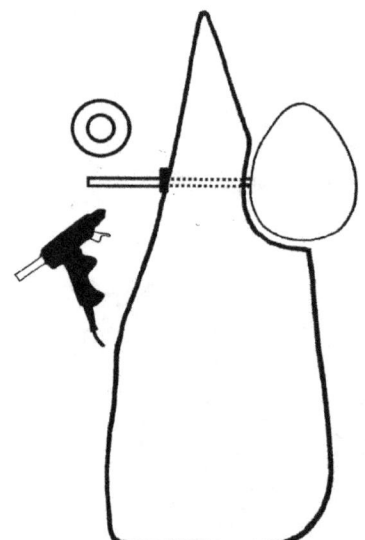

15

Hot glue a washer to the dowel to stop it sliding out.

Be careful; hot glue burns.

Fold down and under the excess cloth from the top as shown. Sew it in place.

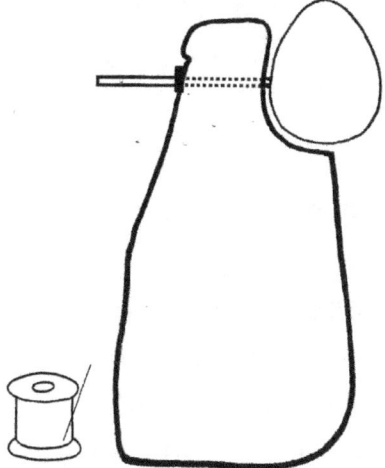

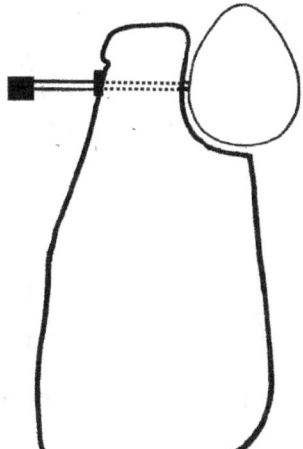

You may need to add a counterweight on to the end of the stick if the head is heavy.

I tape on small fishing weights.

Finish the puppet.

You may want to add a couple of costume details.

You can also paint the costume on the bag. Be careful not to apply the paint thickly. This will stiffen the cloth and make the puppet harder to manipulate.

Sand Bag Puppet

This puppet is inspired by the **3** puppeteer manipulation of the extraordinary Bunraku puppet tradition of Japan.

The puppet and the puppeteers are in full view of the public. One puppeteer manipulates the head and right arm; another puppeteer the left hand and the third puppeteer the feet. The Bunraku puppeteers train for many years and they move together as a team so seamlessly that you don't notice their presence on stage.

The Thin Man puppet is an ideal training tool. It is constructed very quickly. You can experiment manipulating the puppet alone or with more operators. The puppeteers must work closely together to bring the puppet alive.

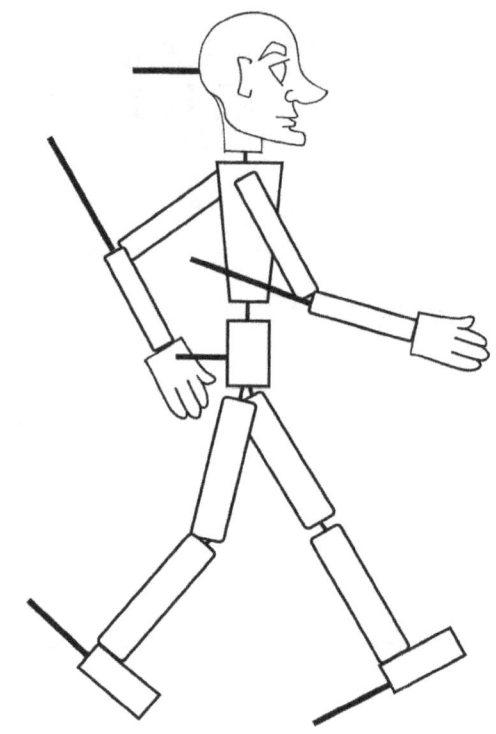

Materials:
newspaper, masking tape, thin dowels, paper that is used to cover the examination beds of doctors (I use this paper because it is thicker than tissue paper but still not as thick as newsprint), paper mache glue, cotton clothesline rope, a small quantity of white cloth, flexible wire.
Tools:
scissors, pliers, hot glue gun, wire cutters, ruler, pencil.

You will construct a head, torso, hips and segmented arms and legs.

An internal rope joins them together.

Consider this:

Consider the size of the puppet you are about to make.

If you are going to operate this puppet alone be careful not to make it too tall.

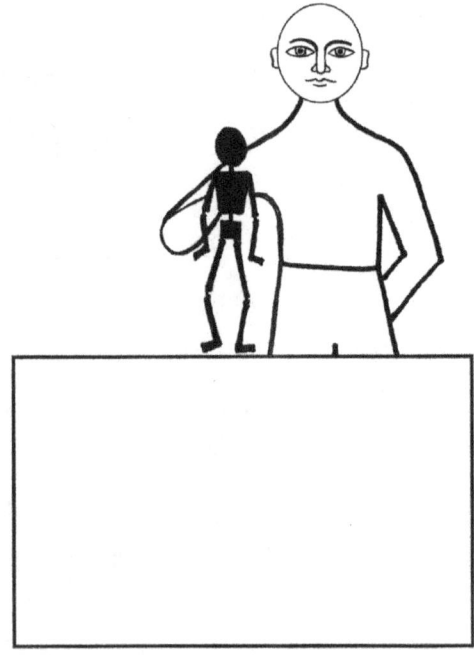

178

Puppets, Puppetry and Gogmagog

Thin Man

1

Cut **2** pieces of rope. I use cotton clothesline rope.

The first piece of rope will join the head to the feet. I generally measure more or less how tall the puppet will be, add extra for the knots and then double the length. It is better to have more rope than less.

The second rope runs from one hand of the puppet to the other (across the shoulders). Add extra.

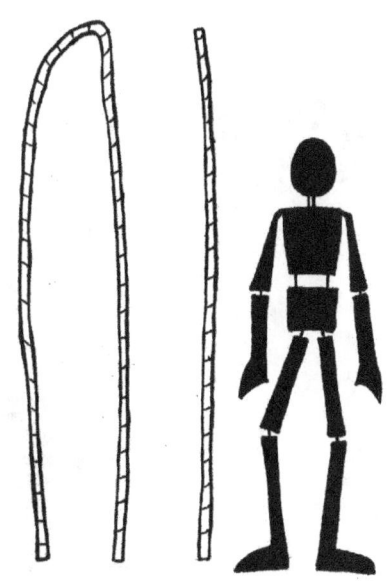

2

Tie the long piece of rope (divided exactly in the middle) as shown on to a small stick.

The length of the stick is a little shorter than the width of the head of the puppet you are going to make.

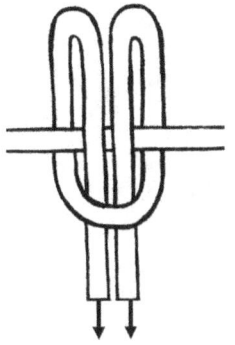
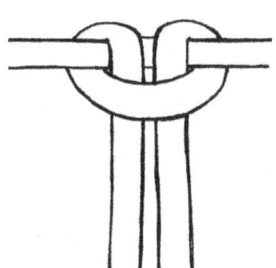

3

Create a head shape around the stick with scrunched newspaper.

Try to keep the stick horizontal.

Tape the newspaper into place with masking tape.

Make sure the **2** long strings descend vertically from the head. These form the neck of the puppet.

Note: in these drawings I have not drawn the masking tape.

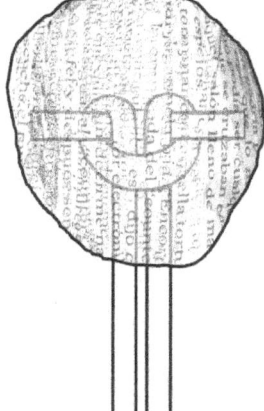

Puppets, Puppetry and Gogmagog   Table Top Puppets **179**

 Lay another small stick on top of the **2** strings. Tape it into place as shown.

This stick forms the shoulders of the puppet.

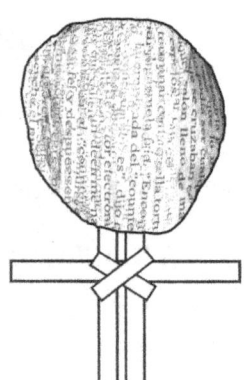

Take the second piece of rope and find the middle point.

Attach the middle point to the middle of the shoulder stick with masking tape.

Keep taping the rope on to either side of the shoulder stick.

This rope is for the arms later on.

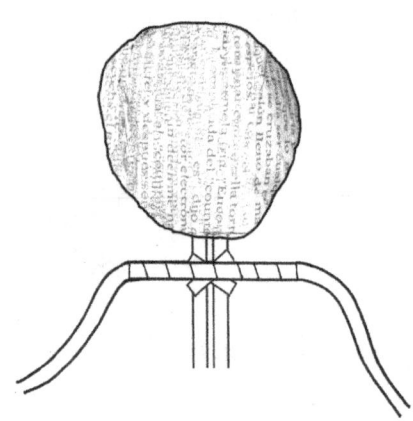

When you add the newspaper to the torso it is important to separate the **2** strings as shown.

These strings will join to the hips. The separation of these strings allows for movement at the waist line but stops the hips swinging wildly around.

Cover the torso front and back with scrunched up newspaper. Tape it into place.

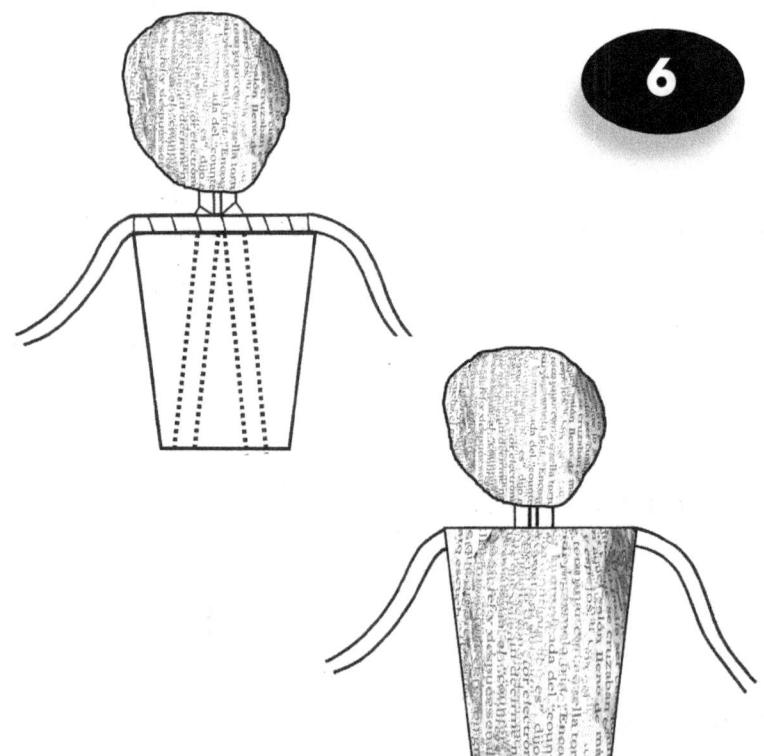

Puppets, Puppetry and Gogmagog

Place another small stick on top of the separated ropes as shown. The distance from the torso is small.

The stick is the base for the hips.

If you want big hips cut the stick longer.

Tape the stick into place with masking tape as shown.

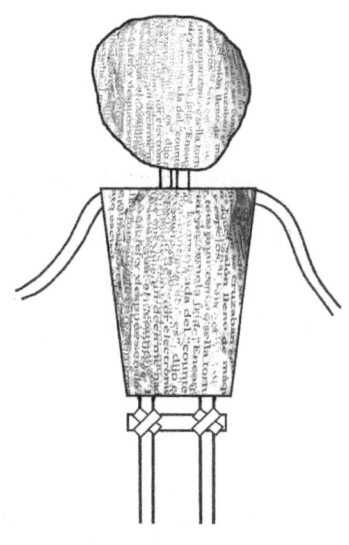

Create the hips with scrunched up newspaper.

Tape the newspaper in place with masking tape.

Make sure the **2** ropes are still separated. These ropes join the legs to the hips so you want to have enough separation between them to accommodate the legs in the next steps.

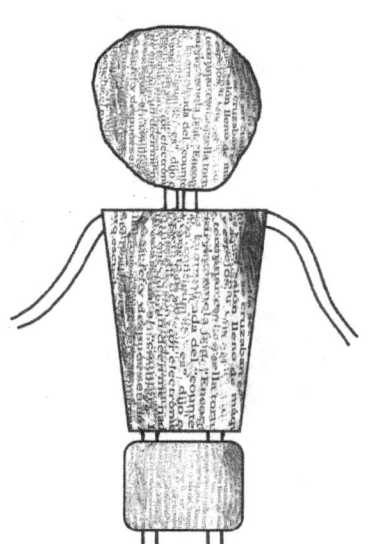

Tie a knot in each of the arm ropes as close to the shoulders as possible.

Tie a knot in each of the legs ropes as close to the hips as possible.

Note: I have exaggerated the size of the knots in the illustration to see them better.

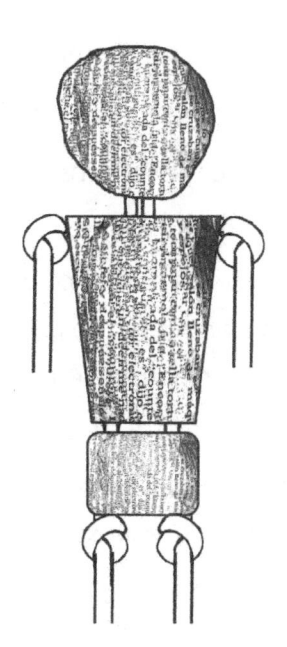

The Legs and Arms

You are going to make the legs and arms out of rolled up newspaper.

You will need to experiment with the number of sheets of newspaper you need to create the rolls. The thickness of the sheet of newspaper in each country is different. I generally start with **4** sheets for the legs and **3** sheets for the arms.

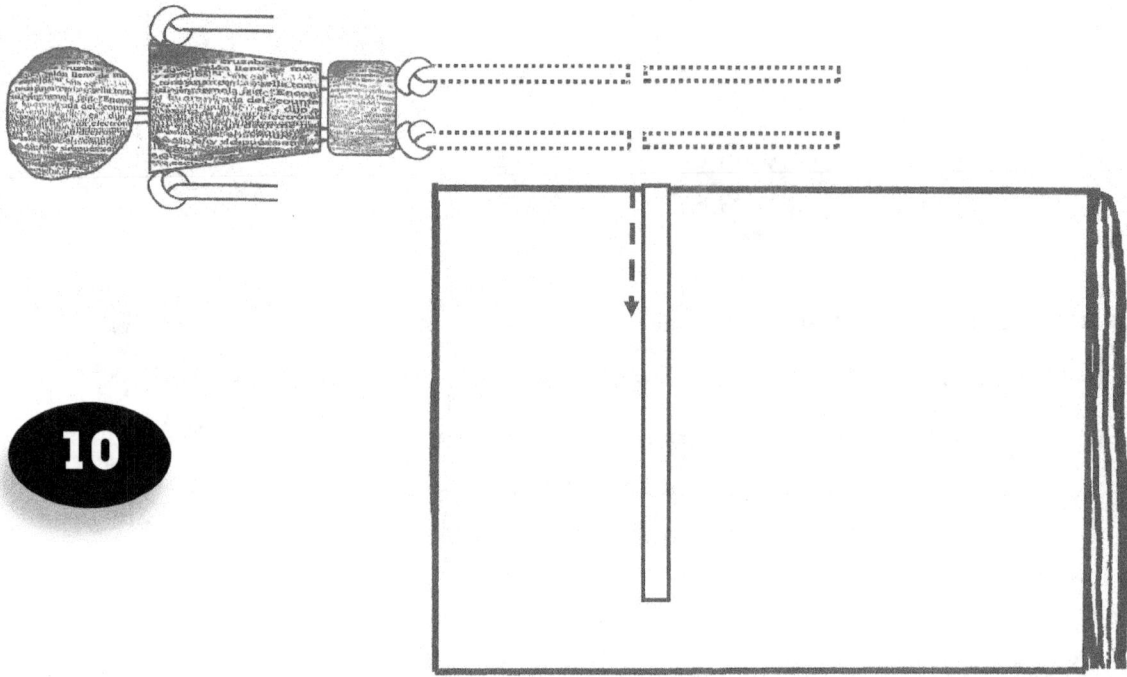

10

Lay the sheets of newspaper together with the fold at the top as shown.

Lay the puppet close to the newspaper as shown.

Visualize the lengths of the thighs and lower legs. Take into account a little extra room for knots in the ropes.

When you are sure of the length of each piece, place a ruler on to the newspaper as shown and tear the layers from the folded edge down towards you. You will do this **4** times to make the **4** parts of the legs.

Do the same for the arms allowing a little extra room for knots. I use fewer sheets of newspaper for the arms. Generally the upper arm goes from the shoulder to the waistline. The wrist of the lower arm reaches the bottom of the hips.

Take a segment of newspaper and roll it around a pencil.

Start with the folded end of the segment close to the pencil.

Tape the roll together and slide the pencil out. Repeat for the other **3** parts of the legs.

Trim the parts of the legs if necessary so that they are all the same.

Do the same for the **4** segments that make up the arms.

Verify that they are all the same length.

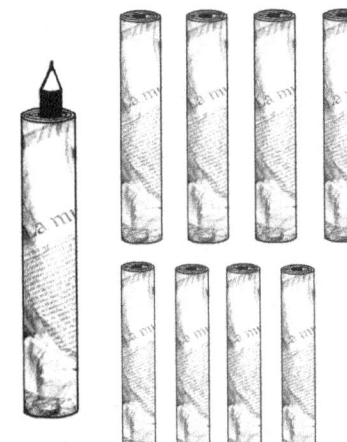

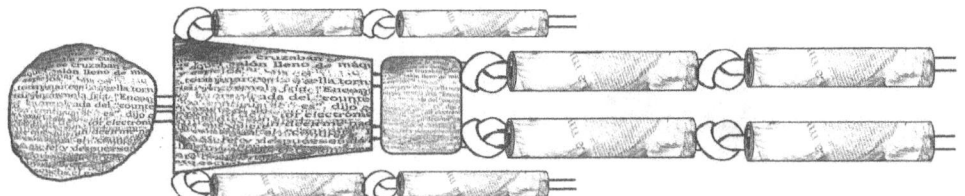

Lay the puppet down flat. Have a good look at the illustration above.

Thread the thighs on to the ropes as shown. Tie a knot at the end of each thigh.

Thread the lower legs on to the leg ropes.

Thread the upper arms on to the arm ropes as shown. Tie a knot at the end of each upper arm.

Thread the lower arms on to the arm ropes.

Leave the puppet as is while you make the hands and feet.

Create the feet and hands from thick cardboard. Include a small wrist on each hand.

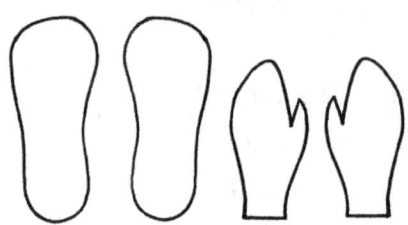

Attach the hands to the lower arms with hot glue.

Pull the arm string a little and glue it to the cardboard hands.

Trim off any excess rope.

Let dry.

Tape over the glue with masking tape.

Be careful; hot glue can cause burns.

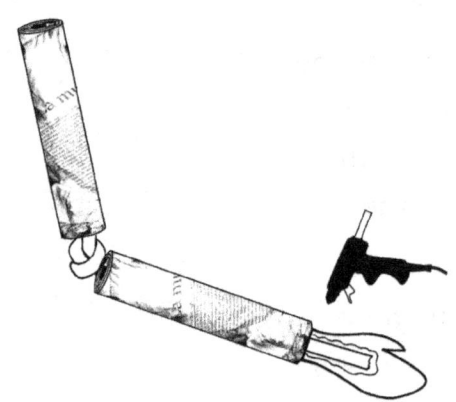

Attach the feet to the leg ropes with hot glue as shown.

The leg rope bends to form the ankle.

Make sure to pull the leg rope tight before you bend it so that the foot does not dangle loosely after being glued into place.

Glue the feet to the lower leg at a right angle as shown. Make sure the toes of the feet do not point inwards.

Let dry. Trim off any excess rope.

Tape over the glue with masking tape.

Be careful; hot glue can cause burns.

> **At this point you can add features to the face and more shape to the body with scrunched up newspaper and tape if you so desire.**

17

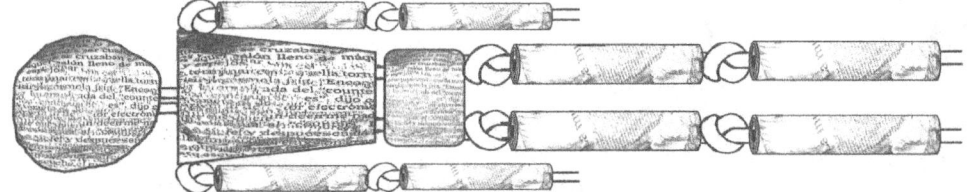

You will now "wrap" the parts of the puppet with paper mache.

I use the paper that doctors use to cover their examination beds. It is stronger than tissue paper.

Put paper mache glue onto the body part first, then "wrap" pieces of the fine paper on top.

It is like adding skin to the puppet.

Have lots of the paper torn onto biggish pieces before you handle the glue.

Let dry. Turn the puppet over from time to time.

> **Now that the puppet is assembled and covered with the paper it is time to apply the "breaks" to certain parts of the body. These "breaks" prevent parts of the body from bending in an unnatural broken way.**
>
> **For instance, the lower leg does not bend further forward than the knee.**

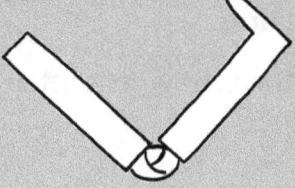

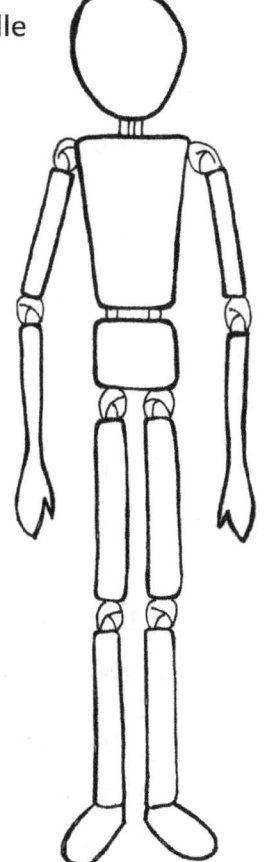

Thin Man

Puppets, Puppetry and Gogmagog — Table Top Puppets

18

Cut **6** small strips of white cloth as shown.

They should be the width of the body parts you are joining together and about 1½ inches/3.5cm long. It depends on the size of your puppet.

19

With the puppet lying **face up**, use hot glue to attach a piece of the cut cloth to the front of each hip as shown.

Pull each tab downwards to create some tension and glue the tab to the top of the thigh.

Tape over the extremities of each tab with masking tape.

20

Do the same with **2** tabs on the front and insides of each arm.

Be careful; hot glue can cause burns.

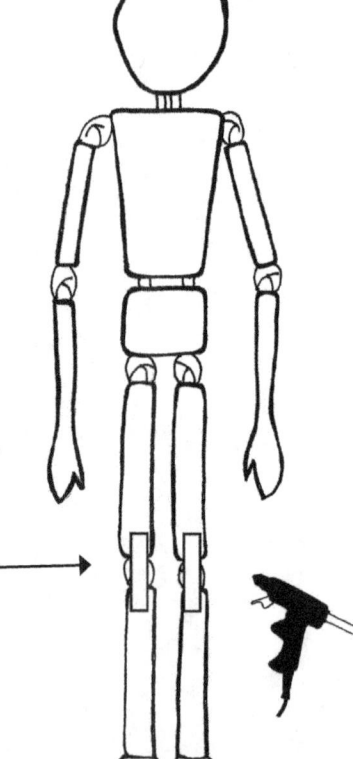

21

Turn the puppet over so it is **face down**.

Attach **2** cloth tabs to the bottom of the thighs with hot glue. Pull the tabs downwards to create a little tension and glue to the top of the lower legs.

Be careful; hot glue can cause burns.

Cover the masking tape on all the tabs with a little paper and glue.

Let dry.

22

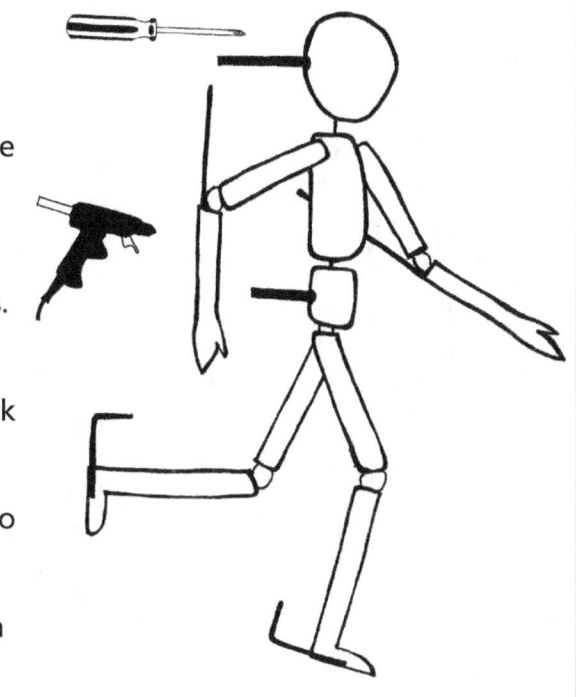

Thin Man

Attach the controls to the different parts of the body of the puppet.

Work a hole into the head of the puppet as shown. I use a thin *Phillips* screw driver for this.

Insert and glue a dowel (¼ inch/6mm dowel) into the hole with hot glue. Make sure the stick is at a right angle to the head.

Do the same with a shorter stick, attaching it to the middle of the hips.

Slide and glue a longer stick into each forearm as shown. I use thick kebab sticks.

Attach the feet wires following the instructions in the next illustration.

Be careful; hot glue can cause burns.

23

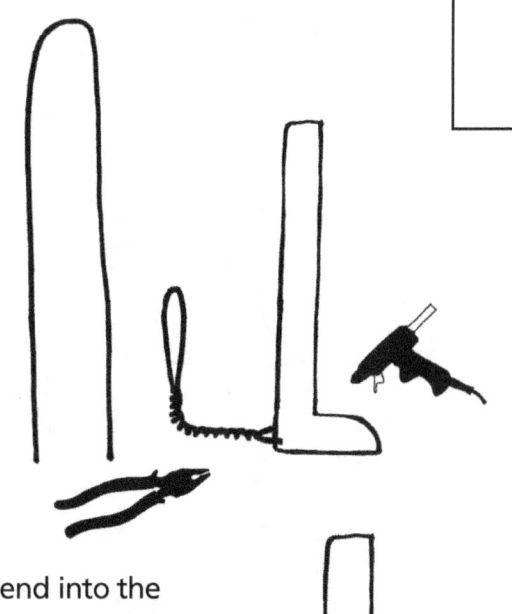

Cut and bend in **2** a piece of wire about 6-8 inches/ 15-20cm long. I use the wire that is used to tie rebar together on construction sites. Coat hanger wire is too thick.

Twist the wire around on itself as shown. Use pliers.

Bend the twisted part at a right angle.

Separate the **2** ends of the twisted wire and force each end into the back of the foot as shown. Glue it in place with hot glue and cover with tape and the white paper mache.

If you don't have enough room on the insides of the feet to do this, simply attach the separated wires to the outside of the foot. Hot glue the wires into place. Tape over the hot glue and apply white paper mache over all of it. Be careful; hot glue can cause burns.

Puppets, Puppetry and Gogmagog

Variation

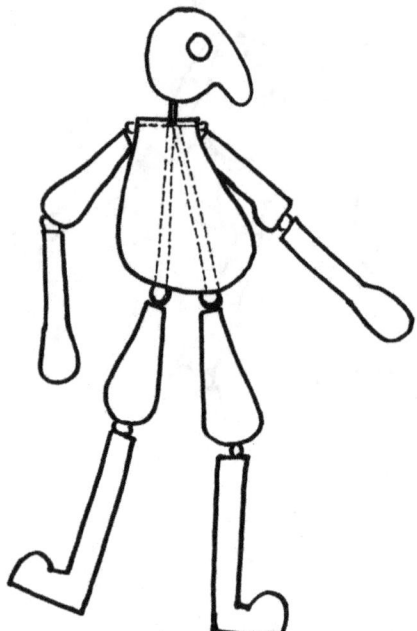

Perhaps you want a huge belly on the puppet.

You can eliminate the hip section.

Remember to divide the ropes from the shoulder stick to the bottom of the belly.

The legs are attached to the belly.

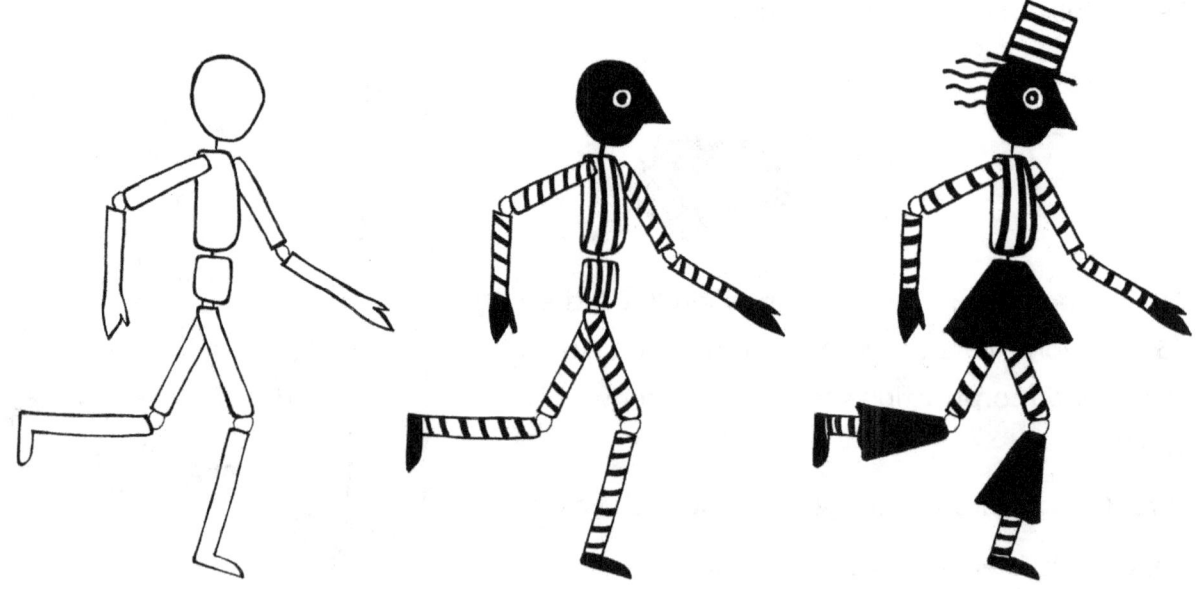

24

You can leave the puppet unpainted. The white bodies look very good against black clad puppeteers.

You can paint the puppet.

You can add elements of costume. Be careful not to impede the movement of the puppet.

Puppets, Puppetry and Gogmagog

A humanette consists of a small body suspended from the puppeteer's neck. The shoes of the humanette reach the playing surface. The head of the puppeteer is the head of the puppet. The hands of the puppeteer (sometimes worn with gloves) are the hands of the puppet. The effect is comical and grotesque.

Humanette

We need to consider the size of the humanette body in relation to our bodies as puppeteers.

The length of the body of the humanette starts at our necks and goes to the surface we are performing behind or on.

It is good to have some small children's clothing to get an idea. I look for clothing that would fit an average **2** year old. I also look for interesting small children's shoes.

Materials:
cloth to make the body, clothes and shoes that would fit and **18** month to **2** year old child (if you sew a special costume it should be this size or smaller), brown paper, pencil or marker, pins, thread, *polyfill*, hot glue sticks, adult sized gloves, 1 inch/25mm black elastic, cloth to make a ruff.

Tools:
scissors, sewing machine, sewing needles, hot glue gun.

Create a pattern on paper for the parts of the body that go under the costume of the humanette.

Make **2** patterns; a t-shaped arms and torso and another pattern for the legs as shown.

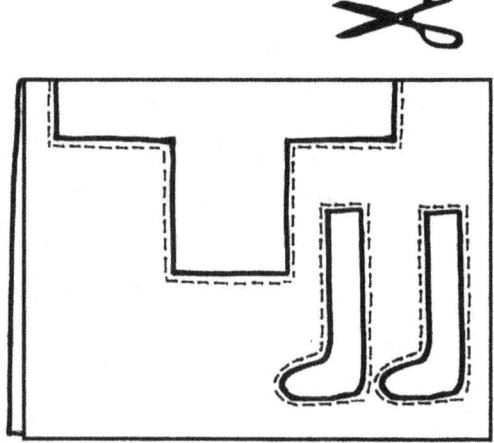

Fold a piece of cloth in **2** that can accommodate the patterns. The body will not be seen so it doesn't matter what kind of cloth you use.

Make sure the top of the torso pattern is placed on the fold.

Cut around the patterns allowing for a seam.

Do not cut along the fold.

Sew the **2** layers of the torso together as shown.

Leave the bottom open.

Sew the **2** layers of each leg as shown.

Leave the tops of the legs open.

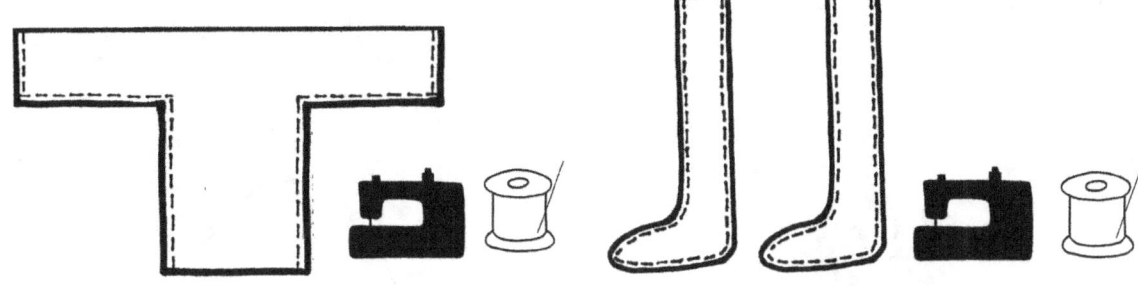

Turn the torso and legs inside out.

Fill the torso and legs with *polyfill*.

Turn the openings at the top so that the feet are pointing towards you.

Sew the openings closed.

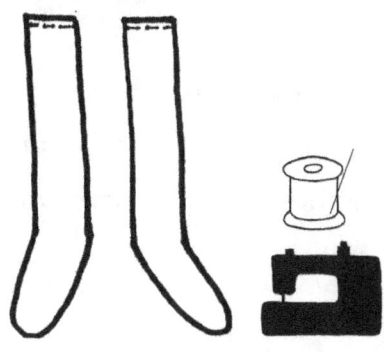

7

Insert the legs into the torso and sew along the bottom of the torso.

You may need to shorten the torso beforehand. Check against the child's clothing I mentioned before.

You now have a stuffed body ready to costume.

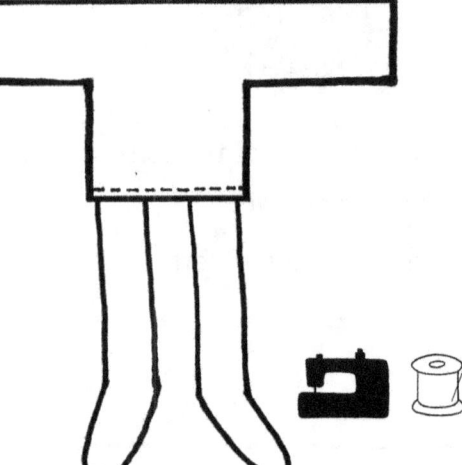

8

Accommodate a shirt or top over the torso.

9

Accommodate pants over the legs.

When you are satisfied with the fit, sew the clothes on to the outside of the body.

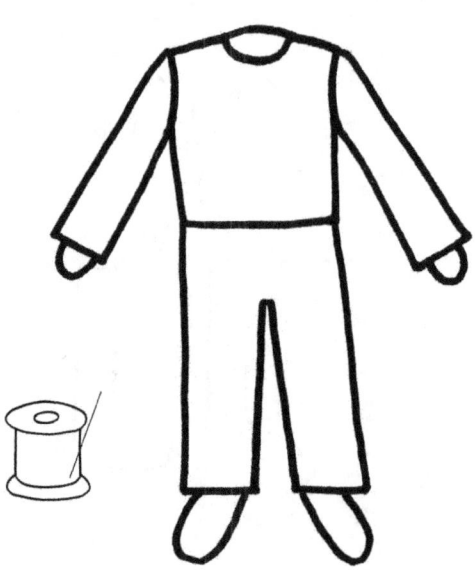

10

Sew a piece of elastic to the neck area of the body. This must fit over your head.

The humanette hangs from this elastic. I use 1 inch/2.5cm black elastic.

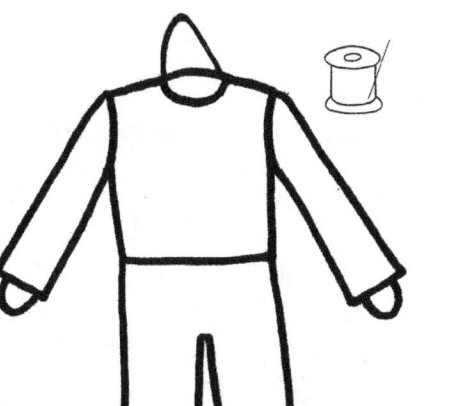

11

Hot glue the bottoms of the feet into the shoes. Use a stick to push the stuffed feet into the shoes.

Be careful; hot glue can cause burns.

Put the humanette on and check against a table that the height is good.

12

Sew human sized gloves to the sleeve holes of the puppet.

Leave a gap at the back so you can insert your hands.

I use cotton gardening gloves. They are easy to get on and off and can also be dyed many different colours.

Create a ruff or something similar to cover the space between the top of the neck of the humanette and your neck.

It is good to cover the elastic.

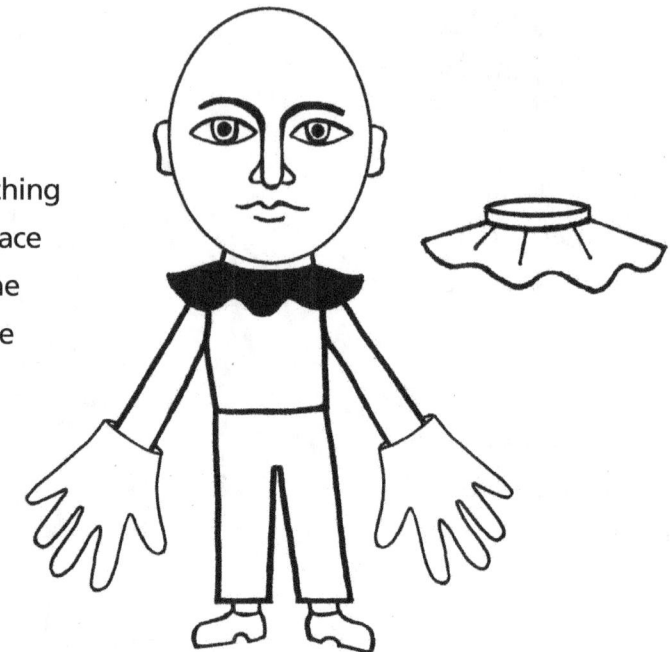

Add more details to the costume as you wish. You might like to add a hat for your head.

As a variation you can also use a mask with your humanette.

Puppets, Puppetry and Gogmagog

Empty plastic water or juice containers of different sizes make wonderful bases for puppets. These containers are readily available and are an economical way to construct comical and grotesque characters. Paper mache is applied directly on to these bases so the results tend to be quick.

Puppets Made Over Plastic Containers

Here are instructions for **2** mouth puppets made over gallon water containers.

Materials:
gallon water containers, masking tape, duct tape, newspaper, brown paper, hot glue sticks, acrylic paints.

Tools:
utility knife, scissors, hot glue gun, paint brushes.

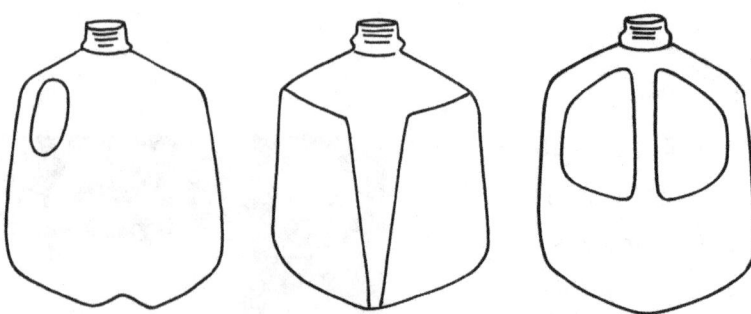

Side, front and back views of a gallon water container.

Draw and cut a vertical line as shown from one side of the neck of the container to the other.

Leave a part uncut at the neck, making sure that the **2** pieces of the bottle are still joined together.

From the side the container will open and close as illustrated.

Create the roof and the bottom of the mouth with cardboard.

See the instructions on page **86** for the **Cardboard Mouth Puppet**.

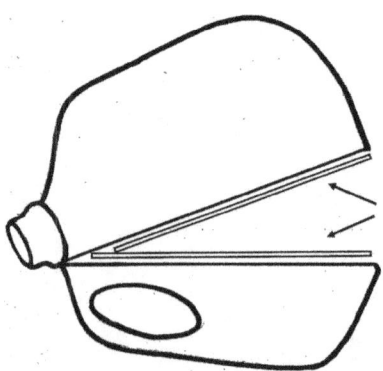

Mouth Puppet Over Gallon Container

Tape the cardboard palates on to the top and bottom edges of the mouth.

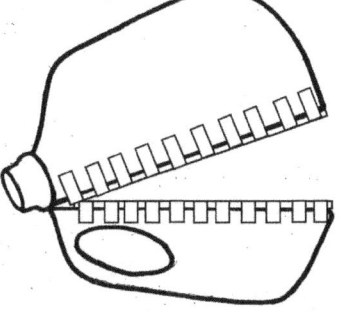

Apply **2** layers of paper mache (**1** newspaper, **1** brown) over the tape. Mache over the cardboard palates as well.

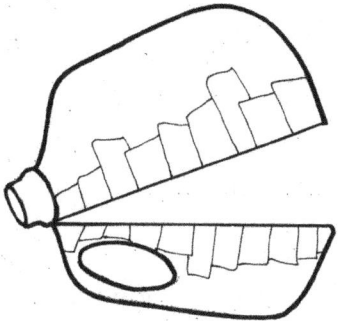

Apply **2** layers of paper mache over the whole container, except for the neck of the container.

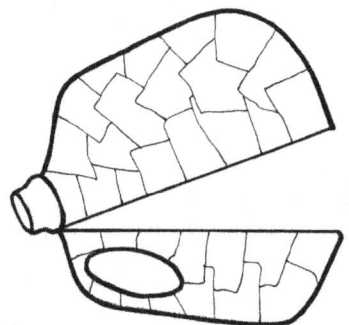

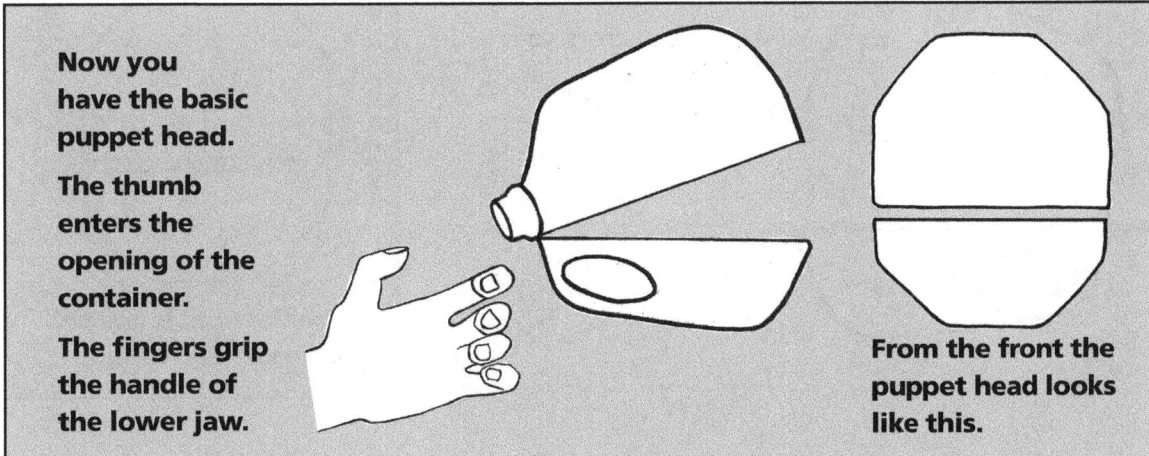

Now you have the basic puppet head.

The thumb enters the opening of the container.

The fingers grip the handle of the lower jaw.

From the front the puppet head looks like this.

Puppets, Puppetry and Gogmagog · Puppets Made Over Plastic Containers

The Eyes and Other Facial Features

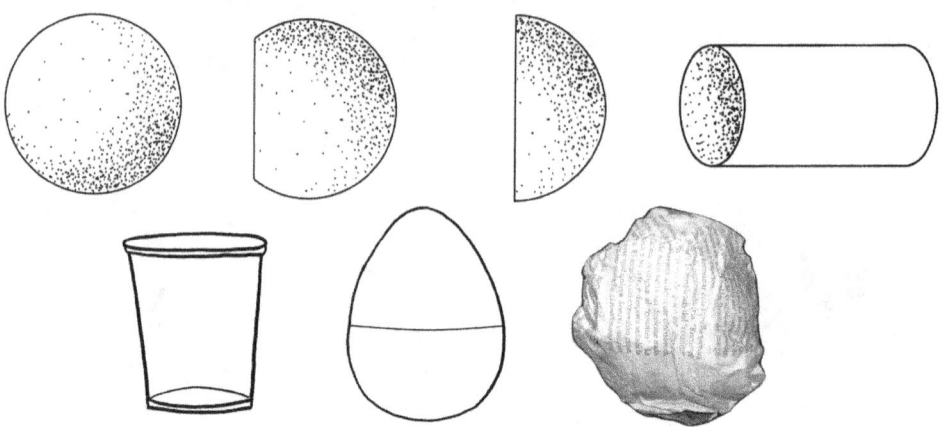

Eyes can be made of polystyrene balls cut in different ways, cardboard toilet paper rolls, plastic glasses or disposable paper cups, plastic eggs or scrunched up newspaper balls.

Experiment with polystyrene balls to make eyes.

6

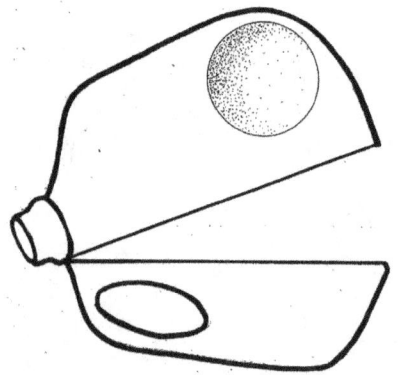

Cut a ball cut in half or three quarters so it will sit easily on the sides of puppet head.

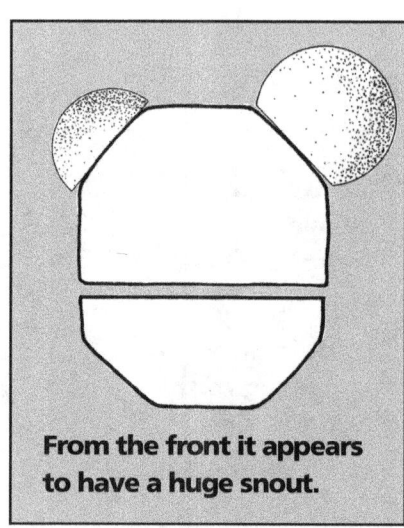

From the front it appears to have a huge snout.

Puppets, Puppetry and Gogmagog

Mouth Puppet Over Gallon Container

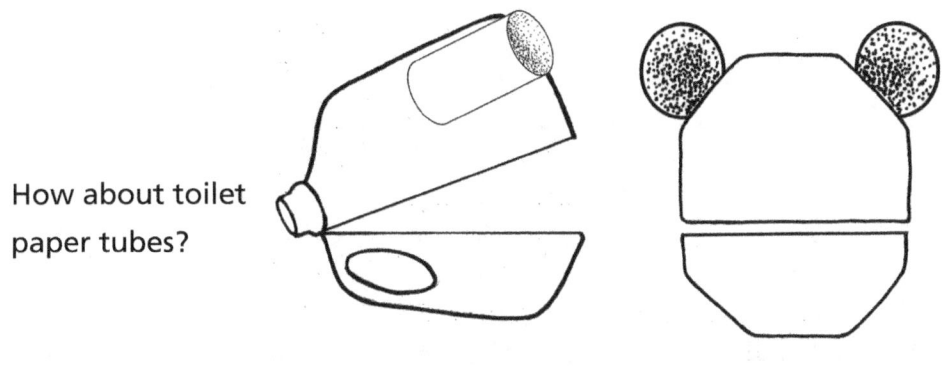

How about toilet paper tubes?

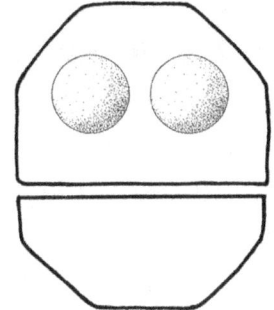

What if the eyes are placed on to the front of the upper jaw or snout?

Another character appears.

7

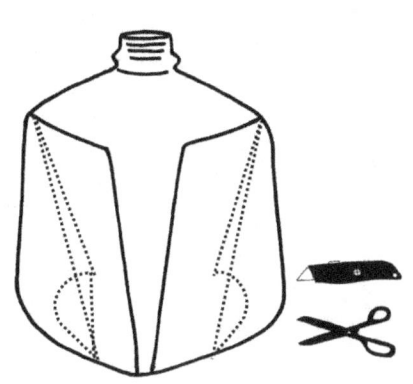

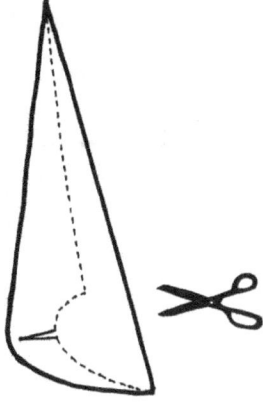

Cut **2** long triangular corners off the sides of another gallon container.

These could be ears.

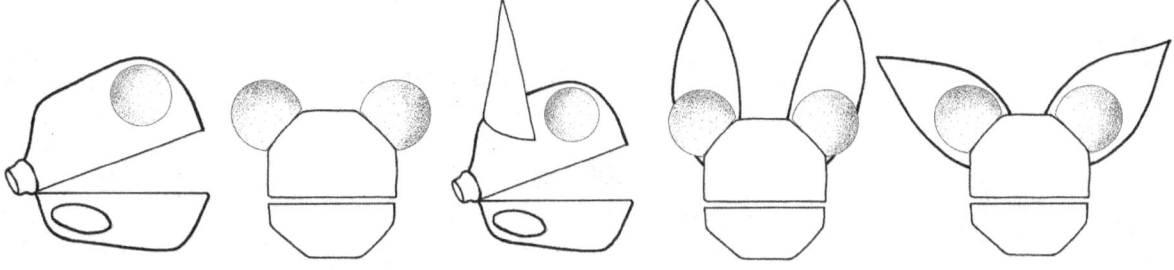

Look at these images so you can get an idea of how the placement of the eyes and ears changes the character. Here the eyes are placed on the sides of the head.

Puppets, Puppetry and Gogmagog   Puppets Made Over Plastic Containers

Here is the same progression; this time with the eyes placed on the front of the upper jaw or snout.

Now you have a completely different character.

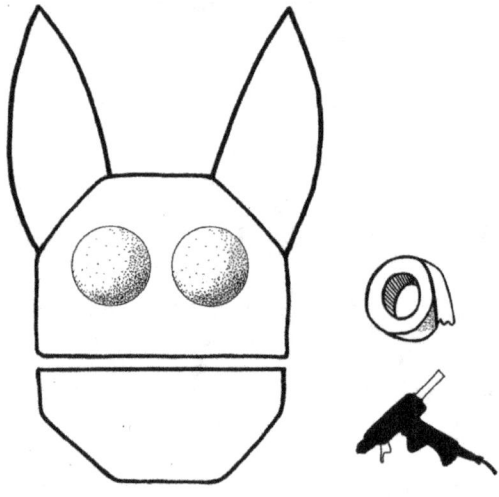

8

Decide on the orientation of your eyes and ears.

Tape or hot glue them into place. The hot glue will melt the plastic so use it sparingly.

Be careful; hot glue burns.

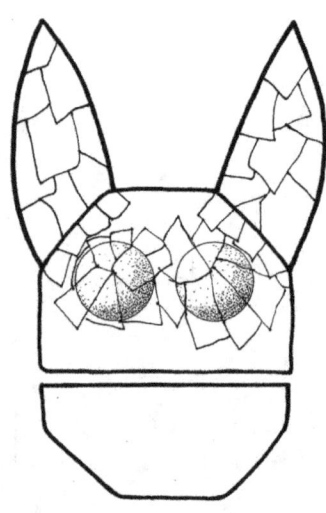

9

Apply **2** layers of paper mache (**1** newspaper, **1** brown) over the eyes and ears and on to the upper jaw.

Make sure you have covered all the tape.

Let dry.

200

Puppets, Puppetry and Gogmagog

Mouth Puppet Over Gallon Container

10

Paint and decorate the puppet.

Apply a base coat of white paint first.

Remember to paint the inside of the mouth; a flash of a contrasting colour looks good as the puppet opens its mouth.

When the paint is dry, you can add a sleeve to the puppet. Follow the instructions on page **92** of the **Mouth Puppet**.

Gallery of Possibilities

Variation: the Gallon Container Cut Laterally

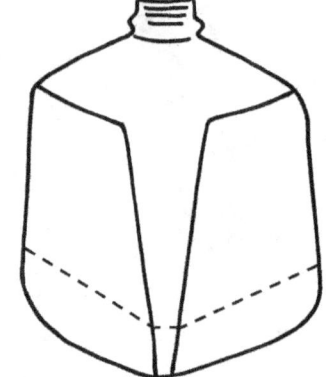

Draw and cut a horizontal line around the bottom part of a gallon water container as shown.

This line divides the top and bottom jaw.

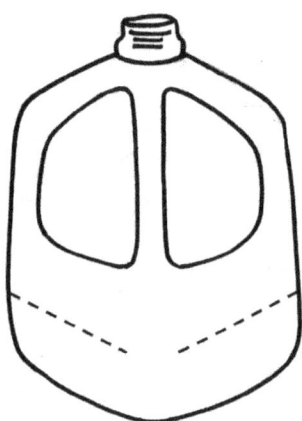

Look at the back.

Continue cutting but leave the central 1½ inches/38mm uncut.

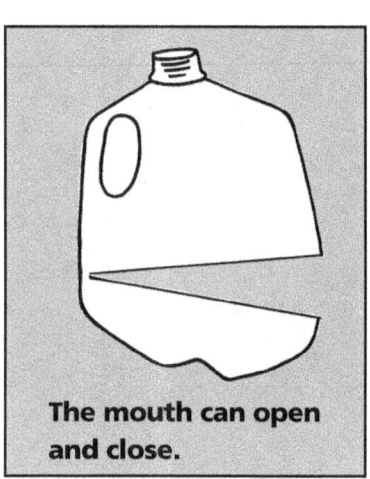

The mouth can open and close.

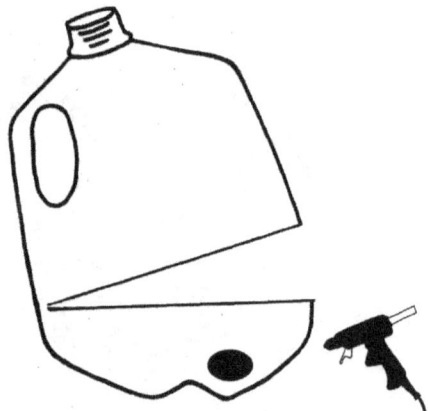

This puppet is manipulated with the handle of the water container.

By moving your arm or wrist up and down the mouth opens and closes in different ways.

Sometimes you need to put a little extra weight in the front of the bottom jaw.

I use fishing weights. Start with a light one first. Hot glue it into place as shown. Add more weight if necessary.

Be careful; hot glue can cause burns.

Mouth Puppet Over Gallon Container

Create the roof and the bottom of the mouth with cardboard.

See the instructions on page **86** for the **Mouth Puppet**.

Tape the cardboard palates on to the top and bottom edges of the mouth.

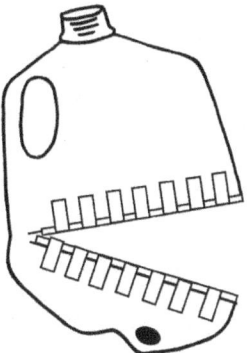

Apply **2** layers of paper mache (**1** newspaper, **1** brown) over the tape.

Apply paper mache over the cardboard palates as well.

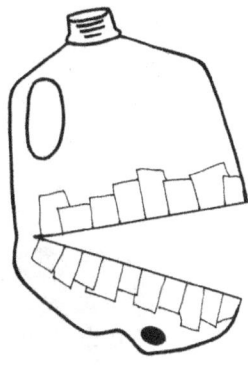

Apply **2** layers of paper mache (**1** newspaper, **1** brown) over the whole container.

Let dry.

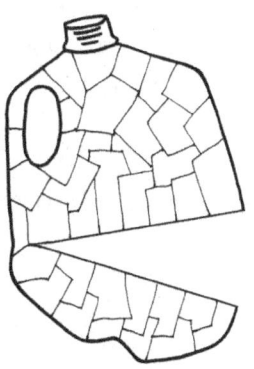

Puppets, Puppetry and Gogmagog — Puppets Made Over Plastic Containers — **203**

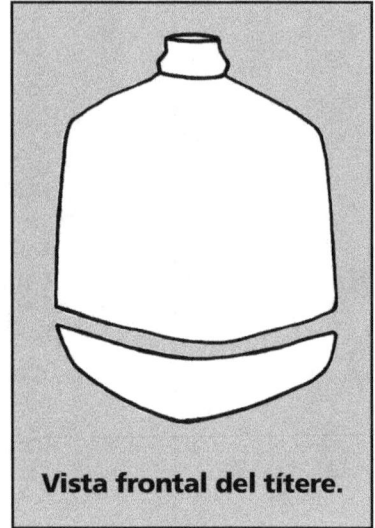

Vista frontal del títere.

Cut the handle from another gallon container as illustrated.

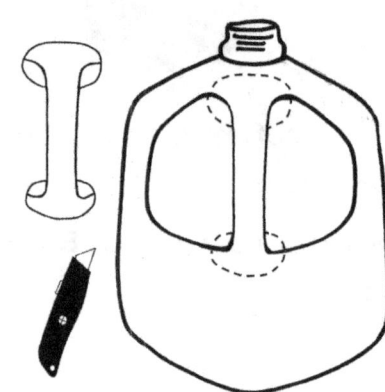

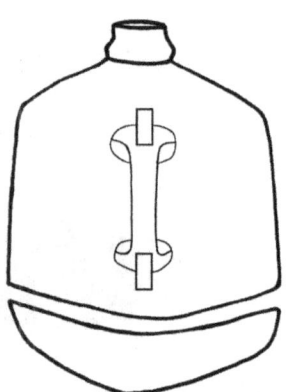

Tape the handle on to the top part of the puppet as a nose.

Take **2** plastic eggs apart and use the tops or bottom for eyes.

Tape them on to the puppet.

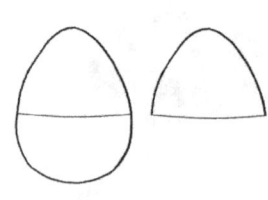

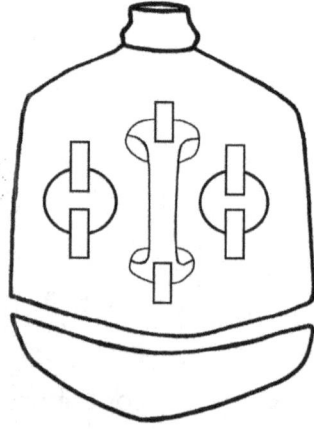

Puppets, Puppetry and Gogmagog

Mouth Puppet Over Gallon Container

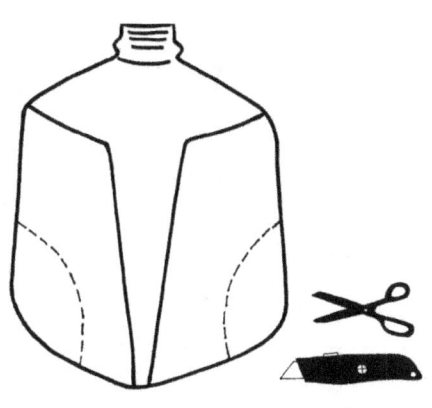

Cut **2** bottom corners off another gallon container for ears.

Tape them to the puppet.

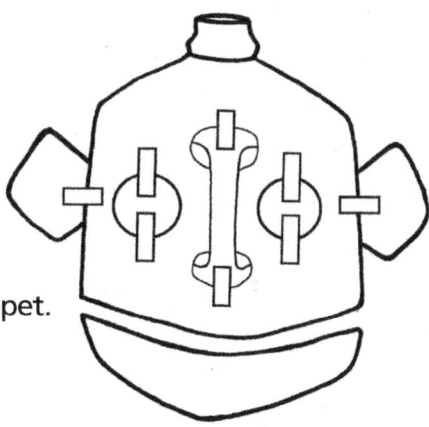

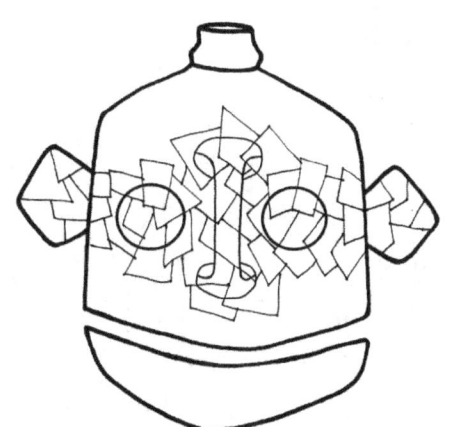

Apply **2** layers of paper mache (**1** newspaper, **1** brown) over the attached nose, eyes and ears.

Make sure you cover all the tape.

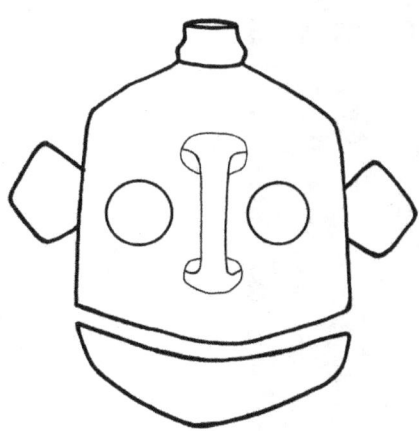

Paint the puppet.

Apply a base coat of white paint first.

Remember to paint the inside of the mouth;

a flash of contrasting colour looks good as the puppet opens its mouth.

When the paint is dry, you can add a sleeve to the puppet. Follow the instructions on page **92** of the **Mouth Puppet**.

Puppets, Puppetry and Gogmagog   Puppets Made Over Plastic Containers

This puppet is made with **2** plastic water containers. A common skirt hides one face. When the puppet is vertically flipped over using the handle of the container, another face is revealed.

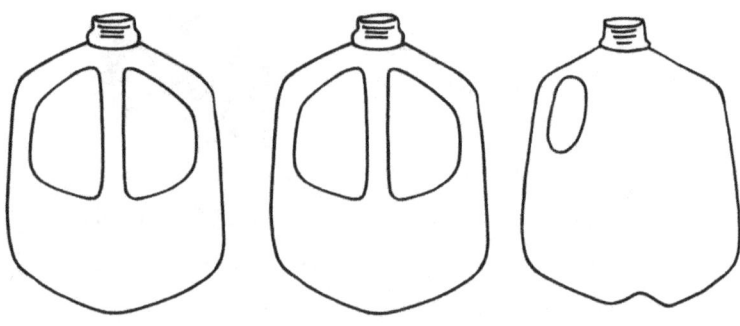

The heads are made with **2** containers. The third container is used to create ears or other facial features.

Materials:
3 empty plastic water containers (gallon size), newspaper, brown paper, duct tape, assorted objects to make the eyes and other facial features of the heads; polystyrene balls, plastic eggs etc., **2** pieces of different coloured cloth to make the small full circle skirt for the puppet, acrylic paints, hot glue sticks.

Tools:
hot glue gun, scissors, sewing machine or needle and thread, paint brushes.

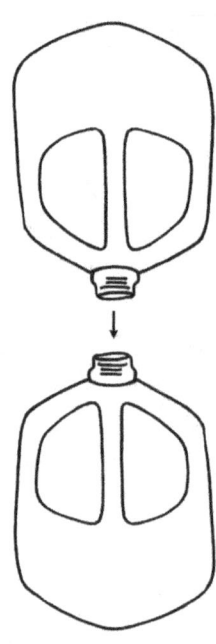

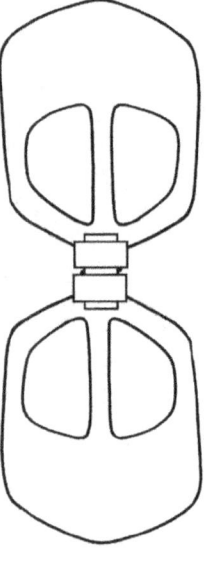

Join the **2** containers as shown with duct tape.

Make sure they are well taped together and can function as a single object.

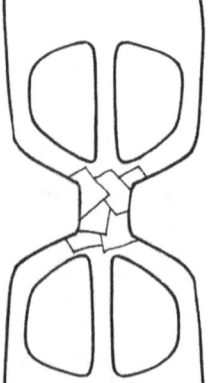

Apply **4** layers of paper mache around the taped neck alternating newspaper and brown paper.

Apply **2** layers of paper mache (**1** newspaper, **1** brown) over the rest of the body.

Let dry.

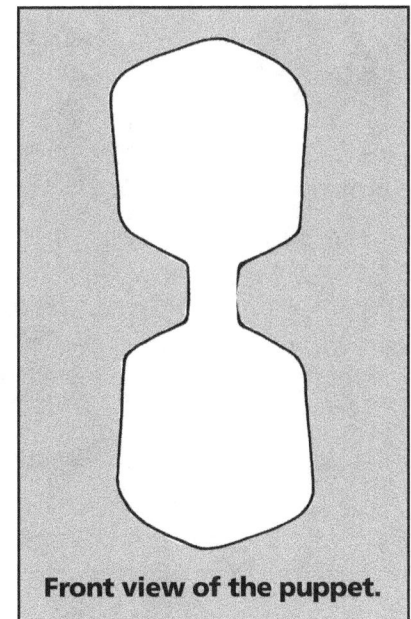

Front view of the puppet.

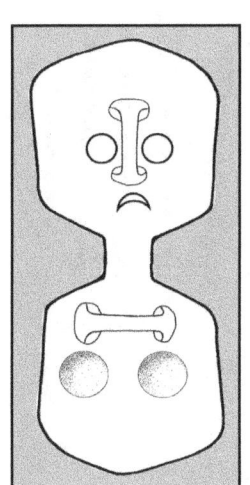

4

Following the suggestions on pages **198-200**, add facial features to the heads.

Remember to turn the puppet over to work each face.

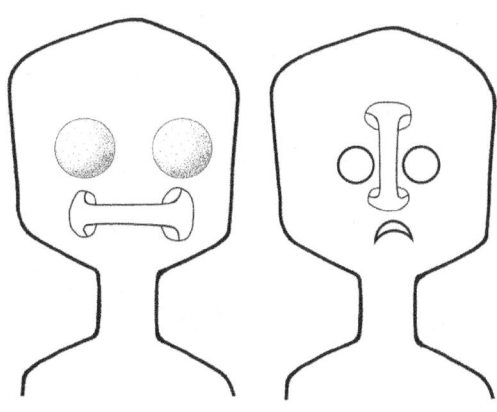

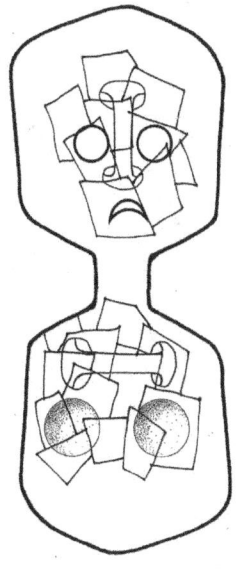

5

Apply **2** layers of paper mache (**1** newspaper, **1** brown) over the features.

Make sure that all the tape is covered.

Let dry.

Two Headed Flip Puppet

Paint the **2** heads of the puppet.

Apply a white base coat first.

Let dry.

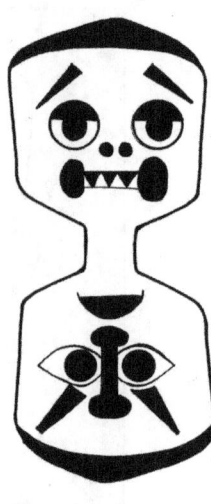

With a pencil draw a horizontal line around the middle of the neck as illustrated.

This line marks where you will glue the skirt of the puppet.

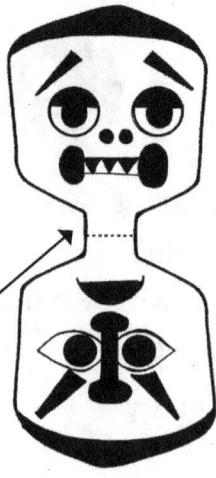

Cut **2** circles of differently coloured or patterned cloth to make the skirt of the puppet.

To measure the size of the circles you should use the puppet as a reference.

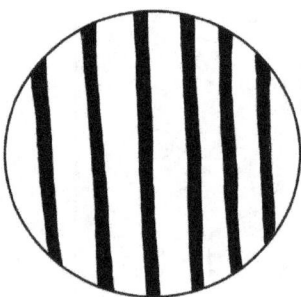

The radius of the circles should cover from the neck of the puppet to the playing surface, completely covering the other head below.

The radius describes the line from the centre of a circle to its outside border.

Fold each circle in half.

You can put the **2** circles together if you like.

Cut a small half circle in the middle of the fold.

This should be no bigger than the neck of the puppet.

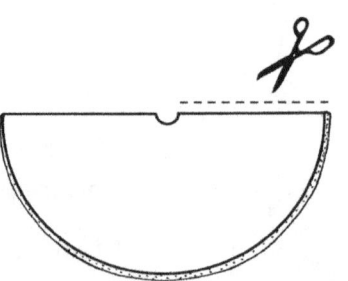

Cut along half of the fold as shown.

Puppets, Puppetry and Gogmagog

Two Headed Flip Puppet

Place the **2** circles right sides together.

Sew the borders of the **2** circles together.

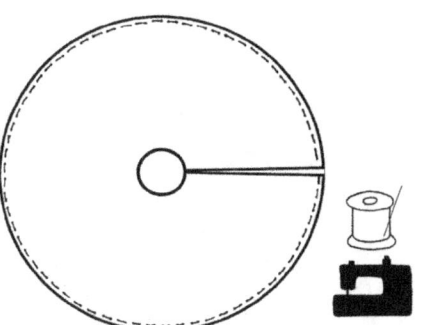

Turn the circles right side out.

If you like you can iron the outer edge/hem of the skirt.

Decide which side (color or pattern) of the skirt goes with the first head.

The open border of the skirt should go to the back.

Hot glue the small circle of the cloth to the neck.

Be careful; hot glue can cause burns.

Turn the puppet over. Now you have the other face to the front.

Hot glue the small circle of the other cloth to the neck.

Try to glue this small circle as close to the first circle as possible.

Be careful; hot glue can cause burns.

Sew the opening at the back of the skirt close.

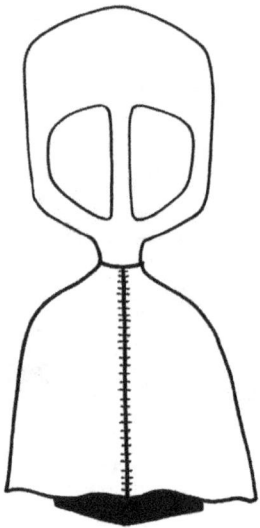

Use the handle at the back of each head to turn the puppet over.

Standing Puppet Over Liter Container

This is a puppet made over a liter container. With or without the addition of legs, it stands alone. Its arms are moved by the fingers of the puppeteer.

This puppet is operated by the puppeteer using the handle of the plastic container.

Materials:
empty liter plastic container, newspaper, brown paper, paper mache glue, hot glue sticks, air dry clay, acrylic paints, duct tape, polystyrene ball, screw eyes, thin dowels, string, epoxy glue.

Tools:
utility knife, hot glue gun, paint brushes.

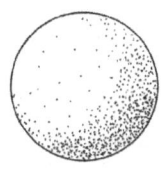
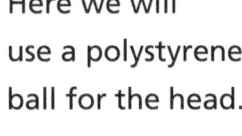
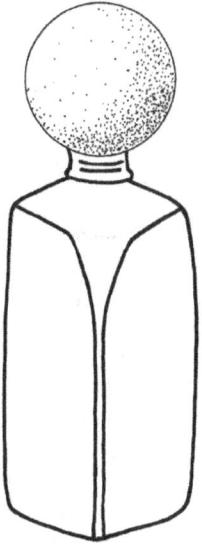

Here we will use a polystyrene ball for the head. Make sure the size of the ball is in proportion to the body.

Fix the head to the opening of the container with duct tape.

Make sure it is securely attached.

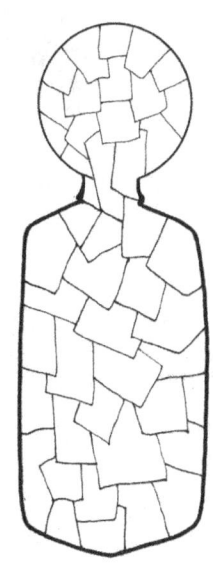

Apply **4** layers of paper mache (alternating newspaper and brown paper) over the head and body.

Include the base and handle.

Let dry.

Puppets, Puppetry and Gogmagog

Knead a little air dry clay. See page **132** for more information about air dry clay.

Remember to keep the package closed when not in use.

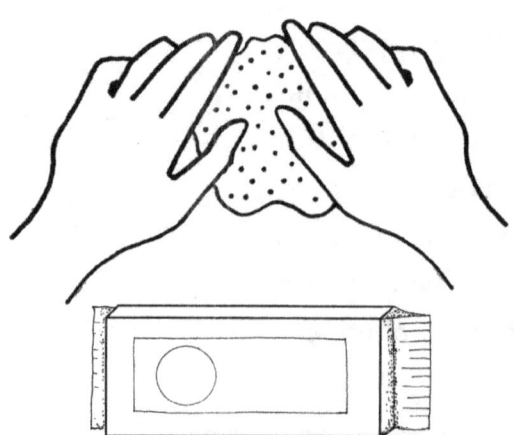

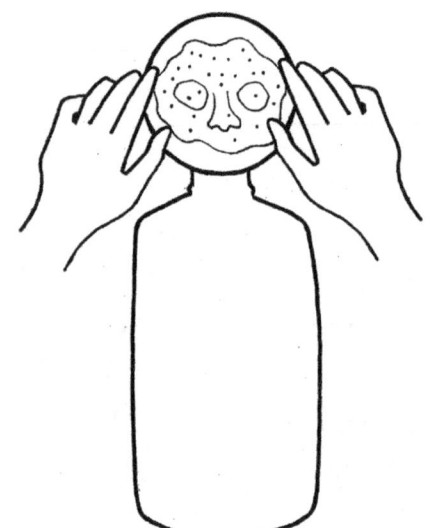

Mold the facial features of your puppet.

Let dry.

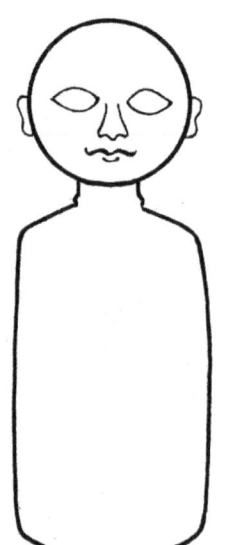

Cut **2** small holes at shoulder level for the shoulder bar. Try to make the holes as horizontally level as possible.

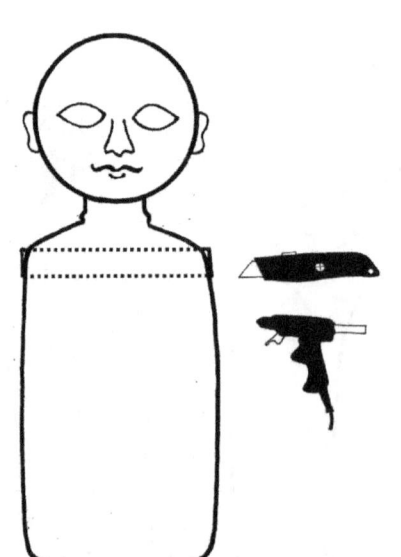

Pass a dowel through the holes and fix in place with hot glue.

I use ½ inch/13mm dowel for this.

Be careful; hot glue can cause burns.

Let dry.

Standing Puppet Over Liter Container

Attach **1** small screw eye to each end of the shoulder bar.

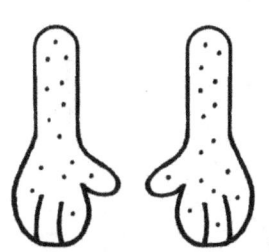

Create the arms and legs for the puppet from air dry clay.

Let dry thoroughly. This may take a day or two.

The arms are the only moving part on the puppet so make them noticeable.

I like a soft curve at the top.

The puppet stands freely balanced on the legs. Make sure that the top of the legs and the bottom of the feet are flat.

I make the top of the legs a little wider so there is a larger area for glue when the legs are attached to the body later on.

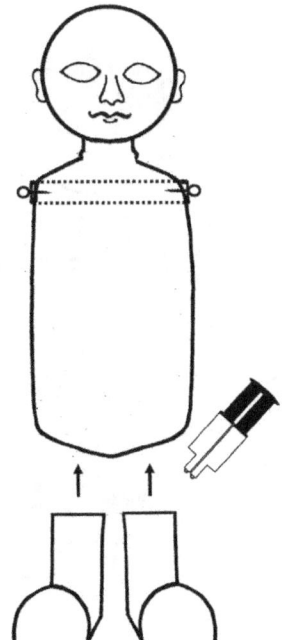

Attach the legs to the bottom of the body with epoxy.

Try various positions beforehand to make sure the body is well balanced on top of the legs.

Let dry.

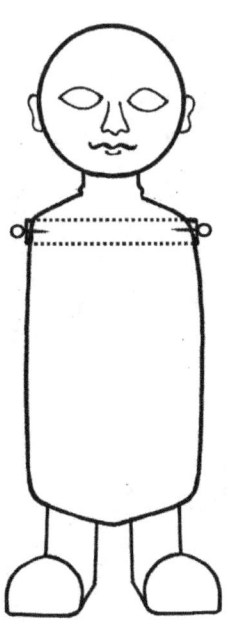

Puppets, Puppetry and Gogmagog

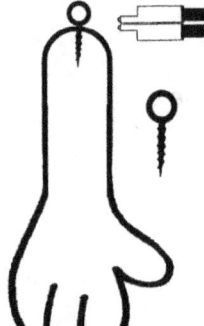

Attach a screw eye to the top of each arm with epoxy.

Let dry.

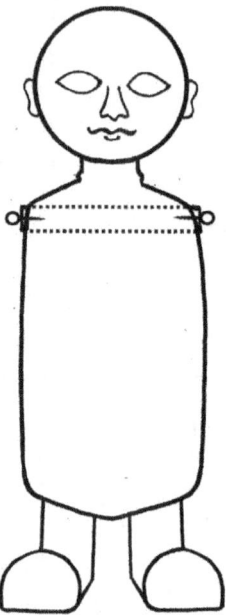

Attach the arms with string through the screw eyes to each end of the shoulder bar.

Make sure you have the arms on the right sides.

Paint your puppet. Apply a white base coat first. The costume is painted on to the body, so the public can appreciate the form of the plastic container.

Add hair at the end if you like.

Puppets, Puppetry and Gogmagog

Bird Puppet Over Liter Container

The bird hops and looks in all directions... a mischievous character.

Materials:
2 plastic juice containers (liter size), 1 hollow plastic ball, **2** small polystyrene balls (or ping pong balls) for the eyes, cardboard, newspaper, brown paper, paper mache glue, hot glue sticks, wire, duct tape, acrylic paints.

Tools:
utility knife, scissors, hot glue gun, wire cutters, paint brushes.

1
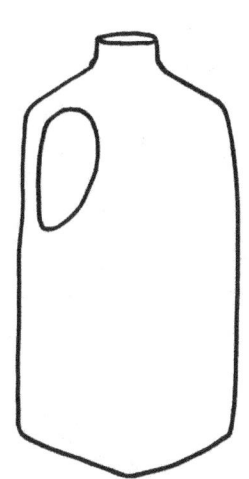
Apply **2** layers of paper mache (**1** newspaper, **1** brown) completely over the first liter container.

This forms the body of the puppet.

Let dry.

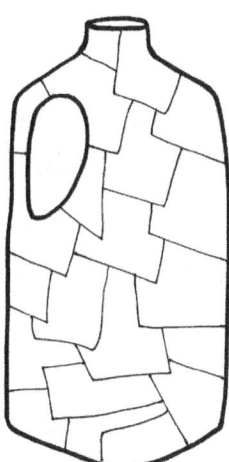

2

Choose a plastic ball for the head.

Make sure it is proportion to the body of the puppet.

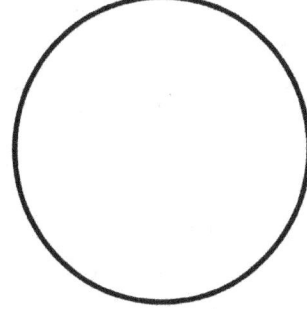

3

Apply **2** layers of paper mache (**1** newspaper, **1** brown) to the outside of the ball.

Let dry.

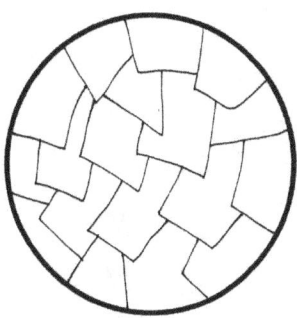

Draw and cut **2** triangles as illustrated.

These triangles form the upper and lower beak. The lower beak is smaller than the upper beak.

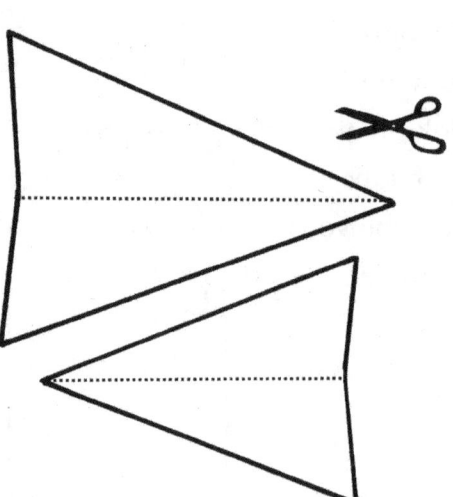

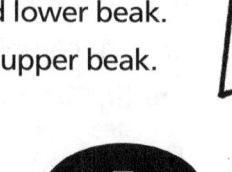

Fold each part of the beak in half as illustrated.

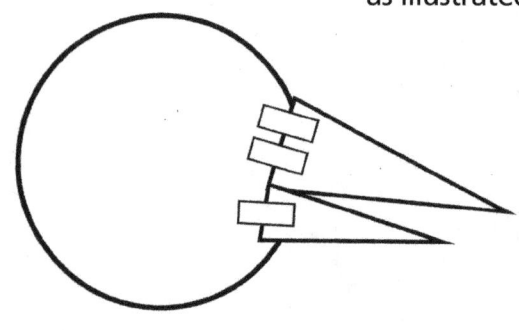

Tape the **2** parts of the beak to the head.

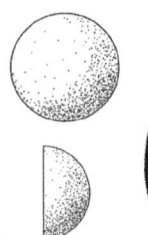
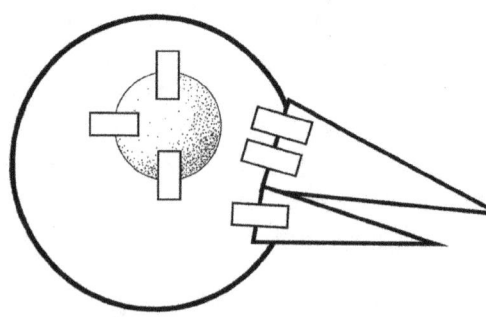

Cut the polystyrene or ping pong balls in half or three quarters so that the flat sides sit well on the head.

Tape the eyes on to the head.

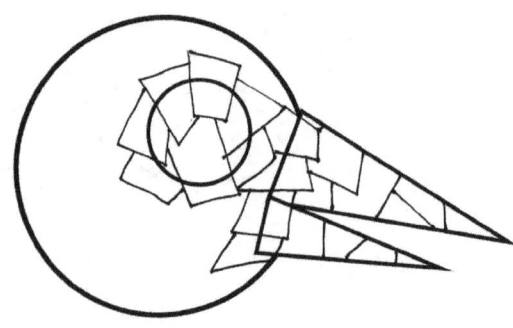

Apply **2** layers of paper mache (**1** newspaper, **1** brown) over the **2** parts of the beak and where they join to the head.

Make sure all the tape is covered.

Let dry.

Puppets, Puppetry and Gogmagog

Drill a hole in the head at the angle illustrated in order to insert the dowel that will form the neck of the bird.

The hole should be the size of the dowel. I use a ¾ inch/19 mm dowel for this.

Make sure that the neck of the bird can move freely in the neck hole of the body.

Insert the dowel into the head at the angle illustrated. Hot glue it in place.

Be careful; hot glue can cause burns.

Apply paper mache (brown paper) on top of the join when the hot glue is set.

Let dry.

Make a hole at the back of the head just above the neck. It should be big enough to easily fit your index finger.

You will use this hole to move the head later on.

Apply **1** layer of brown paper mache around the border of the hole to give it a smooth finish. Let dry.

Bird Puppet Over Liter Container

Puppets, Puppetry and Gogmagog

Puppets Made Over Plastic Containers

217

Form the legs of twisted wire and mark where they will attach to the body.

The legs support the weight of the body so they should be quite large and strong.

Hot glue them into place.

Be careful; hot glue can cause burns.

Apply duct tape over the glue when it has dried.

Try introducing the head into the body.

Make sure that the bird can stand alone.

Find the balance by bending the wire of the legs if necessary.

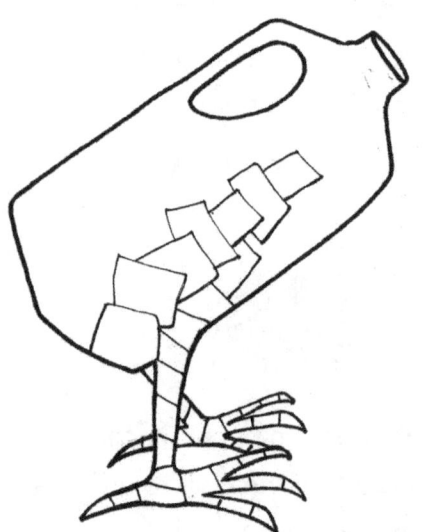

Apply **2** layers of paper mache (**1** newspaper, **1** brown) over the wires.

Wrap strips of paper and glue around the legs and feet to give them more body.

Let dry.

Bird Puppet Over Liter Container

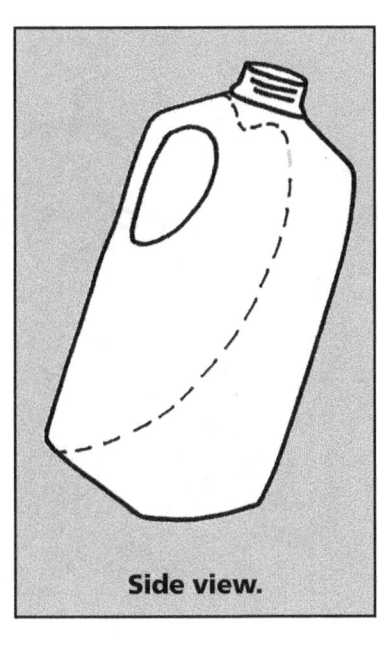

Side view.

From the back of another liter container, draw and cut out **2** wings as illustrated.

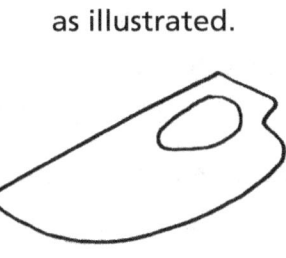

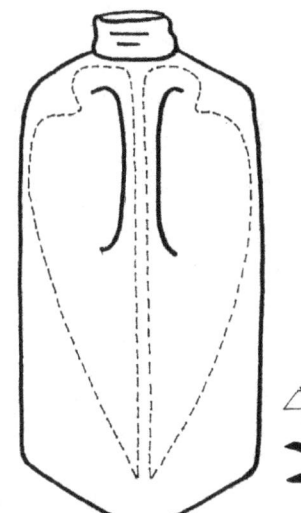

18

If you want to make the wings bigger, cut out cardboard extensions and then glue them on to the plastic wings.

19

Cut out the top part of the plastic handle from each wing.

20

Apply **2** layers of paper mache (**1** newspaper, **1** brown) over each wing.

Do not apply paper mache underneath the curve of the plastic handle.

Let dry.

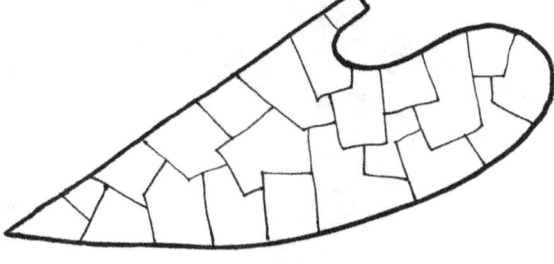

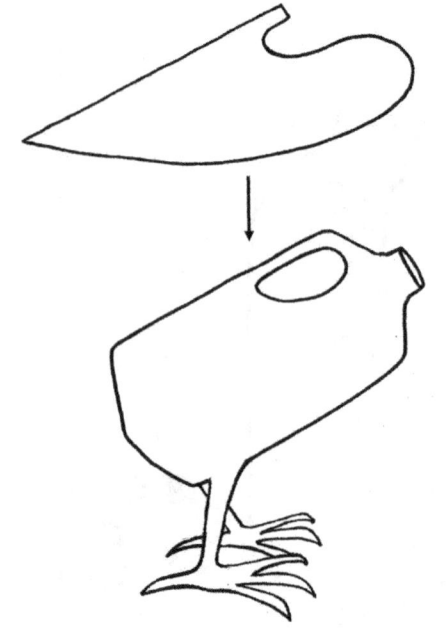

21

Fit each wing on its respective side over the handle of the body of the bird.

Hot glue the wings into place. Be careful; hot glue can cause burns.

Apply a little paper mache over the union.

Make sure your fingers still fit in the handle.

22

Your basic bird is finished. You can add other details at this stage; a crest for example.

Cut a crest from cardboard, attach it to the head with duct tape and apply **2** layers of paper mache over the join.

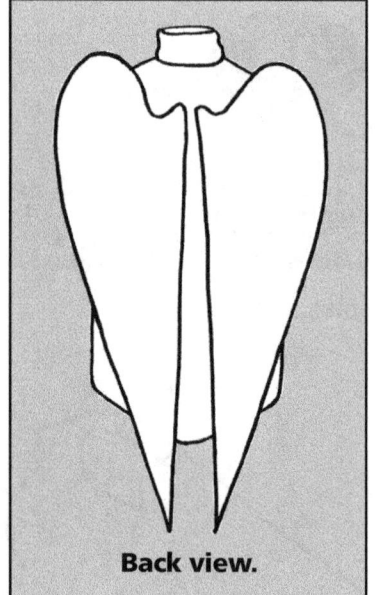

Back view.

21

Paint the head and body of the bird.

Apply a white base coat first.

Puppets, Puppetry and Gogmagog

There was a time when giants walked the earth. In early story and art, great characters were literally of great body. Copious mention is made of giants in religious texts, in the writings of early historians and in myths and legends. My fascination with giants has inspired me to build several. There is nothing like the sight of a giant moving across an open field or peering into the windows of multiple story buildings in small towns. In over 100 countries in the world, people build and carry these wonderful great puppets; celebrating the time when indeed… giants walked the earth.

Giants

There are many ways to build giants. I build them over a tall wooden frame.

A frame giant can be carried by **1** person. The frame and of the giant is carried on the shoulders. The body of the giant itself is built on top of the top platform. The advantage of a frame giant is that it can stand alone. The disadvantage is storage. Below I include the measurements of the frame and close-up illustrations of each level. I do not give blow by blow instructions. If you are unsure how to proceed ask someone with carpentry skills.

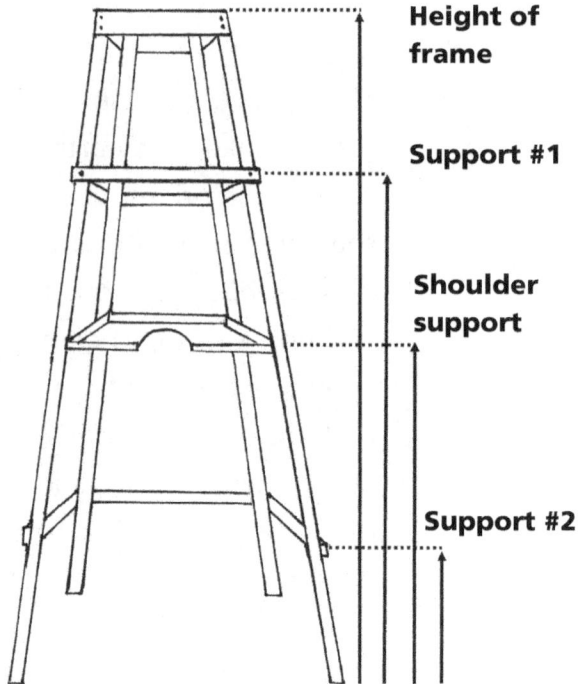

Materials for the frame:
wood: long lengths of 1½x1½ inches by 7 feet; wood for the platform sides, plywood for the top of the platform, wood screws.

Tools:
saw, drill and drill bits, measuring tape, tall ladder.

Height of frame: 7.5 feet/243cm

Each side of the top platform measures about 18 inches/45.7cm.

Support #1 is positioned between the top and the shoulder support.

Shoulder support is positioned about 5 feet/160cm from the floor. It should be 4 inches lower that the shoulder height of the puppeteer.

Support #2 is positioned about knee height from the floor.

Distance between each leg on the floor is about 36 inches/91.5cm.

In the middle point of the top platform drill a hole big enough to fit a bolt.

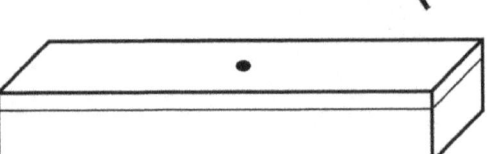

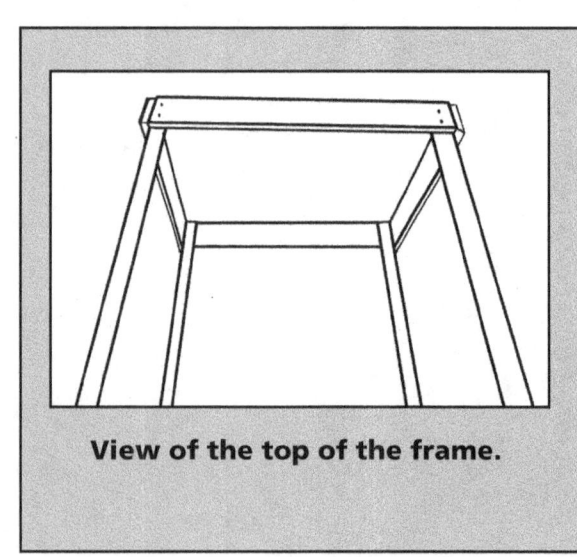

View of the top of the frame.

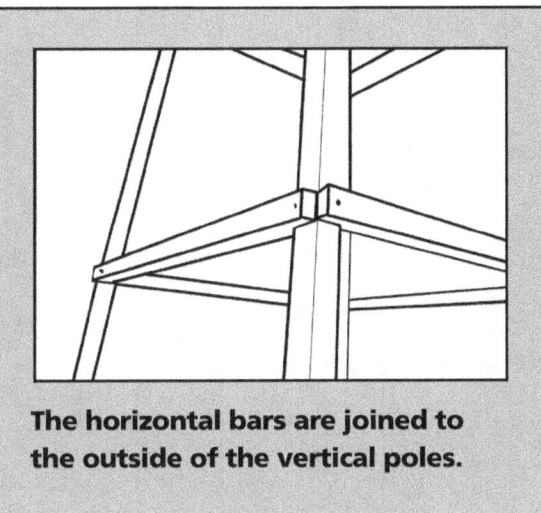

The horizontal bars are joined to the outside of the vertical poles.

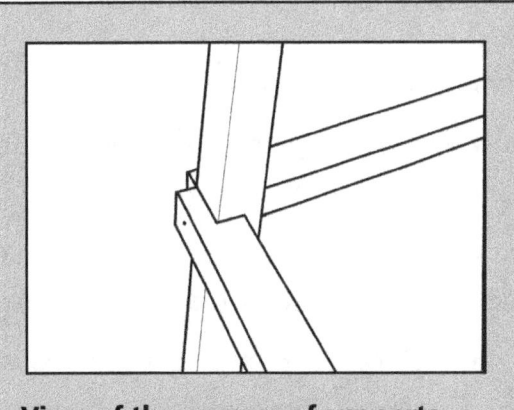

View of the corners of supports #1 and #2 showing the cuts in the connecting lateral bars.

2

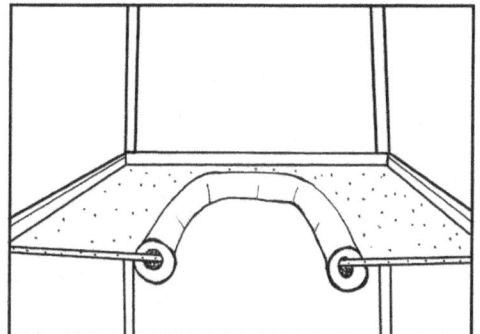

Views of the shoulder support. Foam tubing is added around the area where your neck will go.

It is also a good idea to have extra padding (large blocks of foam rubber) underneath the shoulder platform. Before you attach them, cover them with fabric. You will sweat under the giant and the cloth absorbs moisture.

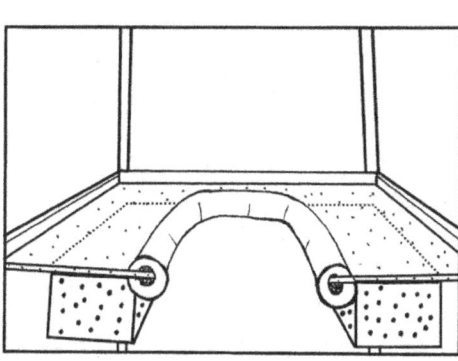

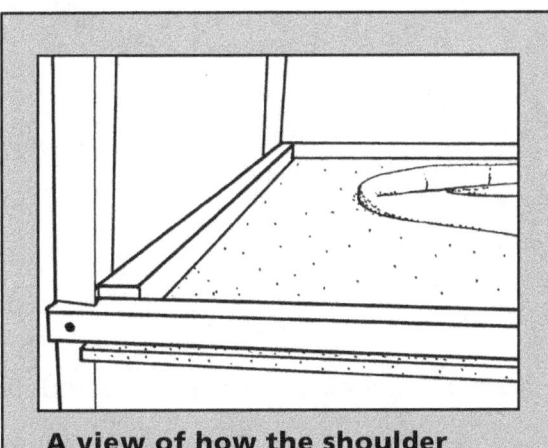

A view of how the shoulder support connects to the corner of the frame.

Giant Made Over a Wooden Frame

Puppets, Puppetry and Gogmagog

Giants **223**

Some things to consider:

How high is your giant? On an open field with wind the giants are more difficult to operate. Take that into consideration.

Do you have room to store the frames? You can choose to attach the head permanently to the frame. If so take that into consideration in terms of storage.

If the head can be removed, do you have room to store it along with the frame?

The giants take up space. Make sure you can get the frame out of the doorway of your work space.

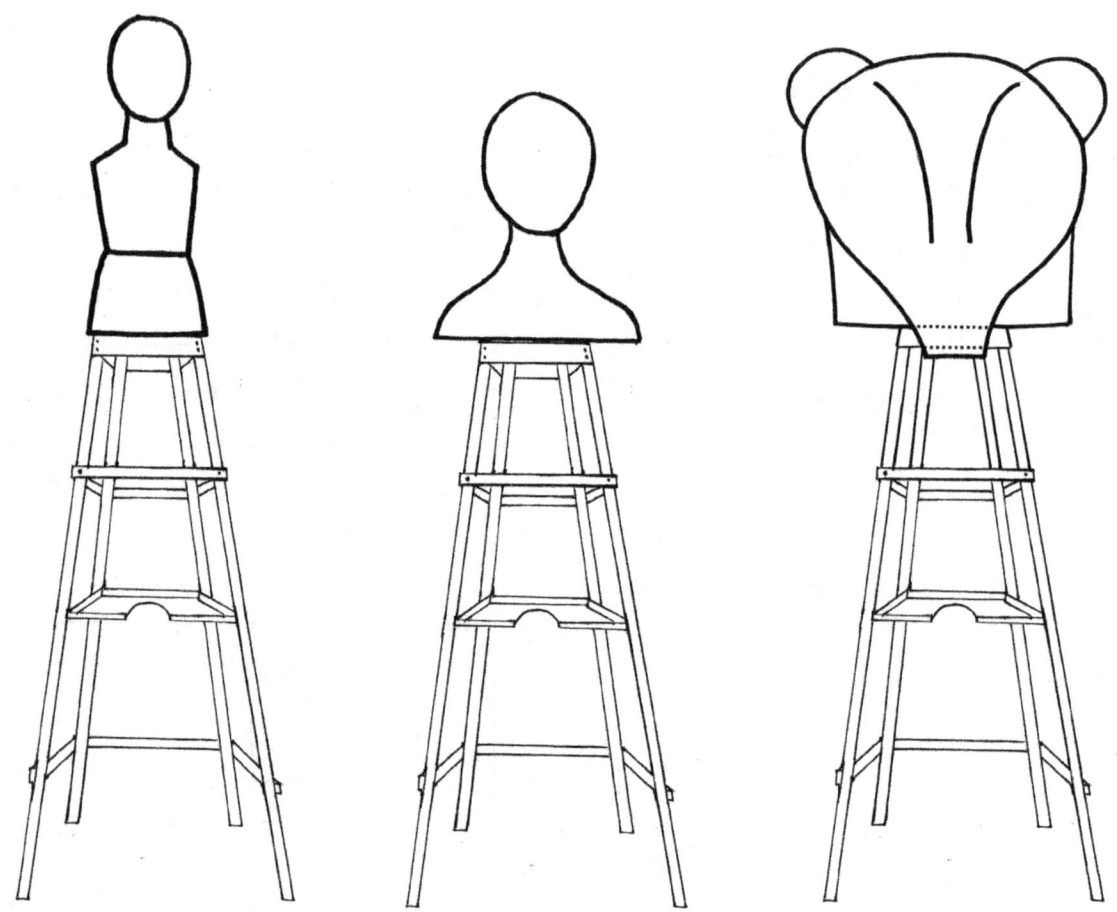

Here are some examples of heads and /or heads and torsos in relation the frame.

Some heads are made of paper mache over molds of clay. Some are made with paper mache over armatures of cane.

Weight is really important. The frame, finished head and costume must be carried by **1** person.

The Head Made Over Clay Mold

Materials:

clay, large plastic containers or objects to fill space, newspaper, petroleum jelly, thin plastic used to cover food, brown craft paper, paper mache paste, strong but flexible wire, duct tape, foam rubber for padding, large balloon, white glue, paint, plywood for the base of the shoulders, bolts, washers, butterfly nuts, 20 plastic bottles (hand variation), packing tape, pvc tubes, flexible dryer hose (arm variation).

Tools:

clay cutters, utility knife, wire cutters, Phillips screwdriver, scissors, saber saw, drill and drill bits, tall ladder.

Consider this:

Heads made over molds of clay can get very heavy. Unless you have a sturdy table on wheels, the mold will generally stay where it is. So choose where you want to work carefully.

Also consider how far you have to reach to work on the mold.

Can you move around it? Think carefully about where you are going to build when working with heavy molds.

Puppets, Puppetry and Gogmagog

 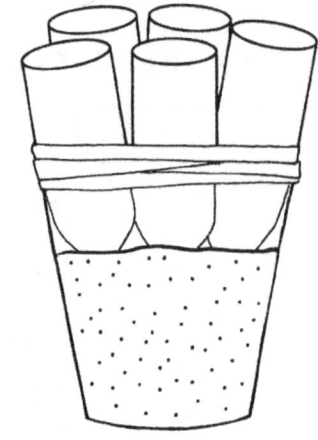 

You can of course make your mold entirely out of clay.

Unless you dig your clay out of a hill, you have to buy it and it is expensive.

So here are some ways to use objects to take up space before you add the clay; thereby economizing on clay.

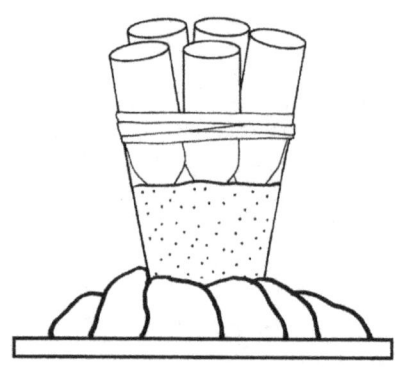 

Add wads of clay around the container to hold it firmly in space.

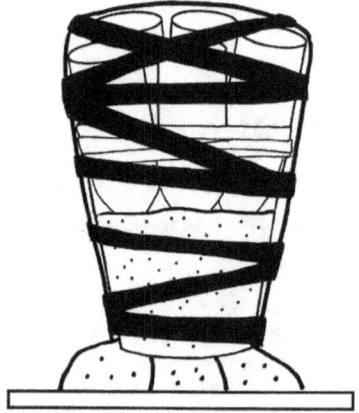 

Cover the whole container in plastic and tape the plastic down.

Cover the whole container with wads of clay until you have a rough form of the head and shoulders.

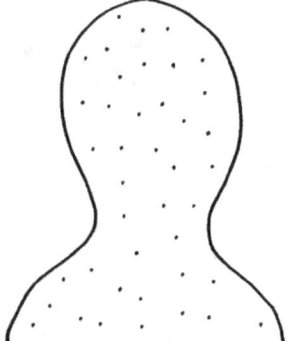

Finish sculpting the head and shoulders.

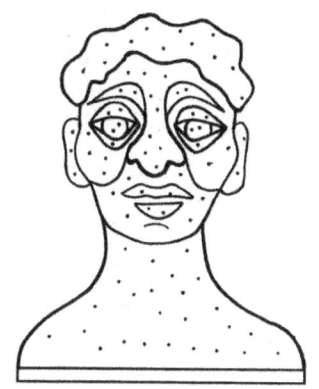

Cover the larger areas with a very thin plastic wrap.

Apply *vaseline* to the areas where there are more details.

Apply **6-8** layers of paper mache, alternating newspaper and brown paper.

Let dry.

Giant Made Over a Wooden Frame

When the mache is thoroughly dry, cut around the base of the shoulder with a utility knife.

Cut the head and shoulders off the mold.

There are **2** ways you can cut the mached head off the mold.

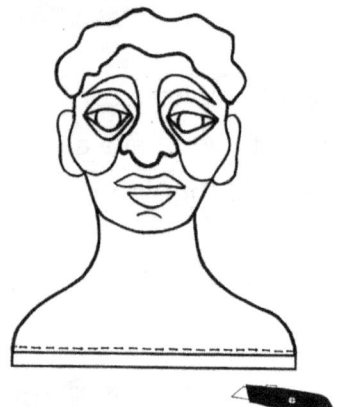

Version 1

Cut from the side of the shoulder, over the top of the head and down the other side.

You will have cut the head and shoulders into **2** parts.

Version 2

Cut from the centre back, over the top of the head and down to the nose.

It is possible that you can start wriggling off the mache from the back.

If that is not possible, continue the cut down the centre of the face.

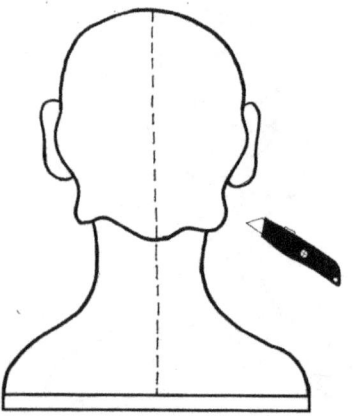

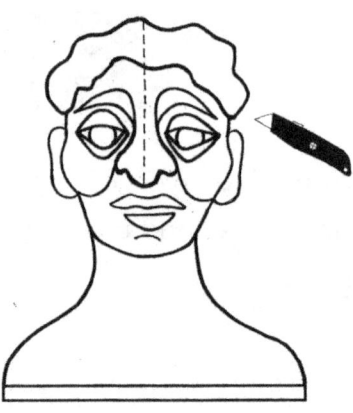

Glue and tape together the cut edges so that the head is one piece again.

Apply **4** layers of paper mache alternating newspaper and brown paper over the join.

Make sure you cover all the tape.

Let dry.

Wire the border of the shoulders. Please see page **17** for wiring instructions.

Let dry.

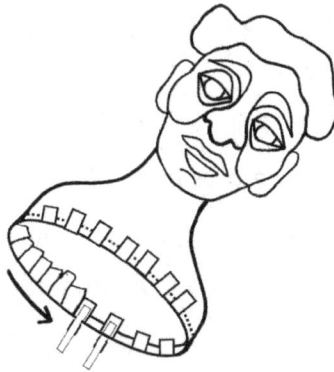

Place the head and shoulders on to a piece of thin plywood.

Trace around the edges and using a sabre saw, cut out the shape as neatly as possible.

Sand the edges.

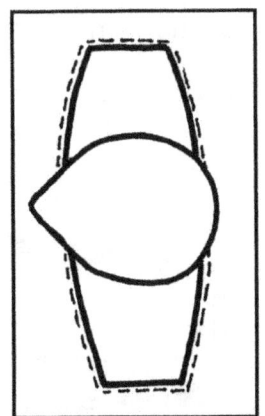

Puppets, Puppetry and Gogmagog

Drill a hole in the middle of the wooden shoulder plate.

This hole should be the same size as the hole in the top platform of the frame.

A bolt should be able the fit through the hole.

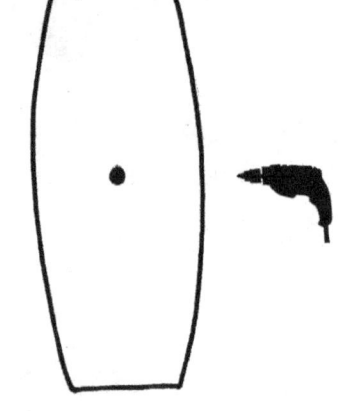

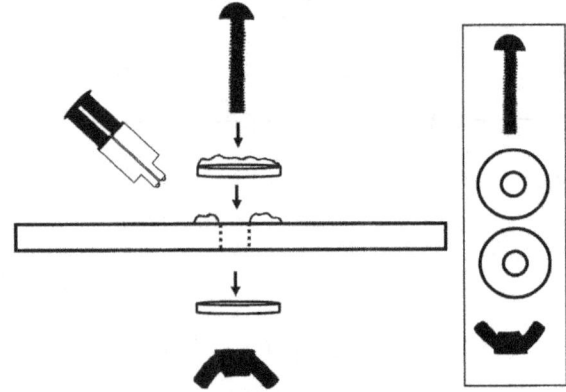

You will now fix a bolt to the wooden shoulder plate.

Apply epoxy around the edge of the hole.

Place a heavy duty washer over the hole.

Apply epoxy on top of the washer.

Pass the bolt though to the other side of the wood.

Let the bolt dry in place. It is now a permanent feature of the shoulder board.

I have drawn the butterfly nut just to show what you will do with it later.

For now keep it and its washer in a safe place.

It is always good to have extra nuts because they can get easily lost.

This is how it will all come together later on.

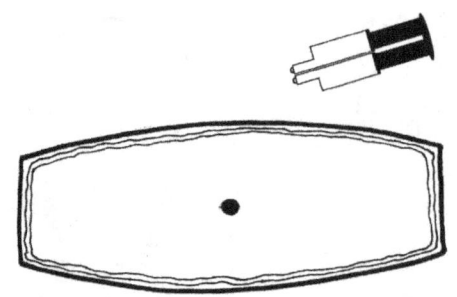

Apply epoxy around the edge of the shoulder board.

Puppets, Puppetry and Gogmagog

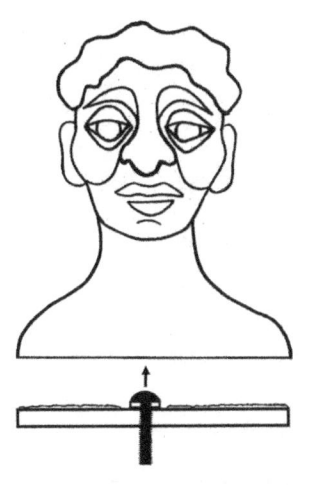

Place the head and shoulders on top of the shoulder board.

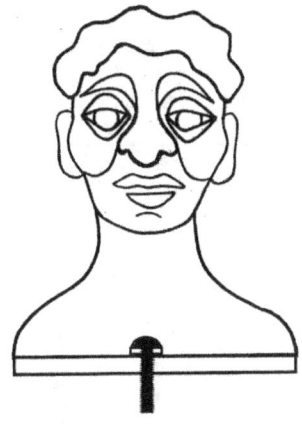

Tape the **2** parts together with duct tape as tightly as possible.

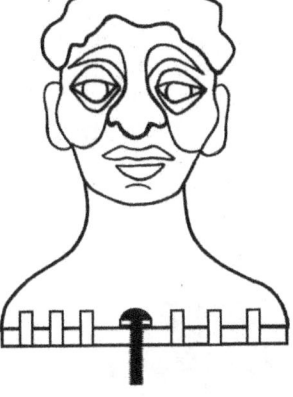

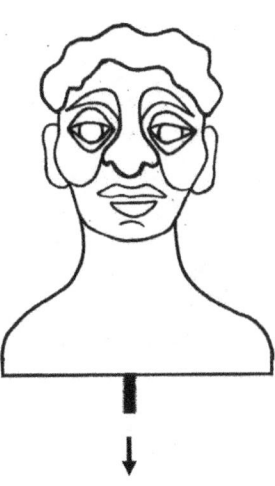

Apply **2** layer of paper mache (**1** newspaper, **1** brown) around the edge.

Let dry.

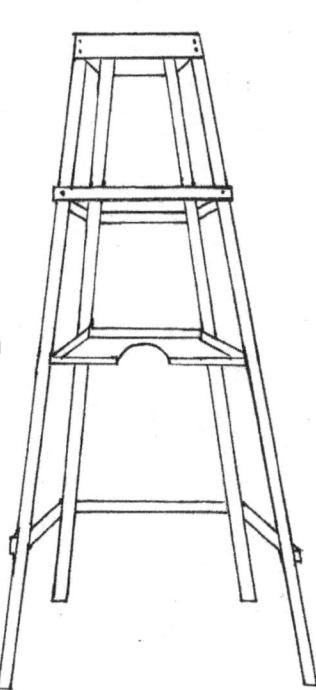

Later on you will be able to attach the head and shoulders to the top platform by passing the bolt of the head through the hole in the top platform.

Then you will screw the **2** parts together using the washer and butterfly nut from underneath the top platform.

This will need to be done with the whole structure is lying down or with a tall ladder.

Giant Made Over a Wooden Frame

Puppets, Puppetry and Gogmagog

| **The Hands** | You can make hands using different methods. Here I describe **2**.

Choose one of the methods to make your hands. |

Version 1

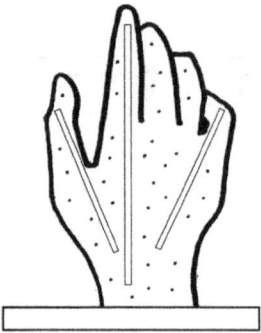

1 You can make a clay mold.

In the illustration you will see that I have inserted some sticks into the clay from the top of the fingers. This is to support the fingers, especially if they are long and thin.

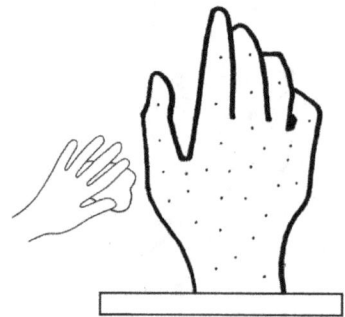

2 Apply a thin layer of *vaseline* over the hand.

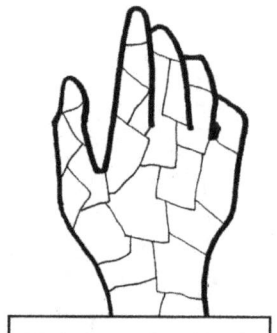

3 Apply **6** layers of paper mache (alternating newspaper and brown paper) over the hand.

Let dry.

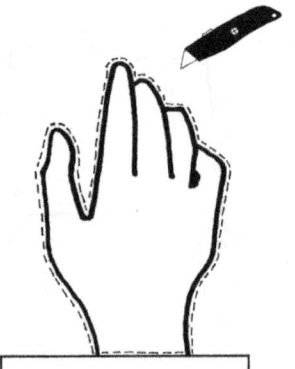

4 Cut the hand off the mold.

First cut around the wrist were it meets the table.

The other cuts will depend on the position of the fingers.

Pry the hands off the mold.

 Unite the **2** halves of the hand with duct tape.

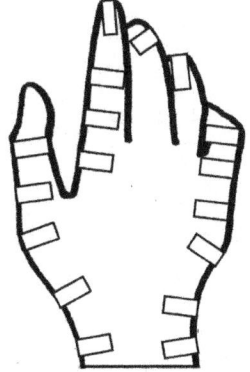

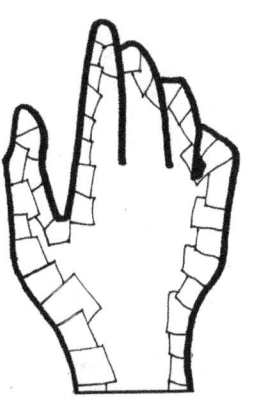

Apply **4** layers of paper mache (alternating newspaper and brown) around the taped areas.

Verify that all tape is covered.

Let dry.

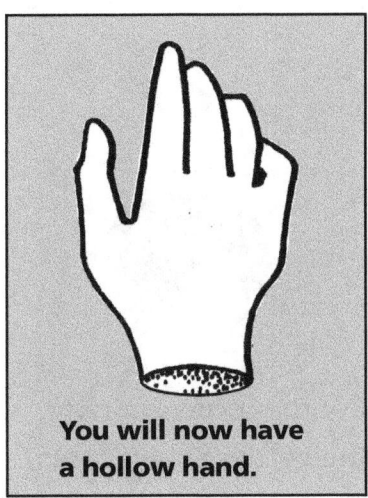

You will now have a hollow hand.

Make a cover for the wrist from thick cardboard and secure it into place with duct tape.

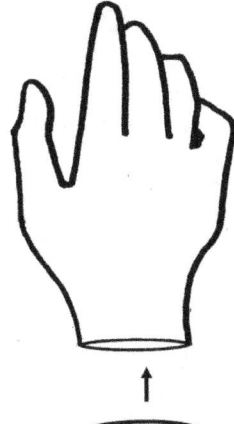

Apply **2** layers of paper mache over the tape (**1** newspaper, **1** brown).

Let dry.

Giant Made Over a Wooden Frame

Puppets, Puppetry and Gogmagog

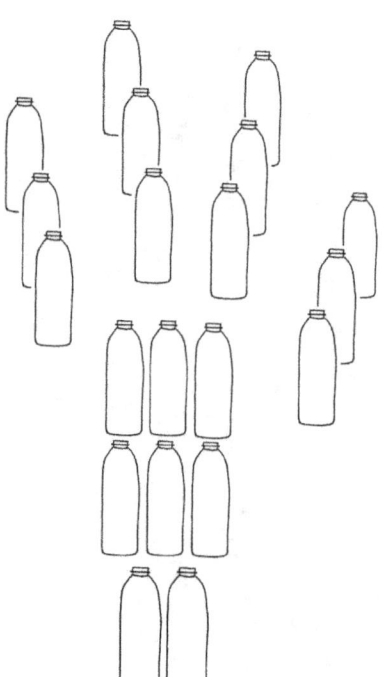

Version 2

This is another way of making hands using small plastic water bottles.

This method is great for hands that look more gnarled, more grotesque.

You will need **20** bottles for each hand.

With this method I prefer to create **3** fingers and a thumb for each hand. This way the hands don't look so bulky.

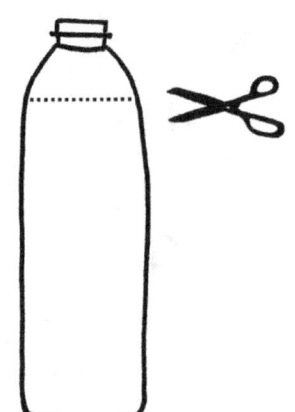
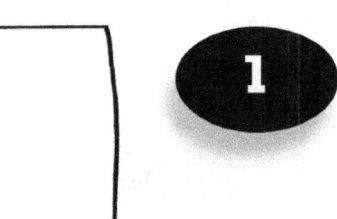

1 Cut the tops off **3** bottles as illustrated.

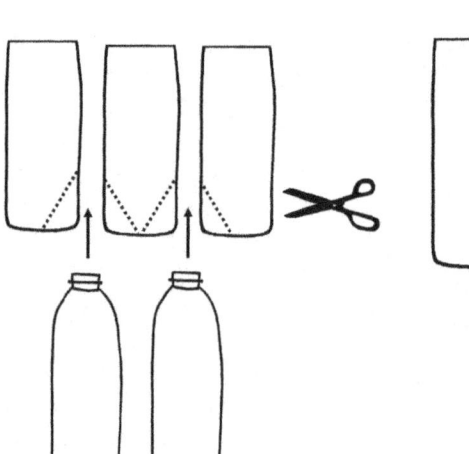
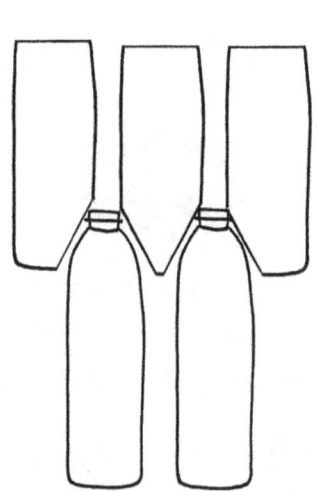

2 Cut the corners out of the bottles as illustrated. This allows room for **2** complete bottles to fit in between the cut bottles.

Now we have a wrist at the bottom part of the palm of the hand.

3

Tape them together as shown.

Use packing tape for this.

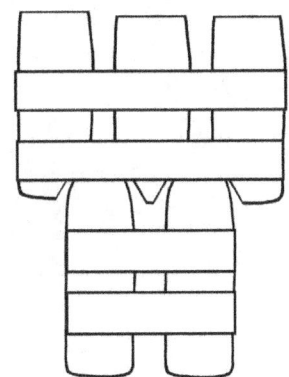

4

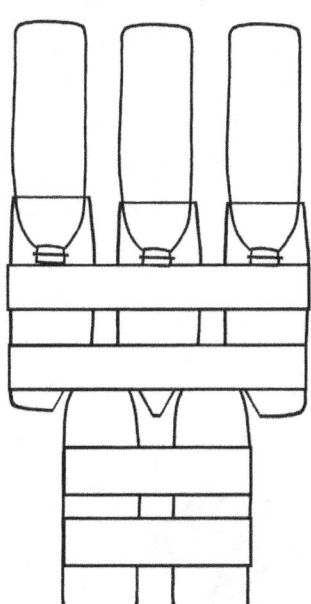

Now you will add bottles to make the top part of the palm of the hand.

Insert **3** complete bottles (tops down) into the **3** cut bottles as shown.

Tape them together.

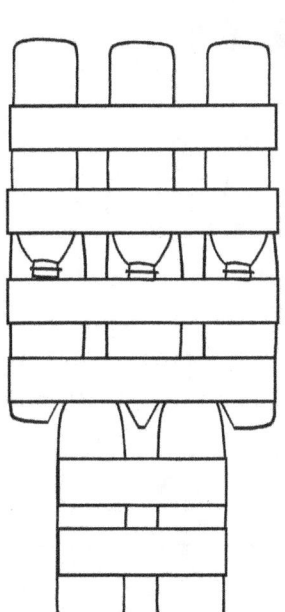

The Fingers

Now for the basic steps for the fingers.

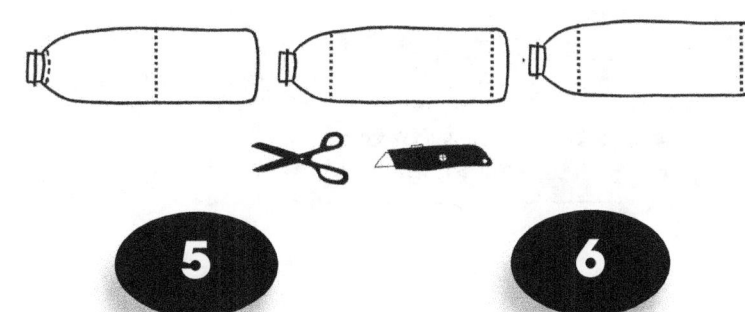

5

Cut the neck off the first bottle. Then cut it in half. This will form the tip of the finger.

6

Cut the top and bottom off the second and third bottle as shown.

Giant Made Over a Wooden Frame

Puppets, Puppetry and Gogmagog

Giants **235**

The 3 bottles now look like this.

7

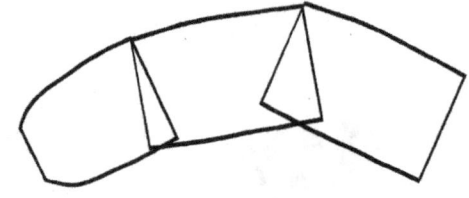

Place the second bottle into the third bottle at an angle you like.

8

Place the first bottle (the tip of the finger) into the second bottle at an angle you like.

9

Repeat with the **2** other fingers and thumb in the same way.

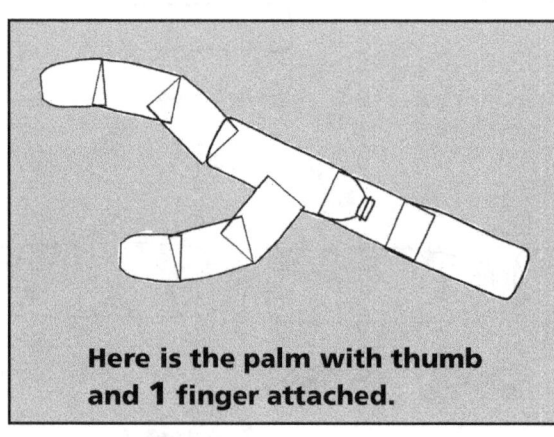

Here is the palm with thumb and 1 finger attached.

10

Attach the fingers to the palm in positions you like. You may have to cut the bottles at the base of the fingers at different angles.

11

When you have the shape you want, cover the hands with packing tape.

Apply **2** layers of paper mache (**1** newspaper, **1** brown)

Let dry.

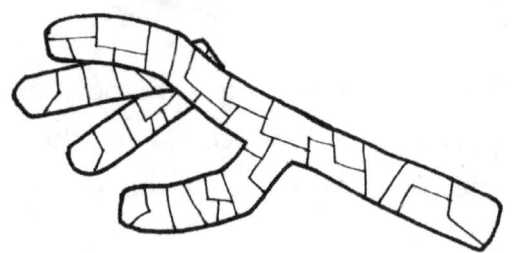

We continue with the steps on page 231.

Now you will make an internal cross bar to be able to attach the arms and hands to the shoulders.

I usually use dowel the thickness of a broom handle for this.

Drill a hole at either end of the middle of the shoulders close to the base. The hole should be the size of the dowel.

Thread the dowel through the shoulders.

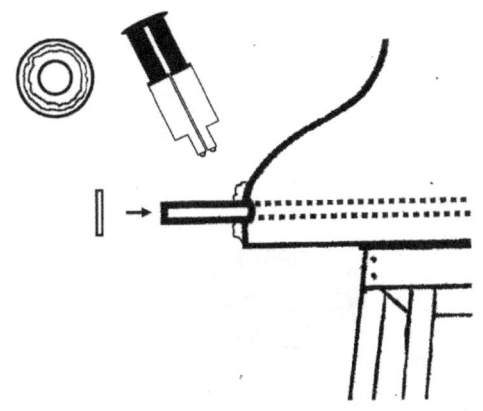

Leave about 5 inches/ 12.7cm of the dowel poking out from each end of the shoulders.

You will now fix the shoulder bar permanently in place.

Apply epoxy to a large washer that will fit over the dowel.

Thread it over the dowel and place it flush with the shoulder.

Tape it firmly into place and do the same with the other shoulder.

Apply a little paper mache around the edges of the washer where it meets the shoulder.

Let dry. Now the shoulder bar will not move.

The Arms

The arms should be in proportion to the head and shoulders and the overall height of the giant.

The forearm will be longer because the hand will fit over it later on. The forearm pole will enter into the hand as far as it will go.

21

Cut **2** pieces of pvc, one longer than the other.

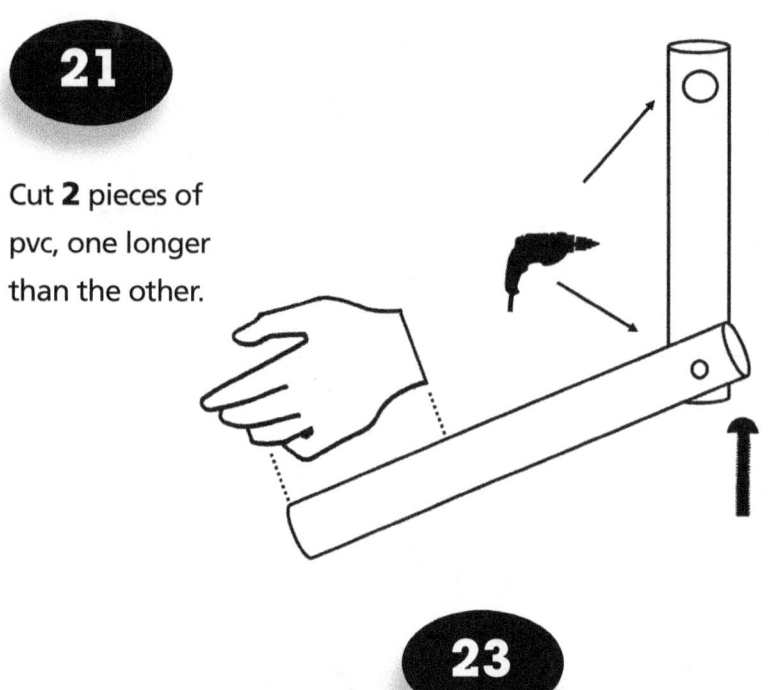

22

Drill a large hole in the top of the upper arm. This should be big enough to accommodate easily the shoulder pole on the shoulders of the giant.

23

Drill a hole through the bottom of the upper arm and one end of the lower arm.

The holes should match because they will be bolted together in the next step.

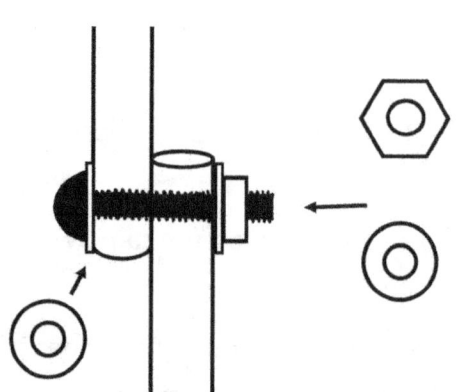

24

Attach the **2** pieces of the arm together with a bolt, **2** washers and a nut as illustrated. This will form the elbow.

Do not tighten the nut yet.

25

Choose the angle of the arm you want and tighten the nut.

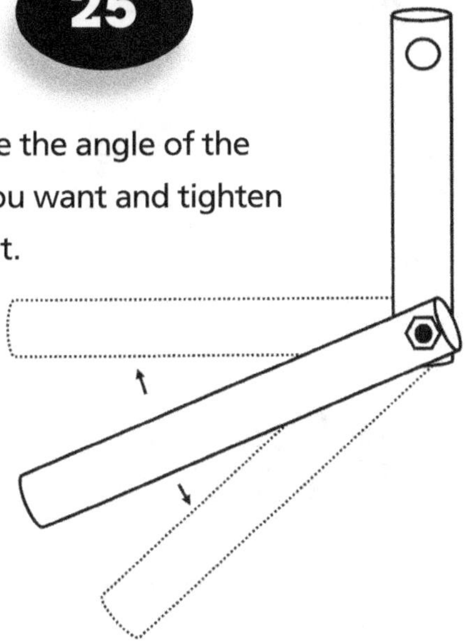

26

Drill a hole in the middle of the wrist of each hand.

The hole should be the size of the width of the pvc.

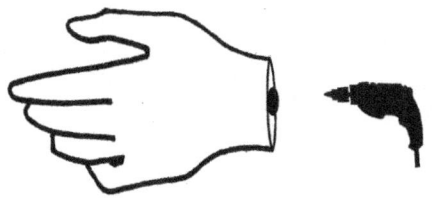

27

Apply epoxy around the edges of the pvc tubing and push it into the hand.

Make sure the hands are facing the right way; thumbs up.

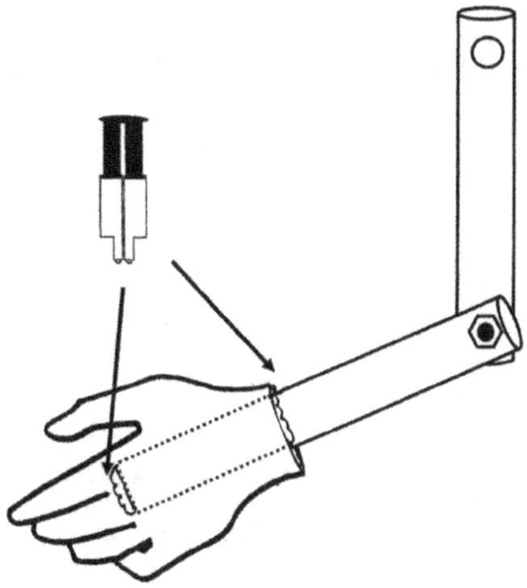

28

Apply more epoxy to the point where the pvc meets the wrist.

Hold in place until it dries.

I have also used hot glue for this.

Apply a little paper mache over the glue once it has dried.

Repeat for the other hand.

Let dry.

29

Now slide the arm on to the shoulder pole.

The whole arm should swing easily from the shoulder.

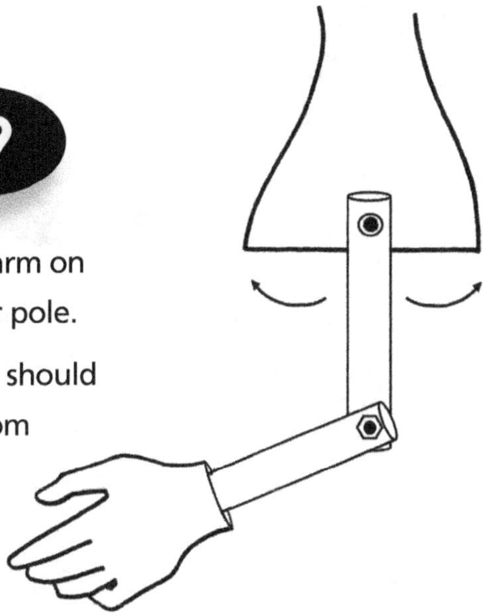

Giant Made Over a Wooden Frame

Puppets, Puppetry and Gogmagog

Giants **239**

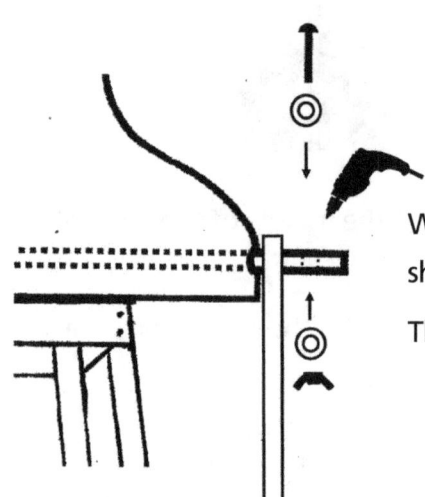

With the arm bar in place, drill a hole through the shoulder bar just to the outside of the arm bar.

There must be room to turn the butterfly nut.

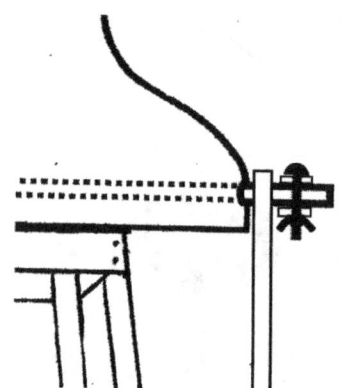

Place the bolt in the hole (washer first) and then screw on the butterfly nut (washer first).

Do the same for the other arm.

Now you have removable arms.

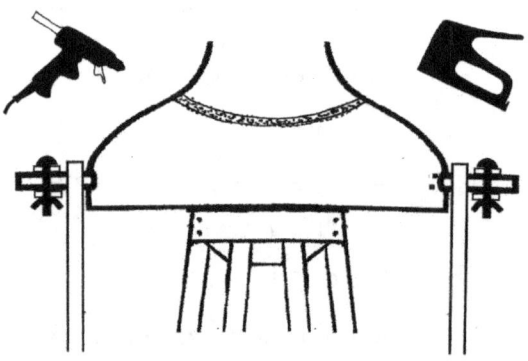

Hot glue a long strip of velcro around the line of the neck where you want the costume to attach to.

When the hot glue is dry, reinforce with a staple gun.

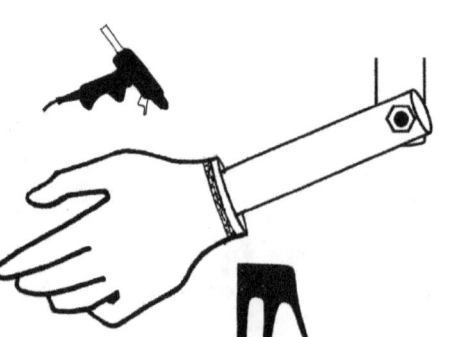

Hot glue and staple (using a staple gun) a long strip of velcro around the wrist as shown.

The sleeve of the costume will be attached here.

Giant Made Over a Wooden Frame

34

When you have the giant on your shoulders, you will need grips for your hands. These make it easy to operate the giant.

I use plastic plastering floats for the grips.

Screw each float on to the **inside** of the front vertical poles of the frame at the height suitable for you or whoever will operate the giant.

I have just illustrated the frame here.

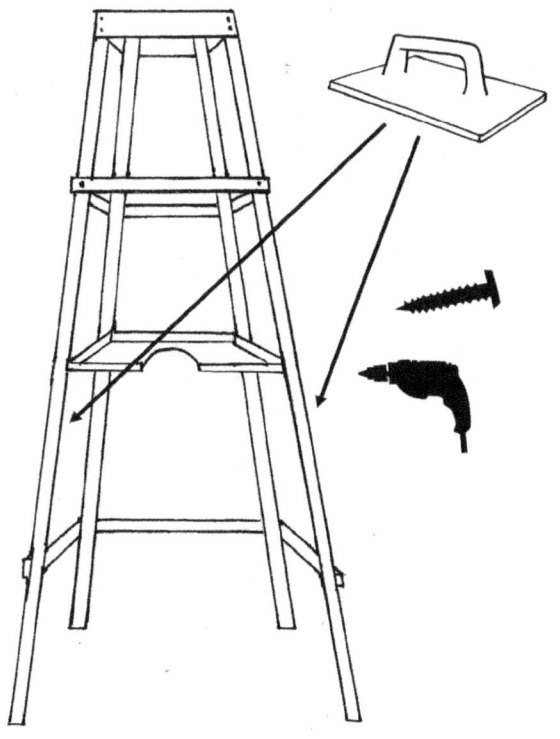

The Costume

35

The costumes for giants are…large. They can add extra weight, so choose your cloth carefully.

There needs to be extra room around the area where the shoulders meet the arms.

Here is a basic pattern I use.

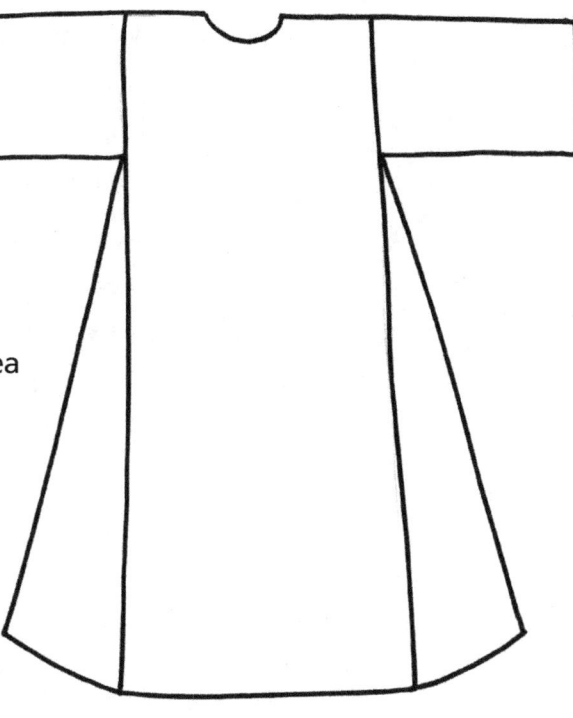

Puppets, Puppetry and Gogmagog

I usually leave the back open. I sew velcro down the whole back opening. It makes it easier to put the costume on the giant.

37

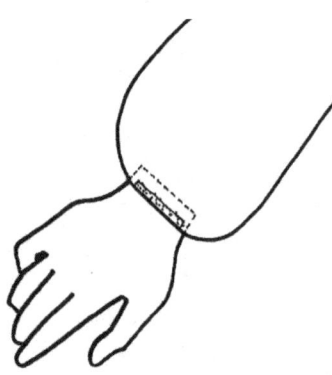

Sew velcro into the sleeves so that they attach well with the velcro already glued onto the wrists.

Leave an opening in the sleeve (on the inside of the wrist so that the sleeve can fit over the hand.

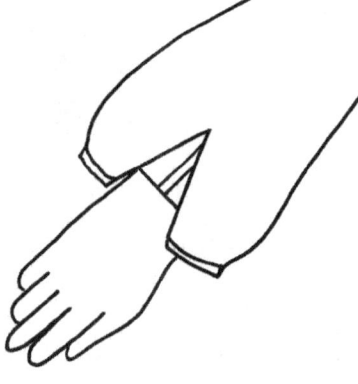

38

Attach velcro to close the cuffs.

Giant Made Over a Wooden Frame

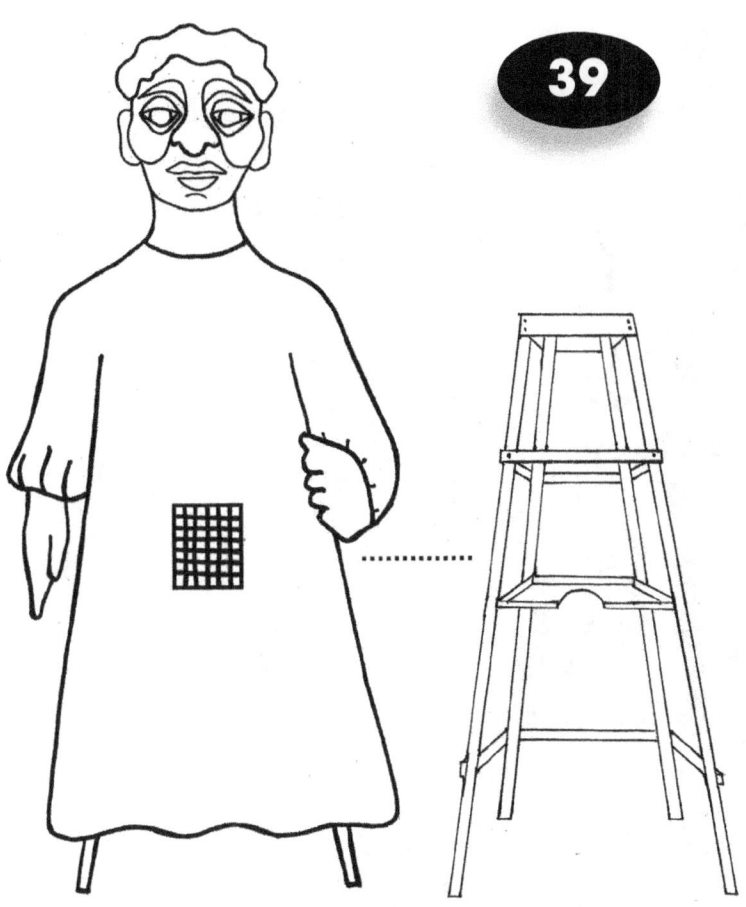

39

Cut a square hole in the cloth at the eye level of the puppeteer who will carry the giant.

Sew a transparent cloth or mesh to cover the hole from the inside of the costume. This way the public cannot see the face of the puppeteer.

40

Add final touches to the giant.

Go walking...

Here is the giant with a torso, illustrated on page **224**.

All the previous steps of construction apply for this giant.

The head and torso are sculpted as one piece in clay.

The arms are fixed in to position.

Variation 1: Flexible Arms and 2 Additional Puppeteers

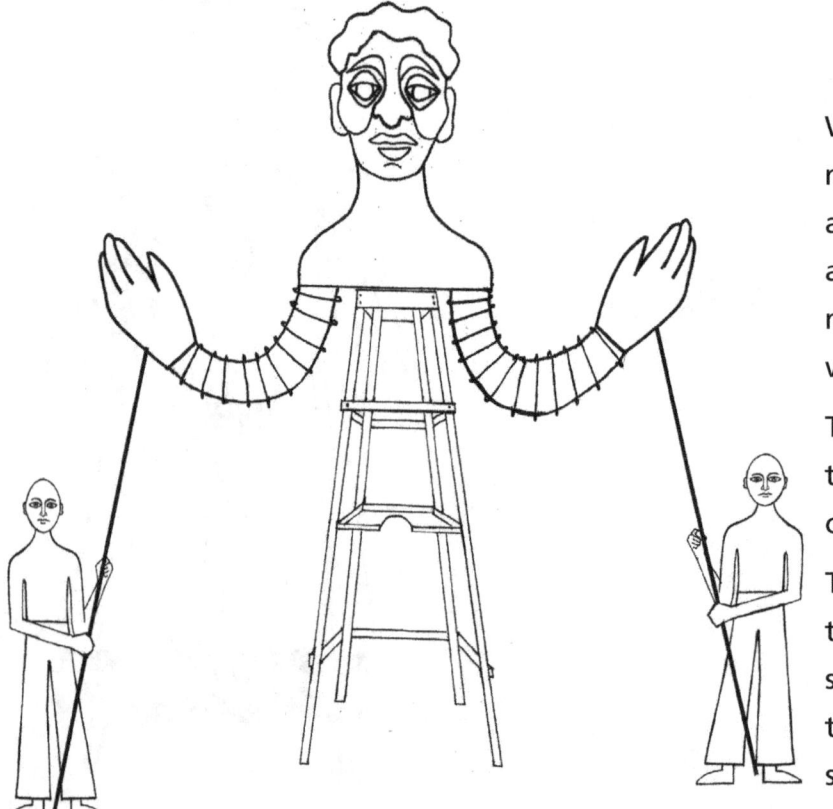

With this way of making the arms, **2** additional puppeteers are needed to manipulate the hands with long poles.

The hands are joined to the shoulders with clothes dryer tubing.

The tubing is joined to the body under the shoulders, directly onto the wooden base of the shoulder plate.

244

Puppets, Puppetry and Gogmagog

Variation 2: Another Way of Using Clothes Dryer Tubing

The tubing can also run from hand to hand through the shoulders.

The shoulder need to be squared off in the construction process.

Holes need to be made at the either of the shoulders to accommodate the tubing.

Giant heads made over cane armatures are very light and surprisingly strong.

The cane I use, properly called cane spline, is wedged shaped and is used for securing the rattan webbing in a groove around chair seats.

It comes from the rattan vine native to Indonesia, the Philippines and Malaysia.

I buy cane in large bundles from a hardware store.

Materials:
hula hoop, ¼inch plywood, wire, cane, newspaper, brown paper, masking tape, duct tape, polystyrene balls, hot glue sticks, long pole the width of a broomstick, epoxy, sheets of white hard foam, bolts, butterfly nuts, washers, paints, cloth for costume.

Tools:
pliers, pruning shears, pliers, wire cutters, hot glue gun, hand saw.

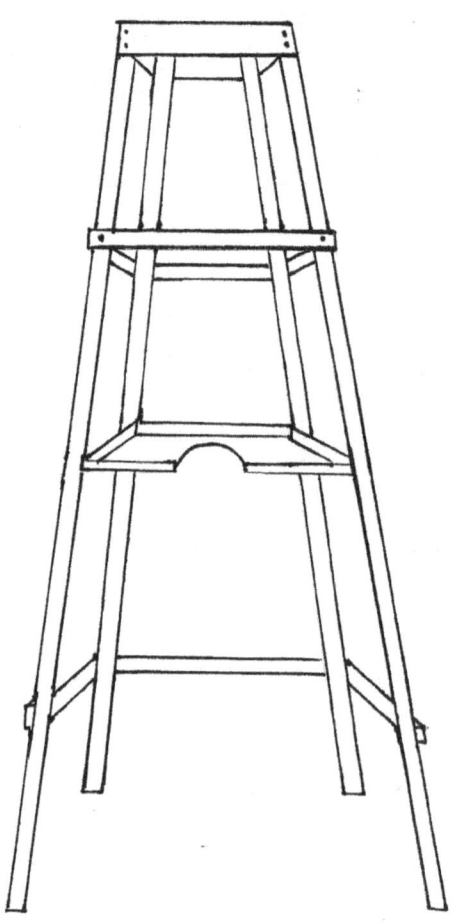

We use the same wooden frame as described in the previous giant process on pages **222-224**.

Start with a hula hoop.

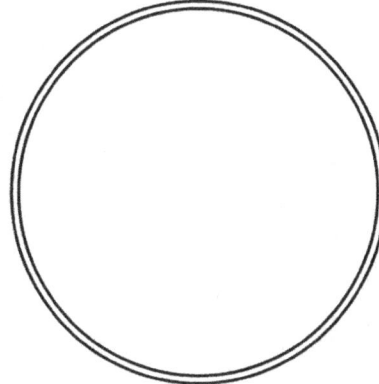

Attach a crossbar made of ¼ inch/6mm plywood.

I use wire.

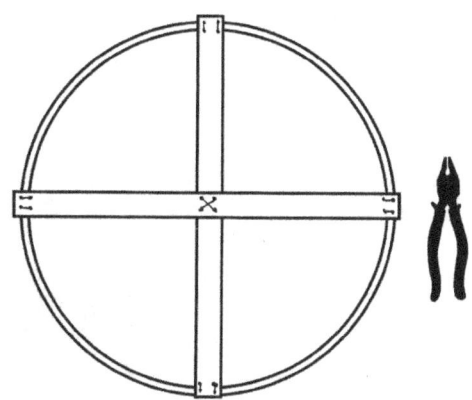

2

Drill **4** holes in the top platform of the frame.

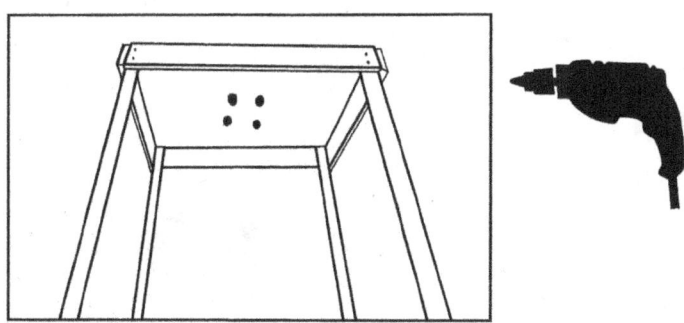

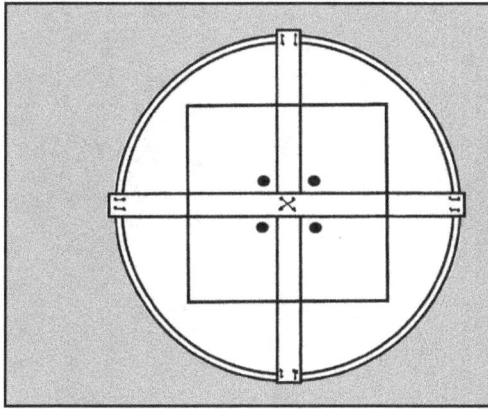

Bird's eye view.

The 4 holes in the top platform are to accommodate the base (the hula hoop and crossbar) later on.

This is how the head will attach to the frame.

Puppets, Puppetry and Gogmagog

Cut the first piece of cane.

This will describe the size of the armature.

Attach each end of the cane to the halfway points on the hula hoop frame with masking tape.

In this and the following illustrations I have not drawn the crossbar.

Using the first cane as a measure, cut **3** more canes the same size.

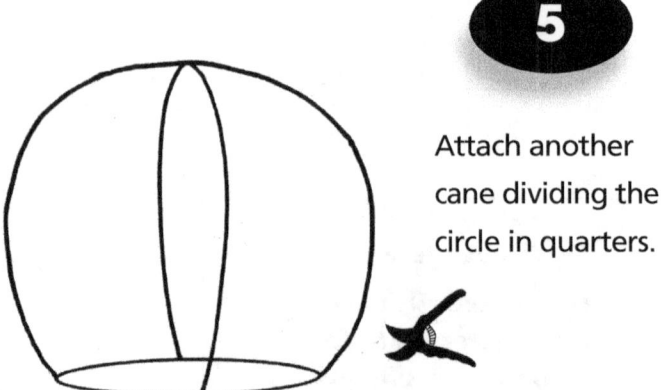

Attach another cane dividing the circle in quarters.

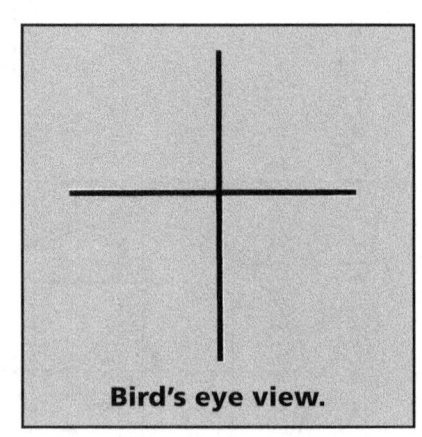

Bird's eye view.

248

Puppets, Puppetry and Gogmagog

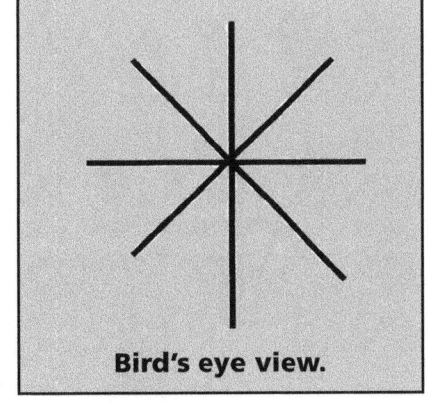

6

Attach the other **2** canes with masking tape, dividing the circle in eighths.

Bird's eye view.

7

Make at least **4** internal circles of cane and attach them horizontally to the vertical canes.

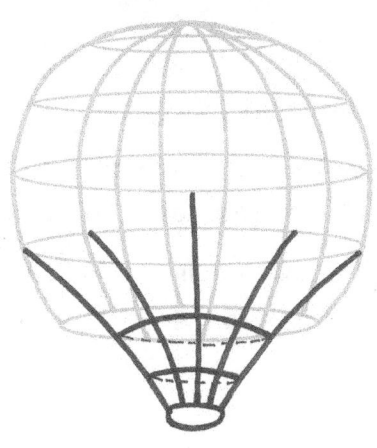

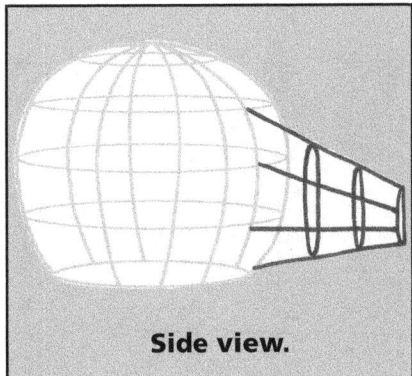

8

Attach lengths of cane to the front of the head with masking tape to create the snout.

Side view.

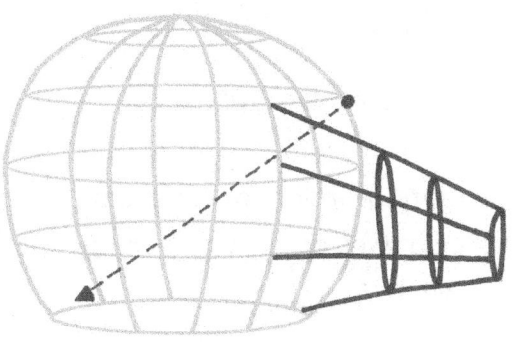

9

If you need to bend a cane inwards, tie string to the point you want to bend inwards. Pull it as illustrated and tie it to an opposite cane.

Giant with Head and Body of Cane

Puppets, Puppetry and Gogmagog

Giants **249**

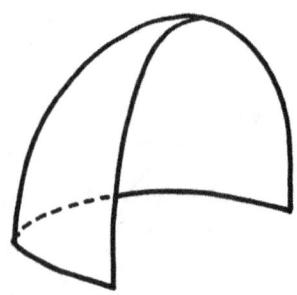

10 Attach ears to the structure with masking tape.

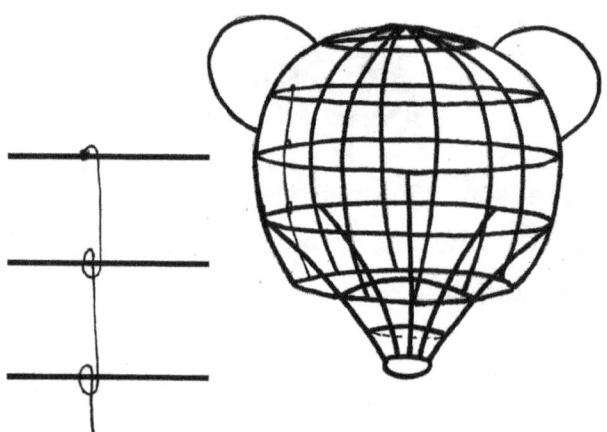

11 If you have large gaps in the criss cross of cane, lace string through the gaps as shown. You will attach paper mache strips to these as well as the cane in the next step.

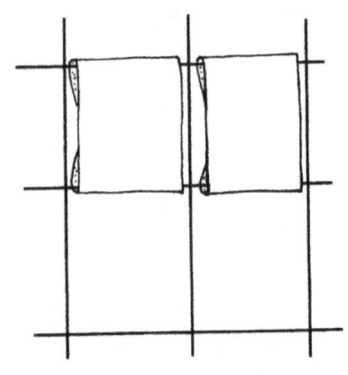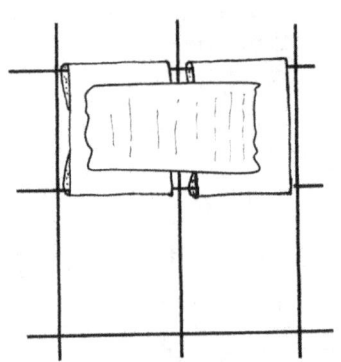

12 Apply the first layer of paper mache (newspaper) in wide strips as illustrated.

The overlapping makes the mache stronger.

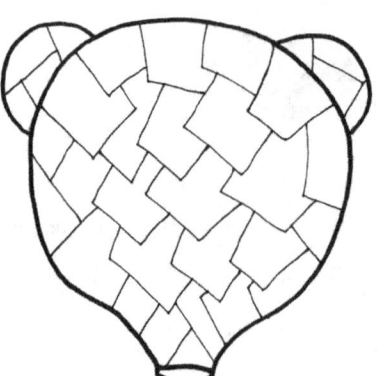

13 Apply the second layer of paper mache, this time with brown paper. Check from the inside for any areas that are not well covered with paper mache. Let dry.

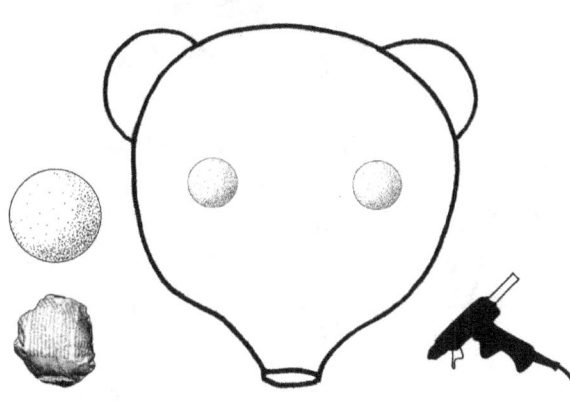

Attach objects for eyes with tape or hot glue.

Polystyrene balls cut in half or balls of scrunched up newspaper work well.

Be careful; hot glue can cause burns.

Mache over the eyes. Let dry.

15

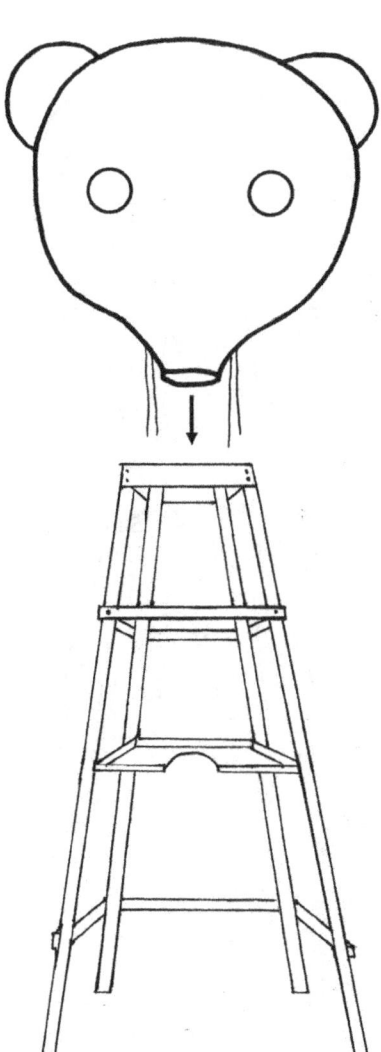

Pass long pieces of wire over the centre of the crossbar inside the head and lower the head onto the frame. Make sure the wires pass through the **4** holes in the top platform of the frame.

Twist them together.

Verify that the head is firmly attached to the platform.

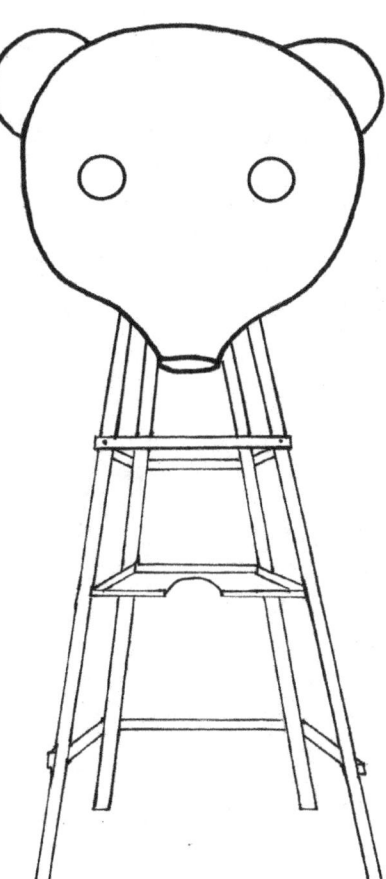

Giant with Head and Body of Cane

Puppets, Puppetry and Gogmagog

16

Drill a hole in the middle of **2** strips of thin wood. The length of each strip is the size of the space between the **2** vertical poles of the frame at the position illustrated.

17

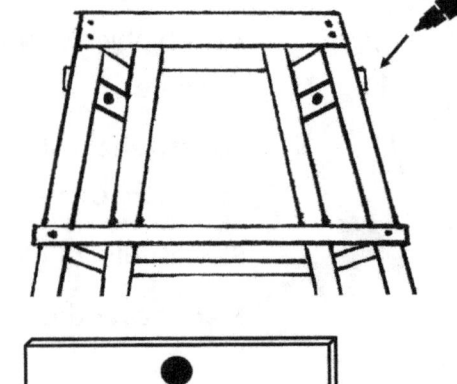

Attach each strip to either side of the frame as illustrated.

Later on you will pass a pole through these holes to make a shoulder bar. Make them as level as possible.

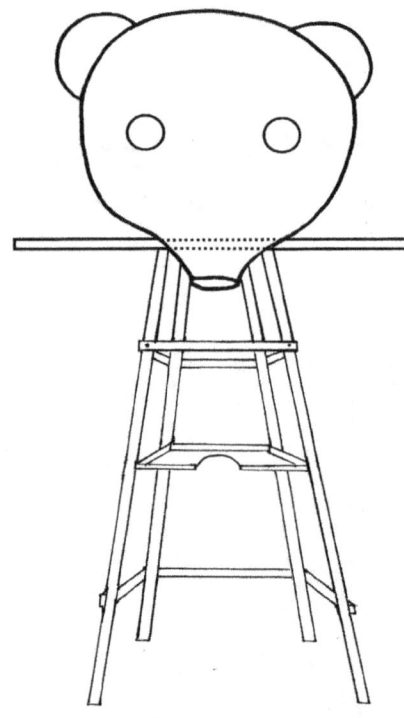

We will now work on creating the cane armature of the body, attaching it to the frame.

First, consider this.

You will be attaching arms to the shoulder pole. These arms swing forwards and backward. So it is important to leave room for them to do this.

The vertical arrows describe the available space to create the cane body, without interfering with the movement of the arms.

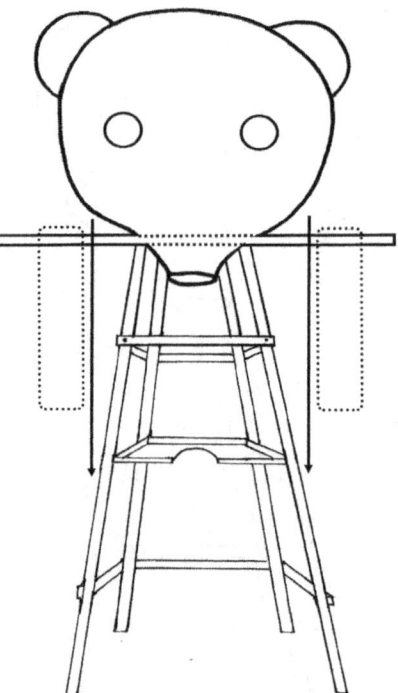

Puppets, Puppetry and Gogmagog

18

With **2** long pieces of cane, make **2** horizontal circles around the positions indicated. This will give something for the vertical canes to attach to later on.

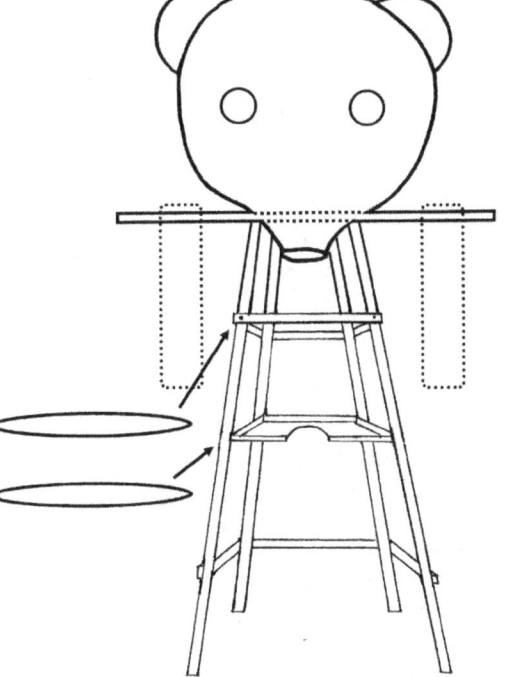

19

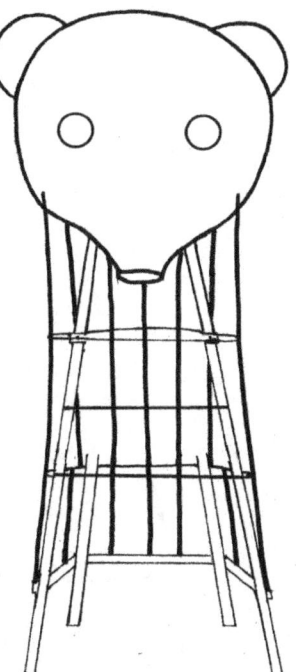

Attach vertical canes from the head to the bottom rung of the frame.

20

Attach the canes to the horizontal circles as you make your way down.

You may have to pierce the mache on the head to do this.

Attach the cane to the head with duct tape.

Elsewhere you can use masking tape.

Here is an idea of the caning process. I have removed the frame from the illustration so you can see the cane well.

Puppets, Puppetry and Gogmagog

Giants **253**

Giant with Head and Body of Cane

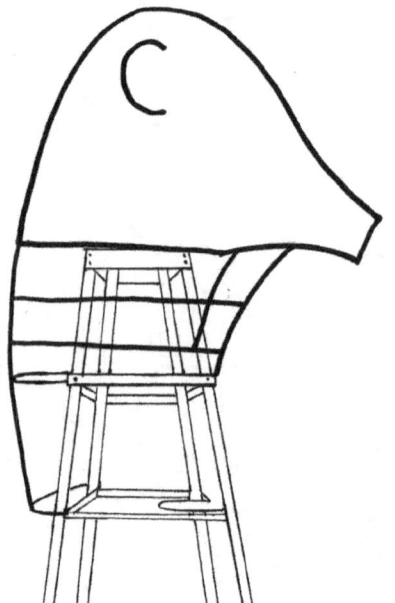

21

Take a look from the side.

Make sure the back canes describe the curve of the back of the animal.

Attach cane from under the snout to the chest area, creating a gentle curve.

22

When you have the giant on your shoulders, you will need grips for your hands. These make it easy to operate the giant.

I use plastic plastering floats for the grips.

Screw each float on to the **inside** of the front vertical poles of the frame at the height suitable for you or whoever will operate the giant.

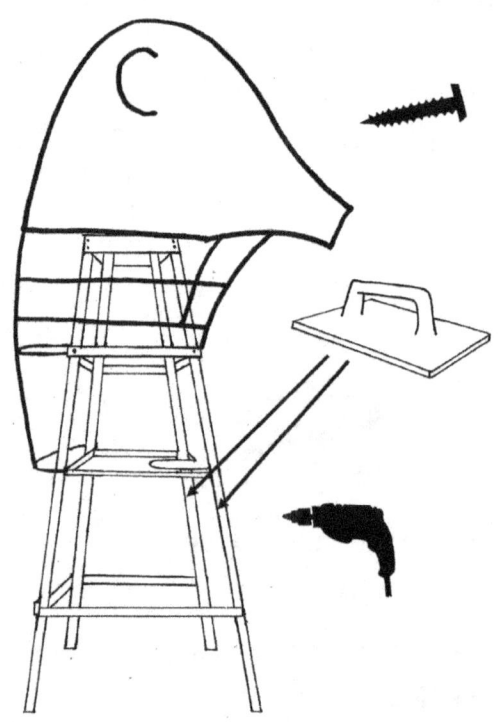

23

Pass the shoulder pole through the holes in the side bars of the frame.

Make sure there is an equal amount of pole sticking out from either side.

Epoxy the pole in place.

This pole should not move.

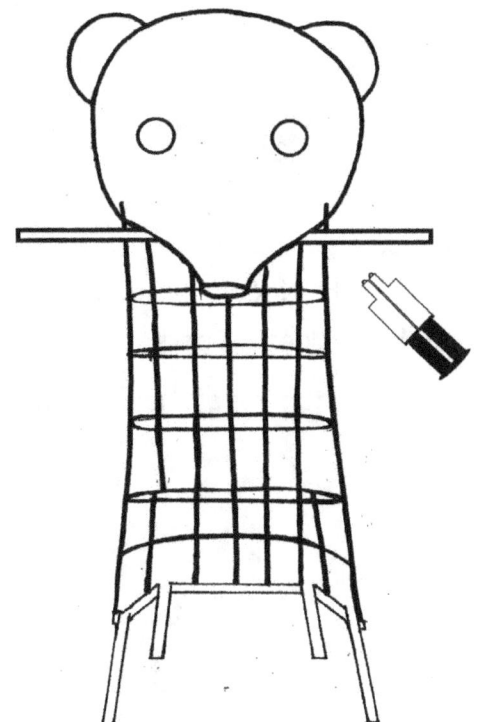

24

Apply **2** good layers of paper mache (**1** newspaper, **1** brown) over the whole cane armature.

Apply the first layer of newspaper the same way as you did for the head; overlapping horizontal and vertical strips of paper.

Apply the second layer of brown paper.

Let dry.

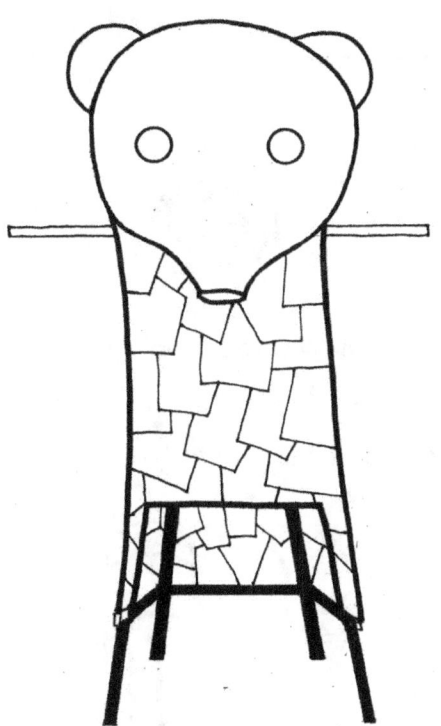

Giant with Head and Body of Cane

The Arms

Cut **2** rectangles (for the upper and lower arms) out of hard foam. I use the foam sheets that fridges are packed in.

Attach the rectangles as shown with duct tape.

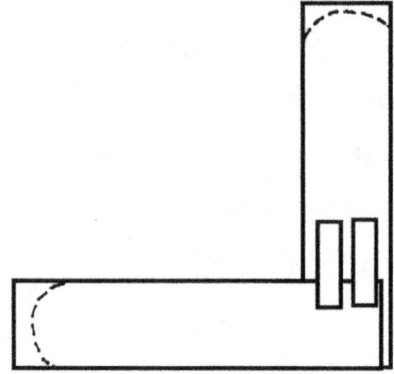

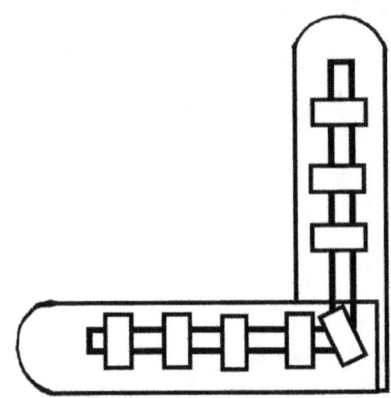

Reinforce the foam but attaching **2** strips of thin wood (lattice) as illustrated.

Tape them securely in place with duct tape.

Now you will create the volume of the arms using lengths of cane.

Attach **2** strips as shown.

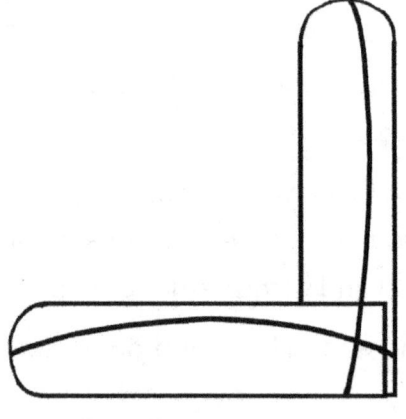

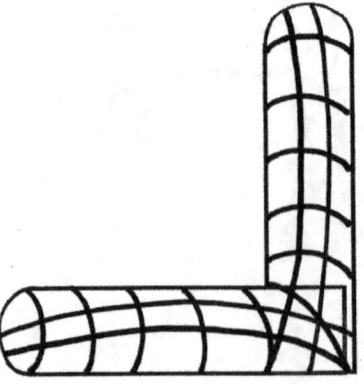

Attach more cane as illustrated, creating curves as you go.

Insert a cardboard tube into the middle of the top part of the arm.

It should be wider than the width of the broomstick you have used as a shoulder bar.

You will have to break through the foam on one side.

The tube facilitates the sliding of the arm on to the shoulder bar later on.

Apply **2** layers of paper mache (**1** newspaper, **1** brown) over the whole arm.

Remember to overlap the newspaper strips.

Let dry.

Create the fastening device following steps **30-31** on page **240** of the previous giant.

Trim any extra pole remaining outside of the bolt.

Giant with Head and Body of Cane

33

Cut a square hole on the front of the body big enough so you can see out of the giant when it is on your shoulders. Cover the hole with mesh.

34

Paint the head, body and arms. You will need a tall ladder.

Paint a white undercoat first.

35

Add elements of costume.

In this case the skirt is detachable. It is attached to the body of the giant with velcro.

The giant Gogmagog, in Guildhall, London.

www.ingramcontent.com/pod-product-compliance
Lightning Source LLC
Chambersburg PA
CBHW082044250426

43661CB00080B/2734

9 780985 338435